DEMONIZING
THE JEWS

DEMONIZING THE JEWS

Luther and the Protestant Church in Nazi Germany

Christopher J. Probst

PUBLISHED IN ASSOCIATION WITH THE
UNITED STATES HOLOCAUST MEMORIAL MUSEUM

INDIANA UNIVERSITY PRESS

Bloomington & Indianapolis

Published in association with the United States Holocaust Memorial Museum

The assertions, arguments, and conclusions contained herein are those of the author. They do not necessarily reflect the opinions of the United States Holocaust Memorial Council or the United States Holocaust Memorial Museum.

This book is a publication of
Indiana University Press

601 North Morton Street
Bloomington, Indiana 47404-3797 USA

iupress.indiana.edu

Telephone orders   800-842-6796
Fax orders   812-855-7931

⊖ The paper used in this publication meets the minimum requirements of the American National Standard for Information Sciences—Permanence of Paper for Printed Library Materials, ANSI Z39.48–1992.

Manufactured in the United States of America

Library of Congress Cataloging-in-Publication Data

Probst, Christopher J., [date]
  Demonizing the Jews : Luther and the Protestant church in Nazi Germany / Christopher J. Probst.
    p. cm.
  Includes bibliographical references (p.   ) and index.
  ISBN 978-0-253-00098-9 (cloth : alk. paper) — ISBN 978-0-253-00100-9 (pbk. : alk. paper) — ISBN 978-0-253-00102-3 (e-book) 1. Churh and state—Germany—History—1933–1945. 2. Bekennende Kirche—History. 3. Christianity and antisemitism. 4. Protestant churches—Germany—History—20th century. 5. Germany—Church history. 6. Luther, Martin, 1483–1546.
  I. Title.
  BX4844.P743 2012
  261.2'6094309043—dc23
                                        2011049610

1 2 3 4 5 17 16 15 14 13 12

Lovingly dedicated to the memory of my grandmother
Esther Goldstein
who passed from this life to the next in June 2006

CONTENTS

ACKNOWLEDGMENTS

This book would have never been completed without the assistance of many friends, colleagues, and institutions. It gives me great pleasure to express my gratitude to them here. I extend my thanks first of all to Dan Stone. His constant guidance, patience, and good humor were invaluable in the early stages of the study from which this book grew. He has become both mentor and friend.

I would not have been able to finance the research required for the book without the generosity of Gabriel Pretus and the Friendly Hand Charitable Foundation, which awarded me the St. Thérèse of Lisieux Ph.D. Scholarship, and Royal Holloway, University of London, which awarded me a research studentship. My aunt, Catherine Sinclair, and my wife's aunt, Peggy Hall, exhibited abundant generosity, as did many friends too numerous to list but without whose support we could not have continued. To them, to my parents, to my wife's parents, and to our families, I offer my deepest gratitude.

This book was made possible in part by funds granted to the author through a Charles H. Revson Foundation Fellowship at the Center for Advanced Holocaust Studies, United States Holocaust Memorial Museum. The statements made and views expressed, however, are solely the responsibility of the author. I am also grateful to the Emerging Scholars Publication Program at the Center for Advanced Holocaust Studies for its support in the preparation of the manuscript and of the book proposal. In particular, Steven Feldman gave helpful advice over many cups of coffee. I enjoyed my time as a Fellow at the Center immensely. I am grateful to staff there, especially Benton Arnovitz, Victoria Barnett, Suzanne Brown-Fleming, Robert Ehrenreich, Steven Feldman, Nicole Frechette, Michael Gelb, Dieter Kuntz, Jürgen Matthäus, Claire Rosenson, Traci Rucker, Joe White, and Lisa Yavnai, and to colleagues who were Fellows with me there.

I offer heartfelt appreciation to my friend and mentor Frank James, for recognizing and believing in my abilities. Thanks to Eckart Conze, Tanja Hetzer, Jochen-Christoph Kaiser, Roland Löffler, Wencke Meteling, and Antje Robrecht for their helpful feedback and warm hospitality during my travels in Germany. I am grateful to members of the faculty and staff of the history department at Royal Holloway. My advisor Rudolf Muhs has been especially helpful and supportive, offering numerous suggestions for reading and ideas for consideration. Jonathan Harris and Marie-Christine Ockenden provided continual assistance with practical matters.

My thanks are due to many skilled and obliging archivists and librarians: Michael Häusler, Johannes Röhm, and Birgit Spatz-Straube at the Archiv des Diakonischen Werkes der EKD in Berlin, Sona Eypper and Christiane Mokroß at the Evangelisches Zentralarchiv in Berlin, Katharina Schaal and the kind and attentive staff at the Archiv der Philipps-Universität Marburg of the Hessisches Staatsarchiv Marburg, the helpful staff of the Theological Faculty Library at Humboldt Universität in Berlin, Hans-Günther Kessler at the Landeskirchenarchiv der Ev.-Lutherischen Kirche in Thüringen (Eisenach), Karin Köhler at the Landeskirchliches Archiv Berlin-Brandenburg, Jürgen König at the Landeskirchliches Archiv der Evangelisch-Lutherischen Kirche in Bayern, Michlean Amir, Ron Coleman, and Vincent Slatt at the United States Holocaust Memorial Museum, Margit Hartleb and Rita Seifert at the Universitätsarchiv Jena, and Howard Falksohn and the helpful staff at the Wiener Library in London. For photographs, I would like to thank Judy Cohen, Gotthard Jasper, Jürgen König, and Caroline Waddell.

Many friends, colleagues, and scholars read drafts of chapters, offering helpful critiques and suggestions, including Rachel Anderson, Steve Cavallaro, David Cesarani, Christopher Clark, John Conway, Steven Feldman, Mary Fulbrook, Matthew Hockenos, Kyle Jantzen, Hartmut Lehmann, Rudolf Muhs, and Dan Stone. Others offered valuable feedback on conference papers drawn from chapter drafts or offered their insights in less formal settings. These include Victoria Barnett, Doris Bergen, Michael Berkowitz, Donald Bloxham, Christopher Browning, Eckart Conze, Martin Dean, Bob Ericksen, Susannah Heschel, Tanja Hetzer, Jürgen Matthäus, Kevin Spicer, Eric Steinhart, and Shulamit Volkov.

I have appreciated the skillful and helpful staff at Indiana University Press, including my editor Bob Sloan, copyeditor Joyce Rappaport, and project manager June Silay, as well as Rhonda Van der Dussen and Sarah Wyatt Swanson. Two anonymous readers provided invaluable feedback on the manuscript.

To our many dear friends in Orlando, London, and northern Virginia, who provided meals, breaks, and immeasurable friendship and moral support to my wife and me over these past eight years, I am deeply grateful. I am also appreciative of the advice and camaraderie of my colleagues and mentors at Howard Community College and University of Maryland University College, including Hanael Bianchi, Bob Bromber, Jerry Casway, Lisa Beth Hill, Dawn Malmberg, Margaret Wedde, and Joe White.

Last and most of all, I owe my deepest debt to my dear wife Rachel. She painstakingly combed through the manuscript at every stage of its production; even more importantly, she offered constant encouragement throughout the process of completing the book. Without her willing sacrifice and unending kindness, none of this would have been possible. Proverbs 18:22.

ABBREVIATIONS

AC	*Apologetische Centrale,* or Apologetics Center
ADW	*Archiv des Diakonischen Werkes der EKD*
BBK	*Biographisch-Bibliographisches Kirchenlexikon*
BDM	*Bund Deutscher Mädel,* or League of German Girls
BK	*Bekennende Kirche,* or Confessing Church
DC	*Deutsche Christen,* or German Christians
DDP	*Deutsche Demokratische Partei,* or German Democratic Party
EZA	*Evangelisches Zentralarchiv Berlin*
HStAM	*Hessisches Staatsarchiv Marburg*
Kd.	*Kamerad,* or comrade
LKA BB	*Landeskirchliches Archiv Berlin-Brandenburg*
LKA Eisenach	*Landeskirchenarchiv der Ev.-Lutherischen Kirche in Thüringen*
LKA Nuremberg	*Landeskirchliches Archiv der Evangelisch-Lutherischen Kirche in Bayern*
LW	Luther's Works
NSDAP	*Nationalsozialistische Deutsche Arbeiterpartei,* or National Socialist German Workers' Party (Nazi Party)

NS-Frauenschaft	National Socialist Women's Organization
OMGUS	Office of Military Government, United States
P.Z.	*Preußische Zeitung,* or *Prussian Newspaper*
RGG⁴	*Religion in Geschichte und Gegenwart,* 4th Edition
SA	*Sturmabteilung,* or Storm Troopers
SD	*Sicherheitsdienst,* or Security Service
Sopade	*Sozialdemokratische Partei Deutschlands,* or Social Democratic Party of Germany
SS	*Schutzstaffel*
UAJ	*Universitätsarchiv Jena*
USHMM	United States Holocaust Memorial Museum
VKL	*Vorläufige Kirchenleitung,* or Provisional Church Leadership of the German Protestant Church
WA	*Weimarer Ausgabe* (the Weimar Edition of Luther's Works)

DEMONIZING THE JEWS

INTRODUCTION

What shall we Christians
do now with this rejected,
cursed people, the Jews?
—Martin Luther, *On the
Jews and Their Lies*

. . . it is the inexorable Jew
who struggles for his
domination over the
nations. No nation can
remove this hand from its
throat except by the sword.
—Adolf Hitler, *Mein Kampf*

On January 10, 1934, German Protestant pastor Heinrich Fausel gave a lecture titled "Die Judenfrage" (The Jewish Question) at a completely filled town hall in Leonberg, near Stuttgart. Most of the second half of the address is dedicated to correcting extreme portrayals of Martin Luther's sixteenth-century rhetoric against Jews, which had gained some cultural currency in the late Weimar and early Nazi years. Even so, Fausel affirms many of the anti-Judaic and antisemitic stereotypes in Luther's writings. He also justifies early Nazi measures against Jews, describing immigration of Jews to Germany as a "threatening invasion" by a foreign people—"decadent Judaism."[1]

Nine years later, as the brutal onslaught of the so-called Final Solution was well underway, Fausel and his wife gave shelter to Herta Pineas. Their efforts were part of a "Rectory Chain" in which a group of pastors and parishioners sheltered at least seventeen Jewish refugees in sixty Württemberg church parsonages. Pineas was a Jewish woman who beginning in 1941 had helped to supply Berlin deportation transports before going into hiding in late February of 1943. She was part of a group of Jewish women— approximately forty to begin with, but dwindling to eight as many of the helpers were themselves deported—who provided scant amounts of food and drink for Jewish deportees and helped them find what luggage of theirs had not been confiscated by the Gestapo. Their work took place under strict Gestapo supervision. At the time of her stay in the Fausels' home, her husband Hermann, who had worked previously as a neurologist in Berlin, was in hiding in Austria. As a result of the Fausels' actions, and those of several other Protestant pastors and their families, Herta and Hermann survived the Holocaust, eventually emigrating to the United States.[2]

Such a course of action quite obviously came at great risk to the Fausels. Perhaps Pastor Fausel's attitudes toward Jews had changed dramatically between 1934 and 1943, leading him to offer shelter to this Jewish woman in fear of her life. Or, did he take this courageous action *despite* his anti-Judaic and antisemitic views? What role did Luther's writings play in his thinking? Fausel's views about and actions toward Jews, to which we will return in chapter four, serve as one window to wider Protestant views about Jews and Judaism during the Third Reich.

While the large-scale complicity and indifference of Protestants toward the plight of Jews in the face of dire events in Nazi Germany have been established previously, Luther's antisemitism as a contributor to these attitudes and actions often is either assumed as a given or left unexamined. I will demonstrate here via carefully situated case studies that a significant number of pastors, bishops, and theologians of varying theological and church-political persuasions utilized Luther's writings about Jews and Judaism with considerable effectiveness to reinforce the cultural antisemitism and Christian anti-Judaism already present in substantial degrees among Protestants in Nazi Germany. Further, I will show that anti-Judaism and antisemitism were intertwined, both in the reformer's writings and in those of his theological descendants in Nazi Germany.

This book, then, is an attempt to contribute to the long-standing and ongoing discussion about continuity and discontinuity in the history of antisemitism and anti-Judaism, particularly of the varieties found in Germany in the first half of the sixteenth century and in the first half of the twentieth century. The stress here will fall on the continuities. Yet, this is not an attempt to trace some straight line from Luther to Hitler. What separates this work from such an endeavor is its theoretical approach, which I will describe shortly.

The history of Christianity has been riddled with varying degrees of antisemitism, leading to oppression, marginalization, and—as in the Crusades and the Holocaust—murder of Jews. Though Martin Luther certainly did not invent antisemitism, one cannot discuss the question of Christian antisemitism without reference to this most prominent figure of the German Protestant Reformation. Luther wrote at least five treatises on the subject of "the Jews."[3] One work in particular, *Von den Juden und ihren Lügen* (On the Jews and Their Lies), has fueled the greatest discussion of the reformer's attitude toward Jews.

Over the last thirty years especially, the role of the Protestant church in Nazi Germany has been evaluated extensively by historians.[4] Further, there is a growing recognition of the role of ostensibly "academic" scholarship as a tool of the Nazi regime to accomplish the "coordination" (*Gleichschaltung*) of the German populace.[5] I will examine here Protestant responses to Luther's *Judenschriften* (his writings about Jews and Judaism) during the Nazi era with an eye to the broader social context, including both the church-political and academic-theological arenas.

When scholars of Nazi Germany and the Holocaust have addressed anti-Jewish attitudes and actions in German history, they have often spoken of antisemitism as a modern phenomenon, one that is steeped in racial rhetoric. Wilhelm Marr's invention of the term in 1879 is usually regarded as the starting point for antisemitism. Anti-Judaism, on the other hand, has often been regarded as a pre-modern, religiously based hatred of Jews.[6]

The historian of the medieval period Gavin Langmuir offers the most helpful definition of *antisemitism*, despite the fact that he must contend with the term's bedeviled past. Langmuir's schema will help us to separate simultaneously in our selected writings the anti-Judaic and antisemitic strands, and to observe how these two ways of thinking about Jews were often interwoven. It will help, first, to explain with greater clarity than previously how the nature of theological discourse shaped German Protestant approaches to the "Jewish Question." Secondly, it will provide an understanding of the nature of anti-Judaism and antisemitism that is more rounded, freeing the discussion from the far-too-rigid dichotomy of pre-modern theological anti-Judaism and modern racial antisemitism.

Langmuir defines the term most succinctly when he declares, "Antisemitism . . . both in its origins and in its recent most horrible manifestation, is the hostility aroused by irrational thinking about 'Jews.'" It is *irrational* thought, he argues, that characterizes antisemitism; *nonrational* thought characterizes anti-Judaism.[7] Whereas irrational thinking is the kind of thought that is in conflict with rational empirical observation, nonrational thinking does not conflict with rational thought and can utilize it in a "subordinate capacity."[8] "Like rational empirical thought," says Langmuir, "nonrational thought comes in many forms, one obvious example being poetry, for instance Solomon's 'Song of Songs' and the fascinating religious interpretations of it. What typifies nonrational thinking is that it typically gives the symbols it shares with rational thought a meaning very different from their meaning in practical or scientific discourse ('your name is oil poured out')." In its essence, then, nonrational language is the language of symbol, the kind of language found in art and affirmations of belief.[9]

Nonrational thought lies in fact at the heart of religion, Langmuir argues. Despite being rooted in a historical event—the crucifixion of Jesus of Nazareth around AD 30—the "nonrational symbol system" of the "Cross" is only "valid" for the Christians who espouse it. In fact, just what the "Cross" symbolizes for Christians can vary in different historical settings, as witnessed by the launching of the First Crusade in 1096.[10] When Luther says in *On the Jews and Their Lies* that "the Jews" have been "accused" of poisoning wells, kidnapping and (ritual) piercing of children, and "hacking them in pieces"—and implies that these accusations might be true—he is arguing *irrationally,* for his charges are in conflict with rational empirical thought. When he presents debate on the interpretation of significant and relevant biblical passages, he is arguing *nonrationally,* for he is interpreting and applying what he regards as divinely inspired truth to contemporary Jews.[11] These realities serve to illustrate a crucial point about the interaction of these two modes of thinking, which Langmuir explains with great clarity:

> . . . if the two kinds of mental processes are very different, we alternate
> between them so rapidly and frequently that their interplay is very hard
> to distinguish. Indeed, so much of our thought of both kinds is so ha-
> bitual, so much a reflex, that most of the time we are not aware of which
> way we are thinking.[12]

With Langmuir, I contend that the distinction between anti-Judaism as "theological" or "religious" hostility and antisemitism as "racial" animus is not empirically demonstrable and thus should be abandoned.[13] While it might be tempting to say that inhabitants of a post-Enlightenment secular era rationalize their behavior along distinctly nonreligious lines and that religious pre-moderns used theological rationales, these lines are not so clearly drawn, as both Luther's *Judenschriften* and their twentieth-century German Protestant appropriations demonstrate. The hard distinction between pre-modern and modern kinds of anti-Jewish hatred militates against a more nuanced approach, one which Langmuir's paradigm can provide. While his interdisciplinary approach has had its detractors, some historians, including Christopher Browning, Philippe Burrin, and Albert S. Lindemann, have embraced at least some aspects of Langmuir's approach.[14]

Historians of twentieth-century Germany in general and of the Nazi period in particular have not hesitated to recognize the irrationality of Hitlerian and Nazi antisemitism, whether they have used the precise language of rationality or not. Jeffrey Herf implies the irrationality of Hitler's view of Jews when he says that Hitler "spoke of a 'world' or 'international Jewry' as an actually existing political subject with vast power that was hostile to Germany."[15] Ian Kershaw describes Hitler's antisemitism, one of his "twin ideological obsessions" (the other being *Lebensraum,* the quest for "living space" in the East), as his "paranoid hatred of the Jews."[16]

On the other hand, many historians of the early modern period or the German Protestant Reformation have been reluctant to attribute to Luther anything other than an anti-Judaism shaped by theology. Most Reformation scholars, to one degree or another, accept a sharp division between a theologically defined anti-Judaism and a racially motivated antisemitism, leading them to discuss Luther's writings about Jews and Judaism primarily in terms of the former.[17]

Pre-modern Europeans, even academic theologians like Luther, could and did relate to "this-worldly" issues, despite living in a world where religion penetrated the public sphere as a matter of course. Sixteenth-century Protestant theological writings addressed all areas of life—social, cultural, political, and intellectual. Conversely, in the twentieth century, the Nazis had a "system" of using words that had "a religious structure yet a secular meaning," including *eternal, miracle,* and *piety.*[18] The Nazis "caricatured fundamental patterns of religious belief, in modern societies where sacralised collectivities, such as class, nation or race, had already supplanted God as objects of mass enthusiasm or veneration."[19]

The very idea of a "modern," "racial" variant of anti-Jewish hatred called antisemitism seems to presuppose that Enlightenment patterns of thinking somehow overwhelmed traditional religious modes of thought. While religious, specifically Christian, beliefs and social mores certainly were on the wane in late Weimar Germany and into the Third Reich, they were far from absent. As we will see, rational, nonrational, and irrational strands of thinking about Jews were all present in varying degrees in the writings of many German Protestant theologians and clergy. In a few cases, they subject the Enlightenment itself to withering attack.

I find that when discussing religious expressions of anti-Jewish hatred, the rational/nonrational/irrational rubric is greatly helpful, whether one is talking about the sixteenth century or the twentieth. Langmuir's schema is especially valuable as a means of demystifying theological reasoning, much of which can in fact be evaluated in a fairly objective manner along rational lines. It presents us with a highly useful tool for examining the history of anti-Jewish ideas as they are expressed in the writings of Luther, the early modern reformer, and of twentieth-century German Protestant theologians, pastors, and bishops. Anti-Judaic and antisemitic ideas about Jews in fact existed side-by-side in both Luther's writings and in those of many German Protestants living during the Nazi era.

Some have tried to exculpate Christians and Christianity from responsibility for complicity in the Holocaust by distinguishing anti-Judaism from antisemitism, with the former term representing a perhaps lamentable but less vitriolic form of prejudice. My employment of the terms, following Langmuir, is quite different. I seek to distinguish two types of hatred against Jews, neither of which is less reprehensible than the other.[20]

The role of Protestantism in Nazi Germany has been explored very thoroughly by scholars, demonstrating widespread apathy toward Nazi oppression and murder of Jews. Yet, German Protestant responses to Luther's antisemitic writings have been addressed only tangentially. I am aware of no works in which Luther's antisemitism has been the central issue.[21] In some, it has not been mentioned at all. The literature has also shown that no major faction in German Protestantism consistently spoke out in unified fashion on behalf of Jews during the Third Reich.

The name of Dietrich Bonhoeffer is perhaps so widely known today because of a deeply ironic fact—that so few of his fellow German Protestants, even within the generally Nazi-wary Confessing Church wing, spoke out on their behalf. Bonhoeffer's chief endeavors in helping unconverted Jews seem to have had a twofold interest. The first part was indirect—his involvement in the July 1944 assassination attempt against Hitler; the second, his part in an elaborate but successful plot to rescue about a dozen Jews ("Operation Seven"), was more direct. Despite a rather traditional anti-Judaic view of Jews up to the early years of the Third Reich, Bonhoeffer seems to have drifted gradually toward a more complex view, one in which he supported their human rights and deeply respected their contribution to Christianity, but in keeping with the prevailing view within the German Protestantism of his day still seemed to call for their conversion. Whatever the complexities in Bonhoeffer's thinking about Jews and Judaism, his remarkable biography has assured that his works are now justifiably regarded as "classic" texts.[22]

Yet, the work of historian Quentin Skinner has demonstrated the value of employing "minor" texts as a benchmark by which to judge the ideological content of such "major" or "classic" texts. The classic texts may in fact be *the worst guide to conventional wisdom: they are often classics because they challenge the commonplaces of the period.*[23] Thus, the works of such well-known figures as Bonhoeffer, Karl Barth, and Martin Niemöller are not dealt with here in any significant way.[24] Rather, books, articles, and pamphlets written by generally lesser-known theologians and clergy will be "dusted off" to give a clearer picture of conventional views about Jews and Judaism in the Protestantism of Nazi Germany. This will help to clarify the historical picture of German Protestantism by shedding light on one important slice of the conventional wisdom of the era. At the same time, we can begin to appreciate the challenge to these commonplaces represented by the work of "major" figures such as Bonhoeffer.

Having said this, there are several figures discussed in this book who were influential within German Protestantism. Paul Althaus was president of the Luther Society and professor of systematic theology at Erlangen University, the third largest Protestant theological faculty in Germany. Heinrich Bornkamm was president of the Protestant League, whose membership numbered in the hundreds of thousands. Thirty-seven thousand copies of Thuringian bishop Martin Sasse's notorious work *Martin Luther über die Juden: Weg mit Ihnen!* (Martin Luther on the Jews: Away with Them!) were printed within two weeks of its initial appearance.[25] Yet, the historical literature about German Protestantism during the Nazi era has demonstrated so far that very few major theological figures directly connected their views about Jews and Judaism to Luther's *Judenschriften*.[26]

Was the generally anemic response to anti-Jewish Nazi policy on the part of German Protestants due at least in part to the denigration of Jews and Judaism in Luther's writings, to a more general traditional Christian anti-Judaism, or to some other cultural, social, economic, or political factors particular to Germany in the first half of the twentieth century? We will observe here that Protestant responses to Luther's *Judenschriften* were an important part of the matrix of ideas about the increasingly beleaguered and persecuted Jewish minority swirling around German society during the Third Reich.

German Protestant responses to the Nazi ascent to power did not coalesce in a historical vacuum. The political antisemitism of the early years of the Wilhelmine period, aggravated by an economic downturn that began in 1873, gradually gave way to a "cultural code" of antisemitism within a nationalist worldview. In Imperial Germany, emancipation and antisemitism became "the signposts of two [co-existing] cultures." During the Wilhelmine years, the two could live in some tension with each other. The evolution of a socially acceptable antisemitism is a crucial part of the social and intellectual context for these years, which were formative for most of the theologians and clergy to be discussed in this book.

Yet, during the Weimar Republic, "the gulf between the two [co-existing cultures of antisemitism and emancipation] became ever deeper."[27] The two most important catalysts for the deepening of this gulf were no doubt Germany's defeat and humiliation in the First World War and the severe economic stresses of this era.[28] During the Nazi years, antisemitism was "fundamentally transformed"; it came to be linked with "the politics of violence, terror and extermination." Yet, the continuity of cultural and ideational antisemitism during the entirety of the period from 1871 to 1945 is inescapable. "Cultural symbols," historian Shulamit Volkov correctly notes, "have a curious tenacity."[29]

During the Third Reich, Protestants, who made up more than 60 percent of the total population in Germany, generally fell into three groups: the Confessing Church, the German Christians, and those who chose not to affiliate with either of these groups, which I will call here the Protestant "middle."[30] The German Christians espoused both ardent German nationalism and vituperative antisemitic sentiment. Far from being a marginal German Protestant group, as argued by some, they in fact were quite influential. The German Christians had the backing of the Nazis in the 1933 church elections for representatives to local church councils of the German Protestant Church (Deutsche Evangelische Kirche), which is one reason why they won a resounding victory.[31]

They remained generally enthusiastic backers of the Nazi regime, but this support increasingly went unrequited.[32] Though they comprised only a small minority of German Protestants (representing a mere 2 percent of the Protestant population), the German Christians made their influence fully felt throughout Germany.[33] At arguably their weakest point, there were 600,000 in their ranks. In 1937, they held twelve of the seventeen deanships in Protestant theology in German universities, along with more than a third of the total number of posts in the theology faculties.[34]

Members of the Confessing Church exhibited varying degrees of opposition to Nazi encroachment on church sovereignty, but only scattered opposition to measures against Jews.[35] Almost from the outset of Nazi rule, the Confessing Church opposed Nazi attempts to form a "Reich Church" based on a nebulous and variously defined "positive Christianity."[36] The key issue for many in the Confessing Church was not the antisemitism of the Nazis, but the efforts on their part to control the churches, something that could not be countenanced by a church grounded in scriptural and confessional unity. The language of the Barmen Declaration of 1934, the founding document and clarion call of the movement, makes this point abundantly clear.[37] While it opposed emphatically both the German Christians and so-called "Aryan" Christianity, the increasingly precarious predicament of German Jews did not appear in the declaration, foreshadowing the reality that many in the Confessing Church would show themselves to be either apathetic to their plight or antisemitic themselves.[38]

Clashes between the Confessing Church and the German Christians generally centered on theological and church-political concerns. This "Church Struggle" (Kirchenkampf), as it came to be called, was very real for its participants, particularly as it concerned the theological ideas at stake, despite the desire of some historians to present it as a mere power struggle. Yet, these divisions often masked an underlying consensus on what to do with or about the German Jewish community.

The majority of Protestants attempted to stay neutral in the Church Struggle—that is, they chose not to affiliate formally with either the German Christian or Confessing Church wings—but most held views of the Volk (the people of the German nation) as an "order of creation."[39] Systematic theologian Paul Althaus, of Erlangen University, was one of the most influential figures of the unaffiliated Protestant "middle," and the leading proponent of a theology shaped by "orders of creation" (*Schöpfungsordnungen*), of which the Volk was most crucial. This doctrine was married to an all-too-prevalent German nationalism. Steeped in the bitterness felt by many Germans toward the harsh terms inflicted upon the fatherland by the Treaty of Versailles and the perceived malaise of the Weimar era, this theological outlook provided fertile ground for both latent and overt anti-semitism.[40]

The German Protestant legend of the Church Struggle as a valiant fight against Nazism, which was propagated after the war mainly by pastors and theologians bent on painting their actions and that of their churches in the most sympathetic light, has been demythologized. Many of the churches in fact cooperated with Hitler, in effect (and in many cases in actuality) promulgating Nazi ideology, including antisemitism.[41] Pro-Nazi and anti-Jewish sentiment within the German Protestant Church during the Third Reich was abetted by an anti-democratic outlook and theological reappraisal spurred on by a decade-old Luther Renaissance, as well as by the now ready availability of a variety of editions of Luther's works.[42] A sizable, vocal minority avidly and openly supported the Nazis in their nefarious goals concerning the Jewish Question.

Since I have thus far painted such a dire portrait of German Protestantism's relationship to Jews and Judaism, it must also be recognized that overt resistance to Nazism and covert assistance for Jews living under Nazi oppression and threat of murder did exist in small corners of the German Protestant scene. The "Grüber Office," based in Berlin, provided Jews (including Jews who converted to Christianity) who were under grave threat from the Reich with advice about emigration, finding employment abroad, social assistance, legal matters, and educational support.[43] As noted earlier, a group of pastors and parishioners sheltered at least seventeen Jewish refugees in sixty church parsonages in a so-called "Rectory Chain" in Württemberg.

It should also be acknowledged that a fair amount of fluidity existed among the three broad groups within the Church Struggle—that is, the Confessing Church, the German Christians, and the unaffiliated Protestant middle. Fragmentation characterized the German Protestant Church during much of the Nazi era. Each wing had its own "moderates" and "radicals," whether we speak of theology or of politics.[44] Many pastors and even bishops changed their affiliations—especially (for many German Christians) after the November 1933 Sports Palace affair and (for many members of the Confessing Church) after the October 1934 Confessing Church synod at Dahlem.[45] Further, individual pastors and theologians could remain part of the unaffiliated middle even while exhibiting sympathy with either the Confessing wing or the German Christian camp. Church historians Heinrich Hermelink (Marburg) and Heinrich Bornkamm (Gießen and Leipzig) chose not to affiliate with either the German Christians or the Confessing Church. Yet, the former exhibited significant sympathy toward the Confessing Church, while the latter displayed ideological affinity with some German Christian ideas.[46] Significantly, and despite substantial ideological, political, and theological tensions, both the Confessing Church and the German Christians remained part of the German Protestant Church.[47]

On April 7, 1933, the Nazi regime introduced its first wave of sweeping repressive legislation, beginning with the Law for the Restoration of the Professional Civil Service. Paragraph 3 (which came to be known as the "Aryan Paragraph"), coupled with subsequently enacted legal decrees, effectively forbade Jews from employment as civil servants.[48] The introduction of the Aryan Paragraph into the German Protestant Church in September 1933 may be regarded as a seminal event in the Church Struggle. Subsequently reintroduced and repealed several times, it became a flashpoint for divisions among German Protestants, and led eventually to the formation of the Confessing Church. Again, it was primarily the issue of church autonomy, theologically considered, that colored the debates about the Aryan Paragraph, rather than the rights of Jewish Christian pastors, who constituted a miniscule percentage of the German Protestant clergy.[49] Debates around the Aryan Paragraph emerge in some of the writings to be examined in this book, but Luther's *Judenschriften* were rarely invoked in the larger debate about its implementation in the Protestant church.

As historians have attempted to explain the passive stance of most German Protestants in the face of Nazi persecution of Jews, the theme of Luther's so-called "two kingdoms doctrine" (*Zwei-Reiche Lehre*) and the closely related motif of obedience to the authorities have garnered the most attention. That Luther taught the existence of two kingdoms, one spiritual and the other temporal, is undeniable. That he taught that ordinary Christian citizens generally should obey authority is clear.[50] It is doubtful, however, that he encouraged the radical quiescence that has been assumed by many historians.[51] I do not wish to solve this conundrum here. In any case, the question of whether German Protestants believed that they were commanded by God to obey the Nazi authorities despite their evil intent is certainly valid, as is borne out by the recurrence of the theme in the pertinent literature.[52]

Other Luther-related themes—German nationalism, Christians and the law, Christian social ethics—have been addressed as well. The reformer's teachings on these issues are without doubt worthy of study. Lutheran views on authority are certainly crucial to understanding the German Protestant mindset in the face of the Nazi onslaught.

Yet, the fact that, first, no systematic two kingdoms doctrine exists in Luther's writings, and, second, that the Luther as "prophet of the state" legend (the "Luther-Bismarck myth") is spurious, should lend pause to those who would want to attribute some causality to Luther's teaching, even as it concerned the Jewish people.[53] The responses to a text (or group of texts) in a particular historical context should not lead us to find an author guilty of offenses committed some four centuries later—provided that the author is not exonerated for the actual "crimes" he may have committed.

Having said this, I will demonstrate in chapter two that Luther's *On the Jews and Their Lies* may be said to contain *both* anti-Judaic and antisemitic rhetoric. Some of his recommendations for social and political action against Jews anticipate the so-called Nuremberg Race Laws, which were passed hastily after the Nazi Party rally in Nuremberg in September 1935 and effectively rendered German Jews as second-class citizens. Luther also recommended to the authorities that Jewish schools and synagogues be burned to the ground. The specter of burning synagogues calls to mind the destruction of hundreds of Jewish synagogues across Germany on November 9 and 10, 1938, commonly referred to as Kristallnacht ("the night of broken glass").

This certainly should not tempt us to reach for overly simplistic conclusions (e.g., "Luther's sixteenth-century antisemitism caused the Holocaust," or even "Luther's antisemitism nurtured subsequent German Protestant antisemitism"). To do so would involve ignoring the many other complex factors of life in Germany—political, economic, social, and cultural—during the Nazi period. No amount of anti-Judaic and antisemitic theological writing—no matter how harsh or deprecating—could have led by itself to the mass murder of Jews in Nazi Germany. Other extreme ideologies, such as ardent nationalism and fervent anti-Bolshevism, certainly played their part. So, too, did massive industrialized killing introduced by the war. And, of course, the onset of the Holocaust cannot really be understood without probing the agency of Hitler himself.[54] Embracing overly simplistic conclusions would also entail disregard for both Luther's theological outlook and the vastly dissimilar cultural and intellectual environment of sixteenth-century Germany. Yet, surely many Protestants in Hitler's Germany might have read Luther's recommendations and sensed the congruities with the gruesome antisemitic program unfolding around them.

I will utilize Langmuir's approach here as a tool to explain more precisely than before the nature of anti-Judaic and antisemitic argumentation in Protestant theological writings about Jews and Judaism from 1933 to 1945. Relatively minor and previously unexamined Protestant writings about Luther's *Judenschriften* will be analyzed in light of Langmuir's theory. We will see that Luther employed anti-Judaic *and* antisemitic arguments and that many Protestant clergy and theologians living in Germany during the Third Reich interpreted and promulgated the nonrational and irrational elements of his thinking about Jews. This approach will help to reveal the general continuities present in German Protestant thought about Jews and Judaism that have often been obscured by a too strictly chronological approach to the discussion of early modern and modern hatred of Jews.

I also will take into account throughout the book the particularities of life in Nazi Germany, especially as they relate to Protestant clergy and theologians. In chapter four, I will examine briefly the solidarity that often existed between clergy and laity. While much more research needs to be done in the area of lay attitudes toward Jews and Judaism, the Church Struggle, and Nazism, I will show that the general pattern, as reflected in theological publications, seems to suggest that their attitudes mirrored those of their pastors. If this is true, then the ideas about Luther, Jews, and Judaism to be uncovered in the chapters that follow were disseminated relatively widely among the members of the largest theological confession in Nazi Germany.

In this study, we will see that Luther's writings about Jews and Judaism indeed were consulted and expounded upon by a considerable minority of Protestant theologians, pastors, and bishops with varying church-political and theological affiliations, from different generations, and from different regions in Germany. On all sides of the church-political and theological divides in the rocky intellectual terrain of the Church Struggle, Protestants were referencing and analyzing the German reformer's sixteenth-century works about Jews and Judaism. While this commonality should be recognized, these works were utilized across the Protestant theological landscape in diverse manners.

Theologians, pastors, and bishops who were active members of the German Christians consistently embraced Luther's irrational antisemitic rhetoric as their own, frequently pairing it with idealized portraits of "Teutonic" or "German" greatness, anti-Bolshevism, and anti-Enlightenment sentiment. Clergy and theologians active in the Confessing Church usually emphasized Luther's nonrational anti-Judaic arguments against Jews, while either maintaining silence toward Luther's irrational rhetoric or tacitly approving State involvement along the lines of Luther's social program. Most were quick to distance their rhetoric (and the reformer's) from the "racial" antisemitism employed by both the German Christians and the Nazis. Pastors and theologians not affiliated with either the Confessing Church or the German Christians exhibited consistently anti-Judaic and at times antisemitic appropriation of Luther's *Judenschriften*. Clergy and theologians from this middle grouping often played upon long-standing xenophobic images, such as the association of Jews with usury.

Luther's treatises about Jews and Judaism were potentially powerful weapons in the anti-Judaic and antisemitic arsenal of Nazi-era German Protestants. A significant minority of theologians and clergy from their ranks mined these treatises for material relevant to surrounding events—especially the Nuremberg Race Laws and Kristallnacht, but also the Second World War. They employed the reformer's treatises in church gazettes, theological journals, apologetic pamphlets and books, and even multivolume works, either focusing directly on the topic of "Luther and the Jews" or utilizing their arguments to support pieces about topical and theological issues, including Bolshevism, the validity of the Old Testament, and baptism of Jews. Some could openly embrace anti-Enlightenment sentiment in respectable and well-received theological writings, signifying decidedly anti-modern tendencies in their thinking.

If individual pastors were influential among their dozens or hundreds of congregants (and those who were published would have had a wider reach), academic theologians, who trained these pastors, held broader sway. This influence probably diminished somewhat after the number of students pursuing theological studies plummeted along with the rest of the population in German universities.[55] Even so, those who published widely and led academic and theological societies helped to mold opinion on weighty manners that certainly included the place of Jews in the Protestant church and in German society more generally. Thus, a substantial number of religious leaders within the Protestant church, including pastors like Heinrich Fausel, helped to shape in an appreciable manner the ways in which many German Protestants viewed Jews and Judaism in the increasingly dire environs of Nazi Germany.

1

PROTESTANTISM
IN
NAZI GERMANY

At the 1927 Königsberg Protestant Church Congress, Paul Althaus gave
a rousing and groundbreaking keynote address on *Kirche und Volkstum*
(Church and Nationality). In it, he offered a carefully constructed new
political theology that railed against a "foreign invasion" (*Überfremdung*)
in the areas of the arts, fashion, and finance, which he believed had led
to a disintegration of the national community (*Volksgemeinschaft*). The
present distress of the German Volk, he charged, was due to the "Jewish
threat." The church's attempts to penetrate the Volk with the Gospel were
opposed by "Jewish influence" in economics, the press, the arts, and literature. Althaus had captured perceptively the mood of Weimar Protestants

and provided theological legitimacy for *völkisch* (nationalistic) thinking in their ranks.

Althaus was one of the most prominent and prolific theologians of the late Weimar and Nazi eras. His carefully constructed doctrine of the "orders of creation" influenced large numbers of German Protestants during late Weimar and the Third Reich. The importance of this innovative theological construct during the Nazi era, its consequences for German Protestant ideology, as well as the influence of its progenitor, require careful examination, which I will undertake shortly. First, however, a few words are in order about some key interpretive issues, the evolution of antisemitism in modern Germany, and some important developments in German Protestantism during the 1920s and 1930s.

Issues of Interpretation

Antisemitism, Anti-Judaism, and Modernity

As I noted in the introduction, scholars who study the history of anti-Jewish hatred often disagree about just what constitutes "antisemitism." Reformation historian Heiko Oberman, for example, distinguished between antisemitism as racially motivated hatred and "anti-Judaism" as hatred motivated by theological conviction. Even so, he recognized the "crossovers and points of transgression" between the two. Many others have made similar distinctions.[1]

Nineteenth-century French Jewish intellectual and early Zionist Bernard Lazare maintained that the term *antisemitism* may only be applied to pre-nineteenth-century events and attitudes anachronistically, given that the term originated with Wilhelm Marr in the last third of the nineteenth century in Germany. Lazare generally used the term *anti-Judaism* to describe theologically based hatred for Jews as it existed in the late medieval and Reformation periods. He usually employed the terms *modern anti-Semitism* and *ethnological anti-Semitism* to denote the form that primarily encompasses racial and/or nationalistic overtones.[2]

Hannah Arendt forcefully argued that antisemitism and "Jew-hatred" are two different yet related ideologies. She regarded as "fallacious" the idea of an "unbroken continuity of persecutions, expulsions and massacres" that is "frequently embellished by the idea that modern antisemitism is no more than a secularised version of popular medieval superstitions."

She also linked the decline of "traditional nationalism" and the "precarious balance of power" of European nation-states to the proportional rise in "modern" antisemitism.[3] Arendt's approach thus reflects a very common distinction between a traditional Christian anti-Judaism and a modern, more secular version of anti-Jewish hatred called antisemitism.[4]

I argued in the introduction that the strict distinction between pre-modern and modern kinds of anti-Jewish hatred should give way to a more nuanced approach. Langmuir's typology, which stresses the fluidity of modes of thought within and across historical eras rather than supposedly static ways of thinking over centuries-long historical periods, can provide this nuance. Some caveats and clarifications about my application of Langmuir's theory are necessary.

First, I do not seek to apply slavishly his theory of history, religion, and antisemitism in its totality here, but rather to appropriate dynamically its most salient argument in the arena of German Protestant theology in the 1930s and 1940s. He has a great deal to say about history and religion that I will not address here. He distinguishes, for example, between religion as "the most enduring and general *social* expression of nonrational thought" and religiosity as "the most enduring form of *individual* nonrational thinking." Religion and religiosity are thus both products of nonrational thinking.[5] I find this distinction both helpful and well reasoned. Yet, it will not find its way into this work in any significant way.

Second, with Langmuir, I do not think it correct to limit the presence of antisemitism to the last third of the nineteenth century and forward, as do those who accept Marr's coinage of the term as their absolute point of departure for the historical phenomenon of antisemitism. This is not to deny that such modern phenomena as "political antisemitism" and "antisemitism as a cultural code" are valid historical frameworks.[6] Though I will not attempt to do so here, Langmuir's approach can be integrated with these constructions.

Third, Langmuir also defined *xenophobic* assertions as "*propositions that grammatically attribute a socially menacing conduct to an outgroup and all its members but are empirically based only on the conduct of a historical minority of the members. . . .*"[7] One example of this phenomenon is the association of Jews with usury. While a small number of sixteenth-century Jews were in fact guilty of usury, the use of the terms *Jew* and *usurer* as synonymous, which was prevalent at the time, qualifies as xenophobia.[8]

Many twentieth-century German Protestants utilized such xenophobic assertions as well, but often these only served to augment nonrational and irrational thinking about Jews.

One might conclude that Langmuir simply replaced the idea of religious anti-Judaism with nonrational anti-Judaism, or that racial antisemitism correlates neatly with irrational thought about Jews. This would be a misunderstanding of Langmuir's schema. The notion of "racial" antisemitism should be viewed as a modern subset of irrational antisemitism. Other forms of irrational antisemitism include the predominant anti-Jewish accusations of the medieval period, including ritual murder and host desecration. "Religious" hatred of Jews correlates even less directly to nonrational anti-Judaism than does "racial" antisemitism to irrational antisemitism. "Religious" or "theological" writings about Jews have often intermingled both nonrational and irrational forms of thought. We will observe many examples of this in chapters three through six.

It is Langmuir's emphasis on typology (the various employments of rationality, nonrationality, and irrationality) that distinguishes it from the essentially chronological usage (modern "racial" antisemitism vs. pre-modern "religious" anti-Judaism). The typological approach works better because of its appropriate muddying of the chronological waters and its emphasis upon the presence (or absence) of human reason. Despite varying historical situations, mixed motives for anti-Jewish hatred have long existed in Christian theological writings. As we will see, anti-Judaic and antisemitic ideas about Jews existed side-by-side in both Luther's writings and in those of many German Protestants living during the late Weimar and Nazi eras.

"Minor" Texts and Conventional Wisdom

Peter L. Berger and Thomas Luckmann, arguing for the "social construction of reality," declare, "Only a very limited group of people in any society engages in theorizing, in the business of 'ideas,' and the construction of Weltanschauungen [worldviews]. But everyone in society participates in its 'knowledge' in one way or another."[9] We will later examine separate subgroups of Nazi-era German Protestants—academic theologians, pastors, and bishops from the Confessing Church, the German Christians, and the Protestant middle—each of whom read and interpreted Luther's anti-Jewish texts in a shared social context.

Since ideas tend to be passed on through socially constructed institutions, my analysis will proceed with an eye to the social context. I will concentrate on clergy and theologians who shaped ideas within German Protestantism, but—in keeping with Skinner's stress on minor as opposed to classic texts—include mainly "lesser" figures from a variety of regions and church-political factions.

I will present a number of socially situated case studies to advance the history of the ideas about Jews and Judaism present in Luther's writings as they were interpreted and passed on by German Protestant clergy and theologians in Nazi Germany. This emphasis on texts is intentional, as I am convinced that the transmission of ideas—especially as it occurs among "minor" rather than "classic" figures—has not been applied rigorously enough to Protestant pastors and theologians in Nazi Germany in the English language literature on the subject.[10]

Despite their general categorization as "minor" figures, the clergy and periodicals consulted are not confined to one region, but represent a fairly significant portion of the Protestant population across Germany in the 1930s. The total circulation of German Christian periodicals overseen by German Christian press superintendent Heinz Dungs (see chapter five) was over 100,000 by 1941. In part because of the bans imposed by the Reich Press Chamber (see chapter four), figures for Confessing Church publications are much harder to ascertain.

Langmuir's stress upon the importance of nonrational expression to anti-Judaic thinking and irrational expression to antisemitic thought, Skinner's emphasis on minor texts, and Berger and Luckmann's concern for the sociological nature of knowledge will form important aspects of the interpretative framework of this book. The socially contextualized case study will be the primary method utilized throughout.

Antisemitism in Germany between 1871 and 1945

Historian Shulamit Volkov writes

> The history of antisemitism in Nazi Germany tends to be written from the perspective of antisemitism in the nineteenth century and vice versa; the history of nineteenth-century antisemitism has been normally written, and perhaps can only be written, from the perspective of the Nazi era.

With piercing clarity, she continues that historians

> are always concerned with the tension between continuity and break.
> . . . In the last resort, the two are always intertwined, only mixed in
> varying degrees. Clearly, from a historical point of view, every event is
> rooted in the past, but at the same time, every phenomenon is at least
> in some way new and unique. *The ongoing debate on break and continu-*
> *ity is thus only about the correct proportions. One cannot hope to decide*
> *between the two; one can only judge their relative importance.*[11]

I am attempting here, as I have already mentioned, to contribute to the
long-term and ongoing discussion about continuity and discontinuity in
the history of antisemitism and anti-Judaism, particularly of the varieties
found in Germany in the first half of the sixteenth century and in the first
half of the twentieth century.

Yet, for obvious reasons—not the least of which being that I will examine works written mainly by individuals who experienced their formative
years during the Wilhelmine era—the best place to begin situating both
their personal history and thought is in the Kaiserreich. Their experiences
and modes of thinking during the Nazi era were both rooted in the past
and unique to the mores and vagaries of the uneasy waning years of the
Weimar Republic and the ascent, rule, and demise of the Nazi regime. We
will discover here, in some measure, a perspective on the right balance between continuity and break in German Protestant writings about Luther,
Jews, and Judaism.

Antisemitism as a Cultural Code

One of the most influential contributions to the historiography of antisemitism in Imperial Germany is Shulamit Volkov's offering in the 1978 *Leo
Baeck Institute Yearbook,* titled "Antisemitism as a Cultural Code." Volkov
makes several acute observations there that will be invaluable for situating
the social and intellectual context for those years that were formative for
most of the individuals discussed in this book.

Volkov recognizes first of all the centrality of continuity to the discussion of antisemitism in Germany *during the modern period* but rejects the
outdated notion of conceiving of modern antisemitism as "yet another
manifestation of 'eternal hatred. . . .'" Paul Massing and Peter G. J. Pulzer both emphasized a "new departure" in the history of antisemitism in
Germany with the emergence of *political* antisemitism in the 1870s. This

period of political antisemitism stretched all the way from (nineteenth-century Berlin court preacher) Adolf Stöcker to Adolf Hitler.[12] Despite this, scholarly consensus was reached on the issue of political antisemitism; the antisemitic political parties had already by the 1890s lost the backing of the populace and suffered "total annihilation at the polls."

Due at least in part to the decline of its political form, antisemitism was no longer taken seriously by its opponents. This underestimation allowed its spread into various cultural groupings and associations, including clergy (especially within Protestantism), students' organizations, and teachers. It had not weakened—it had simply changed forms. Antisemitism was now rife in German society.[13]

Though no "direct link" can be established between the antisemitic political parties of Imperial Germany and Nazism, a "continuous line" can be traced, a line that would trace their disintegration and reappearance in new organizations. There was no "appreciable slackening of antisemitism in Germany during the pre-war years, nor even during the war itself," argues Volkov. "Nazi antisemitism took new forms and showed unparalleled intensity, but it grew upon the institutional structure provided by Wilhelminian society."[14] Modern antisemitism had taken both political and social forms in Germany, but the political version, while perhaps very weak during the 1890s, did not meet with its ultimate demise. It in fact experienced an unseemly resuscitation in Nazism.

Wilhelminian society went through a process of "cultural polarization." At these two poles, two "cultures" were formed that were signified and defined by two ideas: antisemitism and emancipation. By the end of the nineteenth century, antisemitism had become a cultural code. "It became a part of their language, a familiar and convenient symbol." Nevertheless, at this point at least, it was "mainly verbal and of little *practical* importance in deciding the more crucial issues of the day. . . ."[15]

How, then, Volkov inquires, did antisemitism "come to play so central a role in the culture of Imperial Germany?" What were its causes? Despite granting that "pre-capitalist classes of society" experienced distress during the industrial age, Volkov cavils at attempts to center the cause for antisemitism in this setting in the "economic experience" of artisans and other affected groups.[16]

Volkov rightly insists that antisemitism "was not a direct reaction to actual circumstances." To establish an important congruence between Volkov and Langmuir, I will quote her at some length.

In fact, men do not react directly to events. Through a process of con-ceptualisation and verbalisation men construct an interpretation of their experience, and it is only to their man-made conception of reality that they are then capable of responding. Any interpretation of reality is an independent, creative product of the human mind, and it is often all the more powerful for being partially or entirely false. In order to provide the link between conditions of stress and the particular response of Ger-mans in the late nineteenth century, we must probe not only into the actual circumstances of the time but also into the process of cognition which interpreted, and in its own way created, these circumstances; into the process of symbolic formulation that produced the unique antise-mitic ideology and gave it its central cultural role.[17]

Langmuir and Volkov portray "reality" in very similar terms: Volkov call-ing it an "independent, creative product of the human mind" and Lang-muir regarding it as what human beings think about "everything known or unknown that exists."[18]

In the context of the onset of economic depression in 1873 in post-emancipation Germany, a group of successful publicists, including notably Wilhelm Marr, were able to link antisemitism cognitively with an anti-modern worldview. Marr's new terminology, *Antisemitismus*, brilliantly and nefariously made hatred of Jews both symbolic and "scientific": "A new term was needed to express the symbolic process through which anti-Jewish attitudes were made analogous for a whole series of other views." The new term had at least the appearance of resulting from scientific rigor, but also had the ambiguity to allow it to serve as an umbrella for a whole complex of connections, making it a "short-hand substitute for an entire culture." Berlin historian Heinrich von Treitschke helped to make anti-semitism culturally acceptable in bourgeois society and introduced it into the universities. He coined—or perhaps more accurately, recaptured—a phrase that would reverberate right into the Nazi era: "*Die Juden sind unser Unglück* [The Jews are our misfortune]."[19]

As noted in the introduction, in Imperial Germany, emancipation and antisemitism became signposts of two cultures that came to live in ten-sion with each other during the Wilhelmine years. During the Weimar Republic, catalyzed by Germany's national defeat and humiliation in the First World War and the extreme economic pressures of the era, the chasm between the two became ever more pronounced. Fundamentally trans-formed during the Nazi years, antisemitism was linked with political vio-lence, terror, and extermination.[20]

Antisemitic Movements in Imperial Germany

A number of figures appeared on the scene in Imperial Germany whose ideas about Jews and Judaism gained significant airing in Protestant circles. Adolf Stöcker was court preacher in Berlin from 1874. Embarking on a "crusade to win back the working classes from the influence of Social Democracy," he founded the Christian Social Party, which stood for election during the 1880s on an expressly antisemitic platform. He was in fact able to blame Jews not only for social democracy, but for capitalism and the sedition of the working classes as well.[21] Connecting liberal positions to Jewish power, he introduced a "new level of anti-Semitic rhetoric" to German politics.[22] Heinrich Bornkamm, one of the Protestant academic theologians that we will encounter again later, saw this connection in a positive light, declaring that Stöcker saw the "internal interconnectedness (*Verflochtenheit*) of social democracy with liberalism overall, in particular with Judaism."[23]

Other significant figures in the antisemitic movements of the Kaiserreich and the Weimar era include Theodor Fritsch and H. S. Chamberlain. Fritsch attempted to pull together the various "strands of political antisemitism and direct the movement's appeal towards the economically discontented urban lower middle class" and spread his ideas via numerous antisemitic tracts, published from the 1880s all the way through to his death in 1933 and beyond.[24]

Houston Stewart Chamberlain, born in 1855 in Southsea, England, "fell under the spell of Wagnerism" while living in Dresden in the 1880s. Having written three works about Wagner in the 1890s, he was invited by his German publisher to write a study that "would take overall stock of the condition of modern civilisation" at the close of the nineteenth century. The resulting two-volume work was published in 1899 as *Die Grundlagen des neunzehnten Jahrhunderts* (The Foundations of the Nineteenth Century).[25] It, like Fritsch's *Handbuch der Judenfrage* (Handbook on the Jewish Question), enjoyed much success.

In it, Chamberlain marries optimism about advances in racial science to the notion of a superior "Aryan" race in fierce competition with Jews for superiority in the world. Michael Burleigh and Wolfgang Wippermann credit him with "fusing racial-hygienic and Social Darwinist ideas with antisemitism."[26] Yet, it is the author's predilection toward Protestant Christianity—albeit a very nontraditional version—that made this work fodder for praise in German Christian publications. Though not quite declaring Jesus to be an Aryan, he argued that Jesus was not, in fact, "racially" Jewish. The Protestant Reformation is seen as a great achievement for the Teutons. Luther is presented like a Wagnerian hero:

> One can picture this man fifteen hundred years ago, on horseback, swinging his battle-axe to protect his beloved northern home, and then again at his fireside with his children crowding around him, or at the banquet of the men, draining the horn of mead to the last drop and singing heroic songs in praise of his ancestors.[27]

The practice of attributing idealized character traits and physical attributes to German "heroes," "Teutomania," had a long pedigree and was common to racist discourse in modern Germany.[28] Portraits like these helped convey the image of a heroic Luther that would persist right through to the Third Reich.

German Protestantism during Weimar and the Third Reich

Some highly germane developments took place in German Protestantism between the end of the First World War and the rise of the Nazis. The first was the continuing publication of the Weimar edition of Luther's works. This project began in 1883, the four-hundredth anniversary of Luther's birth. Divided into four parts, *Werke* (Works), *Briefwechsel* (Correspondence), *Tischreden* (Table Talks), and *Deutsche Bibel* (German Bible), the Weimar edition became and remains the standard critical edition of Luther's writings.[29] Volume 53 of *Werke,* which contains both of Luther's most controversial anti-Jewish treatises, *Von den Juden und ihren Lügen* (On the Jews and Their Lies) and *Vom Schem Hamphoras und vom Geschlecht Christi* (On the Ineffable Name and on the Lineage of Christ), appeared in 1919. In addition to this authoritative critical edition, many editions of selected works and correspondence appeared as well.[30] Further, topical works regarding Luther's approach to a myriad of issues—including his engagement with the Jewish people—appeared with some frequency.[31]

The second important development was the appearance of two competing theological movements that are referred to as "Dialectical Theology" and the "Luther Renaissance." The latter was a scholarly renewal of interest in Luther that encompassed attempts by theologians to rediscover the reformer—the German who introduced the Protestant Reformation to Europe—in the postwar era. The chief early protagonist of the movement was Karl Holl. Holl delivered a memorial lecture at Berlin University on October 31, 1917—the four-hundredth anniversary of the beginning of the Protestant Reformation—on Luther's view of religion. This may be viewed as the starting point for the movement.[32] Holl's continued and innovative work in the area of Luther studies may be seen as a theological response to the liberal Protestant religious philosophy of Ernst Troeltsch. Emanuel Hirsch was a pupil of Holl, as was fellow German Christian Erich Vogelsang. The erudite Hirsch became the leading light of both the Luther Renaissance and the German Christian movement. Politically, proponents of the Luther Renaissance exhibited a "decidedly conservative tendency."[33] Though the writings of the movement were primarily concerned with theology, anti-democratic sentiments resonated with many of its adherents. This resurgence of interest in Luther carried over into the Nazi era.

Yet, it was not the protagonists of the Luther Renaissance alone that embraced a return to the theology of the Protestant Reformation. Dialectical Theology, led by Karl Barth, Rudolf Bultmann, Emil Brunner, and Friedrich Gogarten, "rejected the dominant tradition of nineteenth-century German cultural Idealism. . . . In its place, it provided a new foundation for Protestant faith with a revival of the theology of the Word of God as proclaimed by the Reformers," primarily Martin Luther and John Calvin.[34]

We will not concern ourselves here with the intricacies of and debates between the Luther Renaissance and Dialectical Theology, as fascinating as they are. The complex theological issues involved were very real at the time, but did not necessarily play important roles in determining views about the so-called "Jewish Question." Yet, those associated with the Luther Renaissance were generally more susceptible to nationalistic and antisemitic sentiments than those in the Barthian camp. This is not to argue, however, that anti-Judaism and antisemitism were completely lacking in the latter grouping. Did the publication of Luther's works and the related reappraisal of reformational theology include the reformer's answer to the "Jewish Question"? As we will see in the succeeding chapters, the works of many German Protestant theologians, pastors, and bishops provide an affirmative answer.

The third development concerns the profound sense of nationalism felt by German Protestants since the birth of the modern German nation. Back in the time of Bismarck, the Protestant church had served, effectively, as an arm of the state. Wilhelm I, who was not only Kaiser, but head of the Prussian church as well, demanded the Protestant church's loyalty to the state and its institutions. From this time forward, for large swathes of the Protestant populace, Protestantism and nationalism generally went hand in hand. Decades later, in the anxious atmosphere of late Weimar, the Protestant population "provided the broadest and deepest reservoir of support for the Nazi party in all social groups during its electoral triumphs of the early 1930s."[35]

Paul Althaus and "Orders of Creation" Theology

Althaus was born the son of a Lutheran pastor and theologian in 1888 in Obershagen, near Hanover. In 1914, he became lecturer (*Privatdozent*) at Göttingen, where he completed his *Habilitation* in the same year.[36] Shortly thereafter, he went off to be a chaplain for the German army in the First World War, serving a German community at Łódź in occupied Poland. It was during this time, argues Tanja Hetzer, that Althaus began to engage himself extensively with German völkisch ideas. The bitterness of Germany's ignominious defeat in the war and the imposition of what many Germans considered the excessively harsh terms of the Versailles treaty led Althaus to support "right wing, stab-in-the-back interpretations" of his homeland's wartime demise.[37]

In 1919 he became full professor at Rostock. He attained the chair of systematic theology at Erlangen in 1925. The post provided him with a prominent platform within German Protestantism, as Erlangen was the third-largest Protestant theological faculty in Germany. Since it was the only Protestant theological faculty in predominantly Catholic Bavaria, nearly all future Protestant ministers in that province would sit under Althaus's teaching.[38]

One year later, Althaus replaced the recently and suddenly deceased Holl as president of the Luther Society, a post that he would hold for thirty years. He published theological works at a prolific rate. At the 1927 Königsberg Protestant Church Congress, he gave the previously mentioned keynote address on "Church and *Volkstum*," offering his new political theology that railed against the "foreign invasion" which he believed had led to a breakdown of the national community. This present distress of the German *Volk* was due to the "Jewish threat." Receptivity to the Christian Gospel was inhibited by "Jewish influence" in economics, the press, the arts,

Paul Althaus as professor in Rostock. Professor Dr. Gotthard Jasper,
Paul-Althaus-Archiv.

Paul Althaus as professor in Erlangen. Professor Dr. Gotthard Jasper,
Paul-Althaus-Archiv.

View of Nürnberger Tor, one of the entrances to the University of Erlangen,
on top of which a banner has been placed stating that Jews are not desired here.
United States Holocaust Memorial Museum, courtesy of
Stadtarchiv und Stadtmuseum Erlangen.

and literature.[39] Althaus had his finger on the pulse of Weimar Protestants.
The lecture indeed "laid the popular basis for a theological legitimation of
the völkisch movement."[40]

Some time in the early 1930s he joined the right-wing Christlich-
deutsche Bewegung (Christian-German Movement). In 1932, Althaus attached himself to the more radical Faith Movement of German Christians,
soon famously welcoming the rise of Hitler with the words, "Our Protestant churches have greeted the German turning point of 1933 as a gift and
miracle of God." Yet, that year he became disillusioned with the politics
and theological extremism of the German Christians.[41]

In autumn 1933, after some in the German Christian movement recommended the implementation of the "Aryan Paragraph" in the German
Protestant Church, the Marburg theological faculty responded with a

Gutachten (advisory opinion) in which they described the policy, which forbade the employment of civil servants of "non-Aryan" origin, as inconsistent with Christian teaching. The theology faculty at Erlangen drafted Althaus and his colleague Werner Elert to write a response. Since the German Volk was being threatened by Jews, the church, they argued, must support it by "demand(ing) of its Jewish Christians that they hold themselves back from official positions." Despite such views, Althaus was regarded by his peers as a model of scholarly affability and moderation.[42]

After the war, Althaus was for a brief period chair of a commission set up by the American occupation authorities to oversee denazification at Erlangen University. This lasted until February 1947, when he was suspended from his teaching post for his pro-Hitler, anti-Weimar rhetoric during the Third Reich and for using his position on the denazification commission to reinstate "anti-democratic" professors. In late December, he was found not guilty by the denazification board. The military government reinstated him as professor at Erlangen in February 1948. He retained his chair until he retired, and died in 1966.[43]

"The Voice of the Blood" (1932)

In addition to being an active churchman and prolific writer of theological texts, Althaus was also a gifted preacher. On Good Friday in 1930, he preached a sermon for a radio address for a Bavarian Protestant morning worship hour. Reprinted in 1932 in a collection of Althaus's sermons, it was titled "Die Stimme des Blutes" (The Voice of the Blood).[44]

The homily is essentially an affirmation of the importance of the crucifixion—and particularly the shed blood—of Christ. Using stirring and effectual personification, Althaus proclaims that Good Friday has a voice that wants to speak, if only his audience would be (figuratively) quiet enough to listen. "The powerful voice of Good Friday is the voice of the blood of Jesus Christ," he exhorts. This blood speaks "words of mediation and reconciliation."[45] He weaves a tapestry of images of the shedding of blood that bolster the effectiveness of his appeal to remember the crucifixion of Christ and its importance. "Here where blood flows, the depths of history come to light." No Volk becomes great or free "without having to spill blood!" Blood has flowed between competing peoples, ethnic groups, political parties, even churches. "There is nothing noble in human history, which did not cost blood. . . . Volk and *Vaterland,* homeland and faith, justice and truth—they all cost blood. . . ." Continuing the nationalistic theme, he illustrates further the importance of shedding blood by appealing first to the words on a German memorial to fallen soldiers and then to a song composed by a German poet during the First World War.[46]

Althaus also intermingles the nationalistic impulse with a traditional emphasis on Jewish responsibility for the crucifixion of Jesus. Not only has the blood of the (biblical) prophets flowed, but the blood of Jesus has also been spilled. He quotes a New Testament passage concerning the Jewish people, "'He came to his own, and his own did not accept him!'" Christ's blood now "speaks"—in fact it "screams." "Against whom does it witness? Certainly first against the Volk from whom Christ came, whom He served. . . ."[47] With increasing intensity, he leads to the seemingly inevitable conclusion, "Until the end of history the terrible word of an unsuspecting realization [looms] over Israel like a thunderstorm: 'His blood come over us and over our children!'"[48] He thus affirms a traditional anti-Judaic interpretation of this passage that espouses the literal fulfillment of these words in the subsequent history of the Jewish people.

Yet, there are nuances as well. "Jerusalem, Jerusalem, you who kill and stone the prophets who are sent to you!" This Jerusalem is not the Jewish people alone, cautions Althaus, warning his audience to beware of "pharisaic pride." "It was not only Jewish blood that revolted against him," he pleads, "it was the rebel-blood of all mankind. . . ." Explicit discussion of race is absent from this work.[49]

If the sermon is to help us to discover Althaus's view of Jews and Judaism in the turbulent climate of the late Weimar era, it presents us with a rather complex picture. On the one hand, there is blunt Christian anti-Judaism that sees the Jewish people as especially cursed not only due to their rejection of Jesus' messianic mission but also because of their unique guilt in his crucifixion. This, coupled with nationalistic overtones packaged in a sermon that stresses the inevitability and importance of the shedding of blood, suggests an unambiguous and deeply held suspicion of Jews.

On the other hand, some elements are present that seem to indicate that this wariness is tempered by Althaus's view of the human condition in general. It is the "rebel-blood of all mankind" that militates against Christ. Secondly, and far more subtly, is Althaus's acceptance of the Jewish lineage of Jesus. The Jewish people are the Volk "from whom Christ came." While this fact is beyond dispute today, it was not nearly so clear in some corners of German Protestantism in the early 1930s, including the radical German Christian movements to which Althaus had belonged. Even so, both of these elements of Althaus's thought would have been cold comfort to German Jews who would just three years later be caught in the crosshairs of the Nuremberg Race Laws. Thus far, Althaus's is a view of Jews that is sharply anti-Judaic—though not especially radical for its time—and laced with nationalistic overtones.

Theology of the Orders (1934)

Two years later, the Erlangen systematician published a foundational work of theology that addressed crucial theological concepts, some of which touched on the very heart of the social and political happenings spurred on by the relatively new but increasingly ruthless Nazi regime. The work was titled *Theologie der Ordnungen* (Theology of the Orders).[50] Althaus deals here with the proper Christian conception of the Volk in the context of the "orders of creation."

The orders (*Ordnungen*) are the "forms of human beings living together, which are essential conditions of the historical life of mankind." They can be spoken of as "orders of creation" because they are "orders of [the] present divine creative work." Examples of proper recognition of these orders of creation include familial responsibilities, including a mother's proper care for her baby, and governmental duties such as a prince's service to his people.

Althaus urges that human beings render obedience to the "specific law of [their] Volk"—not as "natural law" but "in concrete obedience toward [their] Volk's current Law of God." Here, he is rejecting the centuries-old conception of natural law and replacing it with "Volk law."[51] This departure from traditional Christian theology is but one example of the elevation of the Volk in Althaus's völkisch theology.

The exaltation of the Volk in the text continues. The richness of God's creation, Althaus contends, is demonstrated in the "classification of humanity into races and *Völker* [peoples]."

> But the classification is at the same time segregation. The peoples do not only live next to each other, but must also to a large extent stand against each other. Antipathy separates the races and peoples and is not to be obliterated by deliberate suppression of the emotions in the name of human kindness, the brotherhood of all humanity.

Just as the sermonic intensity of Althaus's Good Friday message builds, so the theological passion grows in this text. The love for Volk and *Vaterland*, he intones, is "inescapably bound" to "antipathy, anger, and hate. . . . I cannot stand in this world with my Volk, without standing against others, in acting, thinking, and feeling." Thus, Althaus explicitly roots not only love for Volk but deeply felt, deeply contemplated, deeply effected hatred of others in God's created order. "There is no full commitment to my Volk," he urges, "without fervent passion and wild anger."[52]

Völker before and after Christ (1937)

Althaus developed further his conception of völkisch theology in his 1937 writing *Völker vor und nach Christus: Theologische Lehre vom Volke* (Völker before and after Christ: Theological Teaching on the Volk). In keeping with his "moderate" or neoconservative nature, he rejects the notion that Volk and *Volkstum* belong to the traditional articles of Christian faith, such as God, Jesus Christ, the Church.[53] Yet, he argues that theology has to deal with human beings, history, and "the orders of historical existence, in which our personhood is composed." Christian proclamation must speak to human beings as members of their Volk.

For Althaus, the idea of human beings as part of a Volk goes much further than simply devising a means to speak to people "where they live." As he argued previously, the Volk is God's creation. He ties this belief to an article of Luther's Smaller Catechism, "'I believe that God created me.'" He elaborates:

> The belief that God created me includes . . . my Volk. Because what I am and have, God has given to me from the source of my Volk: the heritage of blood, corporeality, the soul, the spirit. . . . My Volk is my outer and my inner fate. This mother's womb of my being is God's means, His order, to create and endow me.[54]

Despite such ruminations, Althaus issues some qualifiers. Though the responsibility for the Volk is a duty to God, he argues, it is "not the only and entire obligation of our life." One cannot derive everything that he must do in life from the "völkisch imperative." Further, ". . . we are not only responsible for our Volk, but for every human being, if God makes them neighbors to us, also for the other peoples, as far as we come into living relationship to them."[55] Despite the Erlangen theologian's relative theological moderation, strands of nonrational anti-Judaic thought steeped in bloody nationalistic imagery and elevation of the Volk to a divinely sanctioned "order of creation" worthy of vindicated anger and hate would have provided both his readership and his students with justifications for anti-Judaic, even antisemitic, expression.

A capable, measured, and affable theologian, Paul Althaus was no wild-eyed fanatic or rabble-rouser. The respect he commanded from fellow theologians rested on the basis of his great body of theological work, on his position as chair of systematic theology at Erlangen, and on his role as president of the Luther Society. Yet, this sampling of Althaus's writings demonstrates intensely nationalistic, traditionally anti-Judaic, and deeply völkisch tendencies. None of these inclinations was especially unusual for a German Protestant theologian during the Weimar and Nazi eras. In keeping with traditional Lutheran theology, these tendencies were tempered by appeals to universal sinfulness. If only these facts are taken into account, we are left with a modestly complex yet generally middle-of-the-road theologian.

When we reflect on some of Althaus's more forceful pronouncements, along with a few important biographical facts, however, his views do not resemble *consistently* those of a moderate. First, consider the nonrational support for God-ordained hatred of other peoples—embodied in highly charged language such as "fervent passion," "wild anger," and "hate"— which we find in his *Theology of the Orders*. Althaus exhorted that God ordained that Christians should love Volk and Vaterland and hate opposing peoples, all of this in a context of obedience to authorities, whose law is an "order" of God's creation.

Secondly, consider the intermingling of ardent German nationalism and blunt Christian anti-Judaism packaged together in his sermon on the importance of the shedding of blood. Certainly, Althaus's central message is about the sacrificial shedding of Christ's blood on behalf of sinners. Yet, to support this nonrational claim, he appeals to the historical importance of the shedding of blood for noble ideas and institutions, including Volk and Vaterland.

He continued to uphold the conception of a theologically elevated Volk in *Völker before and after Christ*. Yet here, the ever complicated Althaus is less strident than in either of the earlier works. Each Volk must be cognizant of its responsibility to other human beings from other nationalities. The völkisch imperative is not the only demand on the life of the Christian. Had he perhaps moderated his position since his earlier days?[56]

Where it concerns Althaus's position on Luther and the Jewish people, we are left with a difficult interpretive dilemma. Despite the vast quantity of literature that Althaus penned, he was curiously silent on "Luther and the Jews." Thus, there is really no way to analyze directly "Althaus on 'Luther and the Jews.'" We can, however, compare some of Althaus's views with Luther's.

Althaus's view of the state as an order of creation was certainly consonant with that of the reformer. There is no question that Luther viewed obedience to authorities as part of the duty of the Christian.[57] Despite his great love for the German people, he did not, however, exalt the Volk to the same vaunted position as did Althaus.

Althaus's position toward the Jewish people, the crucifixion of Jesus, and the idea of their subsequent cursing by God is certainly similar to Luther's. Yet, as we will see in chapter two, Luther was so much harsher in his condemnation of Jews and Judaism than was the Erlangen theologian. Despite his decrying of the supposedly lethal "Jewish influence" in German society, there are no calls for drastic sociopolitical measures against Jews in the writings we have examined here.

Yet, Althaus lays the theological groundwork, especially in the first two writings, for God-ordained hatred of Jews (and other competing peoples) and an attendant deep love for the German Volk. Althaus is not explicit in recommending what to do about the Jewish people, but neither is he silent on how a German Protestant should have viewed this increasingly oppressed minority. As such, his generally less direct brand of anti-Judaism—coupled with occasional xenophobic ruminations about the "Jewish threat" to German society—served as one side of the coin of Protestant anti-Jewish sentiment in Nazi Germany, while the more stark anti-Judaic and antisemitic pronouncements of Luther and some of his 1930s German Protestant interpreters served as the other.

Althaus's early membership in radical German Christian groups, his public affirmation of the implementation of the "Aryan Paragraph" in the Protestant church, his early euphoria over Hitler's accession to power, and his consistent and ardent nationalism all signify the career of someone far from neutral on the "Jewish Question." Even if Althaus was moderate by 1930s German Protestant standards, he was certainly no friend to the Jewish people. Despite only occasional irrational musings about them, his was a consistent nonrational witness against them, presented at times in a hotly nationalistic, völkisch package. As we will see later, Althaus's doctrine of the "orders of creation" provided theological cover for moderate German Protestant theologians to express anti-Judaic and antisemitic ideas without sounding excessively vulgar or radical.

Luther and the Nazi Era: Prevalent Themes

As noted in the introduction, the tradition of German Lutheran adherence to the authorities and the related theme of Luther's so-called "two kingdoms doctrine" are by far the most prevalent explanation of Protestant apathy and complicity in the face of the cruel Nazi oppression and murder of Jews. Another feature of Luther's thought that has received a fair amount of attention from scholars of German Protestantism during the Third Reich is that of German nationalism, specifically, pride in the German Volk. The view that Germany, the land of the Reformation, was a special *Protestant* nation permeated the thinking of many intellectuals, including theologians, during the nineteenth and early twentieth centuries. Many German Protestants thus viewed Luther as a national hero, the very essence of the German spirit.[58] A. J. Hoover believes that a fervent German Christian nationalism contributed to the implementation of the Holocaust. He cites as one piece of evidence a Protestant churchman who appealed to Luther, a German, as the source for German nationalism and history.[59] The idea of the superiority of the German spirit as embodied in Luther is connected very closely with the next characteristic of the historical literature.

Luther was of such great stature in Germany during the Third Reich that Nazis, their supporters, and their detractors all appealed to him for support of their viewpoint in a variety of ways. Karl Steger, a German Christian pastor in Friedrichshafen who regularly propagandized for the Nazi Party, called on German Christians to fight for the legacy of Luther. Kenneth Barnes notes the irony that while the Nazis used Luther to support their own goals, Dietrich Bonhoeffer quoted him to support his argument that baptized Jews belonged as brothers in the church of Christ.[60]

According to Richard Steigmann-Gall, some leading Nazis actually espoused some views that Steigmann-Gall considers "Christian." In so doing, they sometimes referred to Luther approvingly to buttress their own antisemitic arguments. No less than Himmler, for example, cited Luther's writings on Jews sympathetically.[61] Various other emphases of Luther relevant to Nazi-era Protestantism occur in the historical literature, including Christian social ethics and the relationship of the Christian to the law.[62]

The last characteristic of Luther's thinking that comes into view in the relevant literature is his antisemitism. This feature appears with less frequency than might be imagined. Some examples of Luther's antisemitism reveal the manner in which it was utilized or espoused by Nazis. An example comes from Hitler's friend and mentor, Dietrich Eckart. In one passage, he complains that Luther "spread a halo over 'Satan's Bible'" with his translation of the Old Testament, yet he affirms that when it came to the Jews, Luther had more insight than contemporary Christians.[63]

There are also examples of Luther's antisemitism as it was inherited and embraced by German Protestants. Doris Bergen, for example, makes reference to a religious instruction book that affirmed Luther's antisemitic views. Luther's antisemitic rhetoric was rejected by other German Protestants. Eduard Lamparter, a German Protestant pastor, wrote against antisemitism, including that of Luther, in a church publication five years before Hitler and the Nazis came into power.[64]

There are very few explicit references in the relevant historical literature to anti-Jewish sentiments expressed by Luther. Gerhard Schmidt, a Confessing Christian, wrote that Luther condemned Jews in *On the Jews and Their Lies* and *On the Ineffable Name* while still upholding the authority of the Old Testament.[65] Martin Sasse, Protestant bishop of Thuringia, infamously compiled antisemitic extracts from *On the Jews and Their Lies* in his short book *Martin Luther on the Jews: Away with Them!* and distributed thousands of copies just two weeks after the terror of Kristallnacht.[66] Beyond these isolated references, there are a good number of chapters and articles on the subject of "Luther and the Jews." I will deal with some of these when I tackle the issue in the next chapter.

It is of course very significant that the European Enlightenment occurred between the era of Luther and the Protestant reformers and the rise to power of Hitler and the Nazis. Yet, the importance of rationality was certainly not lost on the German reformer, even if he primarily employed nonrational anti-Judaic modes of thought and more than occasionally succumbed to irrational antisemitism. Similarly, Luther's post-Enlightenment German theological descendants were not above irrational arguments and even explicitly anti-Enlightenment sentiment, despite their general reliance upon nonrational and rational types of thinking. Before addressing Luther's twentieth-century theological descendants, however, it is important to understand how these writings were regarded in their sixteenth-century context.

2

"LUTHER AND THE JEWS"

The most prominent figure of the German Protestant Reformation, Martin Luther was a truly remarkable man. Whether we speak of his posting of the ninety-five theses on the church door at Wittenberg, his refusal to recant his teachings before Charles V at Worms, his marriage to Katharina von Bora in an age of clerical celibacy, or his translation of the New Testament into German, Luther was a genuine trailblazer. Yet, unknown to many—in some cases explained away—is Luther's complex but deeply antagonistic relationship with the Jewish people.

Others have tended to exaggerate Luther's influence through an uncritical reading of history. Erroneously claiming that Luther "called for

Reproduction of *Portrait of Martin Luther* by Lucas Cranach.
Library of Congress.

the destruction of world Jewry," Alan Dershowitz opined, "It is shocking that Luther's ignoble name is still honored rather than forever cursed by mainstream Protestant churches."[1] This sad state of affairs led Reformation historian Heiko Oberman to lament that many would have us choose between "two Luthers"—one, the "bold Reformer, the liberating theologian, the powerfully eloquent German"; the other, an "anti-Semite" who "wrote mainly about Jews," and "preached hatred."[2] Such a choice is, of course, unnecessary.

Luther's *Judenschriften* have been variously defended, debased, and nuanced by historians and theologians, particularly in historical and theological literature about Luther, Nazi Germany, the Holocaust, and the history of antisemitism.[3] In this chapter, I will view Luther's texts about Jews and Judaism in their late medieval social, political, and intellectual-theological contexts, and will evaluate their content along the lines of Langmuir's schema. I will attempt to answer several questions. Should *On the Jews and Their Lies* be said to contain "anti-Judaic" elements, "antisemitic" elements, or both? Must anti-Jewish vitriol be categorized as *either* anti-Judaic or antisemitic? Did Luther favor one sort of argument over the other?

First, I will treat briefly the relationship between Jews and Christians in late medieval Europe, then look at how some of Luther's contemporaries viewed Jews. Next, I will examine four of Luther's treatises that most directly address issues surrounding Jews and Judaism, including *On the Jews and Their Lies*. Finally, I will consider some common interpretive frameworks that have been applied to Luther's *Judenschriften*. I will show that his treatises about Jews and Judaism, though couched in largely nonrational terminology, also include typical irrational medieval slander. That is, they contain both anti-Judaic and antisemitic argumentation.

Historical Context

During the late medieval period, Christians accused Jews of a great number of crimes and religious offenses. One example of this is the charge that Jews blaspheme against the Virgin Mary and Jesus. The late fifteenth-century *Pharetra catholicei fidei* (Quiver of the Catholic Faith) was a "manual for condemning Jews" that included the charge that blaspheming the Virgin is "typically Jewish." A particularly "ferocious" German version of the text was circulated widely in Nuremberg in 1513. Luther, following

Anthonius Margaritha, charged the Jewish people with specific blasphemies against Mary and Jesus as well.[4]

The late medieval Christian also viewed the Jew as a usurer, with the words *Jew* and *usurer* becoming "synonymous" by the late twelfth century. Léon Poliakov ably detailed the medieval history of Jewish usury, a story that entwines their marginalization in society and—in the case of the Holy Roman Empire—their economic worth to the German emperors.[5] Margaritha's *Der gantz Jüdisch Glaub* (The Whole Jewish Faith; 1530) ends with the familiar accusation of Jewish usury (along with theft and other vices) and a request "that the government prohibit them from lending money." Josel of Rosheim, who was protector of German Jewry in the Holy Roman Empire during Luther's day, struggled throughout his career with the thorny issue of actual and supposed excessive Jewish usury—which seldom went unpunished—and hypocritical Christian usury, which often was overlooked by the authorities.[6]

Jews in medieval Europe were regularly charged with profaning the sacred host of the sacrament of the Eucharist.[7] In 1510, the reputable and well-known printing press of Hieronymous Höltzel printed the story of a "wicked Christian" man named Paul Fromm who stole two consecrated wafers from a church in Brandenburg.[8] Fromm abuses one of the wafers in an unspecified "unworthy manner" and is punished by a sudden pitch darkness that overtakes him. He is unable to move for more than half an hour. He then sells the other wafer to a Jew named Salomon.

Fromm then (no doubt terrified at the supposed divinely imposed darkness) tosses the remaining wafer over the city wall of his hometown. It is discovered hanging in a tree, and since he is already suspected of the crime of stealing the wafers, he is taken into custody, charged, and confesses "immediately, without torture." Salomon, meanwhile, "out of congenital Jewish hatred" batters it several times over and pierces it. He curses it and "miraculously" it breaks itself into three pieces; blood appears on the edge of each of the three pieces of the "body of Christ." One year earlier, Salomon had agreed with two other Jews that if he came upon such a wafer, he would give each of them one piece, and he does so.

He takes the remaining piece and further desecrates it, piercing it until blood flows from it. Finally, he kneads the wafer into a piece of matzo dough and throws it into the oven for use in the "Jewish Easter celebration" (i.e., Passover). In the oven, Salomon sees the miraculous specter of a tiny child floating above the bread. The other two Jews similarly desecrate and profane their pieces of wafer. As a result, Fromm, the three Jews, and thirty-eight other Jews are sentenced to death by Joachim I, Landgrave of Brandenburg.

I have recited this particular story in some detail primarily for its illustrative value. It demonstrates that the province of Brandenburg on the eve of the Protestant Reformation was so given to superstition that a respected printing press would publish such an improbable story as "news."[9] As we will see shortly, this story had further repercussions for Jewish–Christian relations in sixteenth-century Germany.

In order to place the vitriol of Luther's *On the Jews and Their Lies* in some intellectual and literary context, it is helpful to see what some other Christian figures were saying about Jews just prior to 1543. Martin Bucer of Strasbourg, for example, was quite inconsistent with regard to the "Jewish Question." One scholar refers to his relationship to Jews as a "case study in striking ambivalence."[10] Bucer was "deeply indebted to the contemporary renaissance of Hebrew letters" and profoundly appreciative of much late medieval Jewish biblical commentary. In 1537, he approved of a letter written by fellow Strasbourg-based Christian Hebraist Wolfgang Capito asking Luther to hear Josel of Rosheim's plea on behalf of the Jews of Saxony, who were being threatened with expulsion by John Frederick.[11] This would seem to indicate some tolerance for the Jewish people on his part.

Nevertheless, approximately one year later, Bucer influenced the Hessian preachers on their "advice" to Landgrave Philipp of Hesse, who suggested that Jews be permitted to reside in his territory, but with stringent restrictions. These restrictions included the following: that they not construct new synagogues; that they not "insult Christianity"; that they discuss Judaism only with specially appointed theologians; and that they attend Christian sermons.[12]

Philipp, in a gently worded reply to the Hessian preachers, categorically rejected all of the articles of their advice, believing them to be excessively harsh. Even so, he incorporated some of their recommendations in his *Judenordnung* (Laws Governing the Jewish Status) of 1539. Events took a malevolent turn, however, when the "advice" of the preachers, along with Philipp's letter of reprimand, appeared in print (presumably by the hand of someone in the Jewish community). Bucer, smarting from the bad publicity that the publication of this private disagreement engendered for him, fired back with the rather harsh anti-Jewish pamphlet partially titled *On the Jews*.[13]

In 1529, Andreas Osiander wrote a tract, published anonymously in 1540, systematically and forcefully refuting the charge of Jewish ritual murder of Christian children (the "blood libel").[14] Osiander was a brash and combative Christian Hebraist, who was based for much of his life in Nuremberg, and was influenced by Johannes Reuchlin.[15] Osiander engaged in the study of the Kabbalah and had a thorough knowledge of rabbinic literature and the Talmud. He thus argued that it is "inconceivable that the Jews should murder children and make use of their blood" when their own kosher laws forbade them even to eat the meat of animals if it contained blood. The treatise appeared just as the investigation of one such supposed murder at Tittingen was ongoing.[16]

Enraged by Osiander's defense of the Jewish community and called upon by the bishop of Eichstätt to rebut it, Johannes Eck, Catholic theologian and Luther nemesis, wrote what amounts to a lengthy retort to Osiander and a denigration of Judaism that Steven Rowan described as "a compendium of every horror story medieval anti-Jewish polemic could encompass." In *Ains Judenbüchlins verlegung* (Refutation of a Jewish Booklet; 1541), Eck bases his passionate argument that Jewish ritual murder is a historical reality in part on what he claimed was his own personal experience. According to Eck, he had actually "placed his own fingers in the wound of a child who had died four weeks before at the hand of the Jews of Waldkirch in the Breisgau in 1503."[17]

The book also includes a call for "new and more stringent laws" against the Jewish people and strong condemnation of usury.[18] Rowan further describes the book as "the absolute nadir of anti-Jewish polemic in the early-modern period."[19] Bearing in mind that the book appeared in the heated atmosphere of the German Protestant Reformation, it is not hard to understand why many historians have regarded the virulence of Eck's work as a means of blighting Osiander with philosemitism, or at least guilt by association with Jewish ideas.[20] What, then, can we conclude regarding the actions and writings of Bucer, Osiander, and Eck on the "Jewish Question" in sixteenth-century Germany?

First, when we approach Luther's rhetoric in *On the Jews and Their Lies*, we must recognize that with respect to both Protestant and Catholic views of Jews and Judaism in Germany in the late 1530s and early 1540s, the air was highly charged. There was a flurry of propaganda on the subject from all sides. Bucer took what we might describe—in its historical context—as a moderately harsh stance in his *On the Jews*. Eck made a more visceral attack with his *Refutation of a Jewish Booklet,* reinforcing medieval superstitions with his own supposed eyewitness testimony of a Jewish ritual murder. Osiander is the only known Protestant reformer to directly refute the charge of the supposed Jewish penchant for ritual murder. A fair analysis of "Luther and the Jews" must take into account what these contemporaries were saying about Jews.[21]

Secondly, we should acknowledge with Heiko Oberman that there were "degrees of harshness and intensities of slander" in the anti-Jewish polemics of the time.[22] Bucer's 1539 recommendations for social restrictions on Jews, for example, are less extensive than Luther's 1543 proposals.[23] It will be helpful at this point to consider how two close associates of Luther answered the "Jewish Question."

In February 1539, Protestant luminaries such as Bucer and Philipp Melanchthon, along with Josel of Rosheim, John Frederick of Saxony, and Joachim II of Brandenburg met in a conference that has been referred to as the "Frankfort Convention."[24] Here we once again recall the Brandenburg affair of 1510. It was Joachim I, father of Joachim II, who sentenced the Jews of Brandenburg to death as a result of the trial and barred Jews from reentry to his province. Later in his reign, however, he relented and permitted a large number to transact business in his territory.

At this convention, Melanchthon presented evidence that the Jews who were executed at Brandenburg because of their supposed desecration of the host were innocent. Whether or not Melanchthon was a special friend to Jews, he was at least concerned with the fairness and accuracy of such a gravely serious charge. Either way, as a result of Melanchthon's presentation and Josel's advocacy, both Joachim II and John Frederick eased restrictions on Jews in their territories.[25]

Despite Melanchthon's important contribution to Jewish safety in this instance, early in 1543 he would send a copy of Luther's *On the Jews and Their Lies* to Philipp of Hesse, along with a "mild recommendation" of its contents. Despite being uncomfortable at least with the violent tone of many of Luther's later writings, he did not repudiate them.[26] Thus, it is difficult to construe his position vis-à-vis the Jewish people. Yet, we can say that the kind of fury that issued from the pens of Luther and Eck is absent in Melanchthon.

Justus Jonas, Luther's close friend and confidant, took a strikingly different view on the subject than did his mentor. In fact, he went so far as to distort Luther's position on the Jews when he translated *Wider die*

Sabbather (Against the Sabbatarians) into Latin. What resulted was a rather pro-Jewish viewpoint that was in marked contrast to Luther's increasingly harsh anti-Jewish stance. There is no evidence that Luther and Jonas ever reconciled their disparate views on the "Jewish Question."[27]

Medieval Christian theologians certainly influenced Luther's *On the Jews and Their Lies*.[28] Yet, perhaps the most direct contemporary influence is a work to which we have previously alluded—Anthonius Margaritha's *The Whole Jewish Faith*. Margaritha was from a prominent Jewish family, the grandson of a distinguished Talmudic scholar. He converted to Christianity and was baptized in 1522.[29]

The Whole Jewish Faith was originally published in 1530, just thirteen years prior to the publication of Luther's *On the Jews and Their Lies*. A third edition of Margaritha's work was published in 1531. It was this edition, argues one historian, that exerted "a powerful influence on Luther." The treatise contains the accusations that Jews commit blasphemy against Jesus and Mary, are guilty of usury and theft, and that they wish to violently overthrow Christian authorities.[30] The fact that Luther appealed approvingly to Margaritha's treatise and even encouraged his readers to read it for themselves demonstrates that it exerted a relatively considerable influence on the reformer.[31]

Finally, Luther viewed Jews as part of an apocalyptic "great coalition" with "papists" and Turks as enemies of God. In fact, he closely associated Jews with Turks in his end-time scenario.[32] Nonetheless, as we will see, the fact that this apocalyptic unholy alliance of the enemies of God includes others besides Jews does not serve to lessen the effects of the anti-Jewish rhetoric of *On the Jews and Their Lies*.

Luther's Writings about Jews

Any analysis of "Luther on the Jews" must begin with a word of caution. While Luther wrote five treatises that directly address the topic, his commentaries, sermons, and "table talk" also contain material about Jews and Judaism.[33] It is not possible here to say everything there is to say about "Luther on the Jews." Accordingly, I will focus primarily upon his *Judenschriften*. Luther's earliest known treatise relating to Jews and Judaism, titled *Daß Jesus Christus ein geborener Jude sei* (That Jesus Christ Was Born a Jew; 1523), was occasioned by the rumor that he was teaching that Mary was not a virgin either before or after Jesus was born. This, of course, was a very serious charge in the religious climate of the early years of the German Protestant Reformation. Luther's twofold purpose was to show that according to Scripture "Christ was born a Jew of a virgin" and that he "might perhaps also win some Jews to the Christian faith."[34]

A few observations about this early treatise are in order. First, it is in the main a biblical and theological treatment of a religious issue. He argues extensively from his understanding of Scripture, for example, that Jews cannot deny that Isaiah was speaking of a *virgin* being pregnant and that "Christ was a genuine Jew of Abraham's seed."[35] Secondly, there are seeds of philosemitism present in the treatise that do not grow into full form in his later works about Jews and Judaism. The Jews, in fact, are "blood relatives" of Christ. Christians should deal kindly and gently with them—the apostles, after all, were Jews who dealt with gentiles in a "brotherly fashion." Christians "must be guided in our dealings with them not by papal law but by the law of Christian love." He further admits that Christians are not morally superior to Jews. "If some of them should prove stiff-necked, what of it? After all, we ourselves are not all good Christians either."[36]

Thirdly, the venom of the later Luther is clearly missing here. Absent are the typical medieval accusations of host profanation, blood libel, and usury that are present in his later works. There are no crude or scatological references. This is not to suggest that direct confrontation is lacking in the work. The Jews are wrong, for example, about Isaiah's prophecy of the virgin birth of Christ and the Genesis prophecy that the scepter (i.e., kingship) would depart from Judah when the Shiloh (i.e., Messiah) comes. The Jews, in fact, are guilty of crucifying Jesus.[37] Yet, never in this work does Luther employ irrational antisemitism.

Fifteen years after Luther wrote *That Jesus Christ Was Born a Jew,* he composed an open letter, titled *Against the Sabbatarians,* to his "good friend" Count Wolf Schlick zu Falkenau. A member of a prominent Moravian family, Count Schlick reported that many Christians in Bohemia and Moravia were developing "sabbatarian tendencies." Just what these inclinations entailed is not perfectly clear, but they no doubt involved the observance of the Jewish Sabbath. Crucially, Luther blamed the sabbatarian tendencies primarily on Jews themselves, and this is where he directed most of his attacks.[38]

Luther's arguments against Jews in this treatise contain elements also found in his other tracts directed at them. They have not kept covenant, they have sinned and rejected the Messiah; they are in exile and—most tellingly—they do not reside in "the land" and no longer possess the temple. While there are "reasonable" and "obdurate" Jews, as a whole they "are given to babbling and lying."[39] This rather mild slander (again, "mild" in its historical context) is one indication of a gradual increase in the harshness of Luther's tone toward Jews. The argumentation is very similar to the earlier tract, but the tenor has become decidedly less sympathetic.

The immediate occasion for the reformer's most notorious treatise, *On the Jews and Their Lies,* was a May 1542 request from his friend Count Schlick to refute a Jewish apologetic pamphlet, which the Count enclosed with his letter.[40] While at the end of *Against the Sabbatarians* Luther hinted that he might write such a treatise as this, he begins here by saying, "I had made up my mind to write no more either about the Jews or against them."[41] It is difficult to say to what degree the contents of the aforementioned Jewish apologetic pamphlet induced Luther to change his mind.

The treatise is rather lengthy (approximately 135 pages in the Weimar edition). Thus, it will be useful to outline it briefly.[42] It falls into four major parts. In the first section, Luther describes and decries the "false boasts" of the Jews. In the second part, he presents debate on the exegesis of significant and relevant biblical passages. In the third part, the reformer repeats the supposed Jewish blasphemies against Jesus and Mary. In the fourth and most infamous section, Luther makes recommendations to church and state authorities for actions against Jews in Germany.

The treatise is scathing in tone, a fact that can be seen most readily in Luther's deprecating, sometimes crude language and in his scornful sarcasm.[43] Luther in places calls the Jews "a defiled bride, yes, an incorrigible whore and an evil slut," a "whoring and murderous people," and "bloodthirsty bloodhounds and murderers of all Christendom." While the gentiles give them everything they have, including "land and people and everything," still they "curse, spit on, and malign" the *Goyim.* While Luther is aware of the objection that the Jews of biblical times and the Jews of his day should be distinguished from each other, he nonetheless frequently applies scriptural condemnation of the Jews of ancient Israel to contemporary Jews.[44]

Indeed, he often intermingles Scriptural deprecation with typical late medieval pejoratives. In one illustrative example, he says that Jews are "stiff-necked, disobedient, prophet-murderers, arrogant, usurers, and filled with every vice, as the whole of Scripture and their present conduct bear out." Thus, it is not only their ancestors' behavior that is deplorable, but their own as well. In fact, Luther's "incorrigible" Jewish contemporaries are more "conceited" than "David and other pious Jews" of biblical times.[45] Similarly, with famed medieval Hebraist Nicholas of Lyra, he argues "that their present exile must be due to a more heinous sin than idolatry, the murder of the prophets, etc.—namely, the crucifixion of the Messiah."[46]

Secondly, he levels a myriad of accusations at Jews. They are guilty of stealing and usury. Three Jews with whom he had met "called Christ a *tola*, that is, a hanged highwayman." Their Talmud says that it is no sin for a Jew to kill a gentile.[47] They curse Christians in their synagogues. They practice witchcraft, "conjuring signs, figures, and the tetragrammaton of the name, that is, with idolatry, envy, and conceit."[48]

They defame Christ and Mary in various manners, calling Jesus a "sorcerer and a tool of the devil," denigrating his name through kabbalistic numerology, even calling him a "whore's son." A "malicious rabbi" supposedly called Mary a "dung heap." Jews are even purported to believe that Mary conceived Jesus during her "menstrual uncleanness," implying that Jesus is thus insane or a demon.[49] They have been "accused" of poisoning wells, kidnapping and piercing children, "hacking them in pieces," and using the blood of Christian children (i.e., in ritual fashion) to "cool their wrath." Luther strongly implies that these "accusations" may be true, despite Jewish denials:

> Whether it is true or not, I do know that they do not lack the complete, full, and ready will to do such things either secretly or openly where possible. This you can assuredly expect from them and you must govern yourself accordingly.[50]

Nearly all of these accusations were common in late medieval antisemitic rhetoric.[51]

The most widely known aspect of the treatise, its anti-Jewish social program, appears in the fourth and final section. Luther here makes seven severe recommendations concerning Jews. Their synagogues and schools should be burned to the ground; their houses should be "razed and destroyed"; their "prayer books and Talmudic writings" should be confiscated; their rabbis should be "forbidden to teach henceforth on pain of loss of life and limb"; they should be denied safe-conduct on the highways; usury should be prohibited to them and their gold, silver, and cash should be taken from them; and finally, they should be subjected to harsh labor (as retribution for their supposed laziness).[52]

As scathing, sarcastic, and denigrating is *On the Jews and Their Lies,* his *On the Ineffable Name and on the Lineage of Christ* sinks to even lower depths of polemical rhetoric. The first section of the treatise, comments Mark Edwards, "is singularly devoid of any edifying theological, exegetical, or historical comments."[53] Perhaps this is overstatement, but there is indeed precious little in it that is commendable. Nothing in the earlier Luther can prepare the reader for the venom of this work. It is not difficult to imagine why it was not published in English translation until 1992.[54]

In the first section, Luther translates and comments upon the fourteenth-century monk Porchetus Salvaticus's *Victoria Adversus Impios Hebraeos* (Victory Against the Impious Hebrews). The portion that Luther translates claims Jews fabricated a slanderous tale about Christ in which he finds a stone in the Jerusalem temple with the *Shem Hamphoras* (the "ineffable name" of God) written upon it, keeps the name to himself, and uses it to perform miracles. In other words, it presents Jesus as a wicked magician. The tale includes far-fetched and bizarre occurrences, slander of Christ, and at least one historical inaccuracy.[55] Luther's retorts—based upon the notion that such a tale is truly Jewish in origin—are laced with crudity, sarcasm, and scatological references. The bulk of the second section is generally less strident and is reminiscent of the exegetical argumentation of *That Jesus Christ Was Born a Jew,* at least in its content.[56] Even so, there are still some crude references and harsh denigration of Jews.

The work is steeped in late medieval anti-Jewish paranoia. Contrasting "their Messiah" to Jesus, he says that theirs will be like "Kochab [*sic*]" who will "not allow himself to be crucified, but kill the heathens and *make the Jews masters of the world.*" As in *On the Jews and Their Lies,* he assails the "present day Jews" with typical late medieval rhetoric. They are the "most vicious and malicious fellows" who are guilty of usury, "spy out and betray all countries," "poison water," and "steal children." There is no ambiguity as to their culpability here—they are most certainly guilty of such things.[57]

The language of denigration is much cruder here than in *On the Jews and Their Lies.* At the heart of Luther's repudiation of their purported *Shem Hamphoras* tale is a coarse wordplay. Their *Shem Hamphoras* ("ineffable name") is really *Sham Ha Peres* ("here is filth"), the kind of filth "that comes out of the belly." In other places, they are "full of shit" (*beschissen*), "sow Jews" (*Säujuden*), and their biblical interpretations are "Judas piss" (*Judas pisse*).[58]

Still, there is much cogent biblical exegesis in the work. This helps to illustrate Edwards's contention that, while perhaps neurotic at this point in his life, Luther was not psychotic.[59] These are not the random ramblings of an insane man, but the angry denigrations of a highly accomplished reformer and biblical exegete.

"Luther on the Jews": Typical Interpretations

Church historian Wilhelm Maurer's thinking concerning Luther's anti-Jewish diatribes has been very influential—particularly among church historians and theologians—for a very long time. Influential Luther historians such as Oberman and Edwards, for example, modified, but never fully challenged, Maurer's thesis that Luther's diatribes were essentially theological in nature.[60] It will be helpful to sketch his view.

Maurer posits that Luther relied upon medieval exegetes such as Nicholas of Lyra, but contends that the "young" Luther went beyond late medieval exegesis with respect to the "Jewish Question" (*Judenfrage*) by widening it to the "Humanity Question" (*Menschheitsfrage*). The Jew, while still an example of divine punishment for disobedience (à la Augustine), nonetheless becomes a symbol for the judgment of the entire sinful world.[61] To Maurer, this "eases" the situation "without question." The struggle between Church and Synagogue loses its "exclusive character," becoming a "special case of the struggle which the church actually has to conduct with the world."[62]

Not only is the "young" Luther to be hailed for supposedly easing the tension between Church and Synagogue, but he is also supposed to be responsible for a new Christian missionary endeavor to Jews. This evangelistic endeavor was not to involve forced conversions as in late medieval Christianity, but presumably the Christian love which Luther recommends be shown to Jews and their gradual recognition of their Messiah. Yet, neither the sixteenth-century Lutherans nor even the "older" Luther would cling to this missionary vision.[63]

In the end, Maurer centers Luther's "excessive polemic" against the Jewish people in the reformer's doctrine of justification (*Rechtfertigungslehre*). A constituent part of this doctrine is the "anger" or "wrath" of God. Luther, following Paul, believes that rebellious, sinful men exist in a state where God's wrath is "revealed from heaven against all ungodliness and wickedness of men." Indeed, sinful men are "storing up" wrath for themselves until the "Last Day" of God's judgment.[64] Outside of Christ—indeed the cross of

Christ—the sinner is subject to the wrath of God. Luther seems to indicate that his anger is merely representative of God's anger against the Jews.[65] From this background, argues Maurer, the "excessive polemic" against them must be understood. He explicitly rejects viewing Luther's position concerning the Jews in terms of "philosemitism" and "antisemitism."[66]

While following Maurer in his essential position, Oberman challenged assumptions about late medieval and Reformation thought concerning Jews. Reuchlin, supposedly the prophet of Jewish emancipation, was a Christian Hebraist not out of sympathy for Jews, but to "prove the superiority and the universality of Christian faith."[67] The thinking of the archetypal Christian humanist Erasmus—reputedly the European father of tolerance—was "permeated by a virulent theological anti-Judaism." The terms *Jewish* and *Judaic* were a paradigm for *legalism* or externalized religion, which was anathema to Erasmus. For him, even a baptized Jew never became a "full-fledged Christian," but remained a "half-Jew."

"This was a religious world that viewed truth as indivisible, banned deviation as error, and dreaded patent heresy as blasphemy fatal to a life with God."[68] Oberman grasped with great clarity the religious realities of the late medieval and early modern historical context. How, then, did he portray Luther's diatribes against the Jewish people? The "motive" for these treatises, he says, was "to reclaim the Scriptures in their entirety from the perversities they were suffering at the hands of the Jews. . . ." Hence, like Maurer, Oberman believes that Luther was guilty of a primarily theological anti-Judaism. While Luther (along with Reuchlin and Erasmus) was not a conscious antisemite, nor did he think in "racial categories," he nevertheless left no room for Jews *as* Jews.

Thus, his opposition to Judaism "in effect became opposition to Jews," a view that allowed the image of the Jew to enter the service of "racial" antisemitism.[69] Oberman is not prepared to call Luther's vitriol antisemitic. He chooses instead to label it as anti-Judaic, but recognizes in it an image of the unconverted Jew that would serve modern "racial" antisemitism quite well.

Mark Edwards—on some level—sees the value of Maurer's (and Oberman's) delineation between Luther's theological rationale and his deficient sociopolitical recommendations vis-à-vis "the Jews."[70] On the *historical* level, however, he concedes that this "theological" explanation is "unsatisfactory." To Edwards, Luther clearly believed that social and theological realities were interrelated.

It is not only (church) historians of the early modern period who have tackled Luther's *Judenschriften*. In 1968, modern church historian Kurt Meier produced a relatively short but potent work about the Protestant church's position toward Nazi Jewish policy in the Third Reich.[71] He dedicates approximately twenty-five tightly argued pages to the interpretation of Luther's *Judenschriften*. While in some respects an extension of Maurer's position, it also contains some important qualifications.

Meier agrees with Maurer that Luther's stance toward the Jewish people is "rooted (as far as it does not concern medieval remainders) . . . in [Luther's] doctrine of justification. . . ." Yet, he discounts Maurer's assertion that Luther merely stressed the "antinomy of Law and Gospel" and that "everything else that Luther said . . . on the matter can be ascribed to the practical-legal consequences. . . ." He rejects the implication that these consequences are somehow self-standing, and that they do not derive from— or at least stand in correlation to—Luther's "principally theological judgment."[72] Meier's qualifications are important. Despite regarding Luther's position toward the Jewish people as "principally theological," he recognizes that the implications for Luther's stance were very real.[73]

Edwards's analysis of Luther's series of serious physical illnesses during the latter part of his life marks another important explanatory framework for Luther's *Judenschriften*. Throughout his life, the reformer experienced hemorrhoids, heart congestion, fainting spells, dizziness, "roaring in the ears," an "open, flowing ulcer on his leg," and severe constipation. During the last fifteen years of his life, he lived through "more frequent and more serious illnesses," including uric acid stones, which caused him "great agony."[74]

Luther also struggled with all sorts of mental anxieties. While it is certainly difficult to clinically diagnose a man now dead for more than 450 years, Edwards lists as symptoms Luther's "frequent bouts of depression," his "death-wish," his "vulgar and scatological language," his "outbursts of rage and vilification," and his "visions of and contests with the devil."[75] He questions, however, applying the term *mental imbalance* to a sixteenth-century man with a "biblically based view of the world" that was hardly unusual. Further, Luther's later polemics contain lucid, "persuasive exposition of doctrine and exegesis of Scripture." Nevertheless, as previously noted, Edwards speculates that Luther was neurotic, even while denying the notion that he was psychotic.[76]

Edwards presents a view of Luther's harshness toward the Jewish people that accords with the literary evidence. "The trend towards greater harshness was relatively gradual and extended over a number of years. . . ."[77] As noted earlier, *That Jesus Christ Was Born a Jew* (1523) was arguably philosemitic (for its era), *Against the Sabbatarians* (1538) was mildly slanderous of Jews, and *On the Jews and Their Lies* and *On the Ineffable Name* (1543) were virulent in tone.[78]

The question arises naturally as to *why* Luther became harsher and harsher in his outlook on the Jewish people. Nevertheless, close examination of Luther's thinking on "the Jews" over the span of his lifetime might reveal that there is less of a distinction between the "old Luther" and the "young Luther" than this increasingly harsh tone might intimate.[79] Further, to attribute to this apparent change in tone any number of causes—sickness, old age, frustration with the lack of Jewish conversions—is tempting, but perhaps it should be a call for further research rather than the typical speculation that occurs in the historical literature. As Edwards rightly noted elsewhere, Luther consciously used "vulgarity and violence" for effect, and they were typical of his polemic against not only Jews, but "Turks" (Muslims) and Roman Catholics as well.[80]

Betsy Halpern-Amaru believes that views such as Oberman's, which in spite of their condemnation of antisemitism contain an "apologetic tone," do not place Luther's thought in the broader context of the "Jewish Question" in Western civilization.[81] She argues that in his writings "on the Jews" Luther presents two typologies (or, "portraits," "witnesses") of *Judenspiegel*. The first such "mirror image" represents the hope for the conversion of the Everyman. If the "blinded Jew" can believe, so can the Everyman. The second "mirror image" represents the theologically defined (unconverted) Jew. To confront this type of *Judenspiegel* is to battle evil.[82] It is crucial to realize, in Halpern-Amaru's schema, that both types of Jews are "unreal," "exegetical devices," or "religiopolitical foils." They only have real significance as "reflections" of Luther's own inner struggles. Nonetheless, in recognition of Luther's late medieval context, she rightly argues that these symbols of "the Jew" are not Luther's "creation," but his "heritage."[83]

Conclusions

At the outset of the chapter, I asked whether Luther's *On the Jews and Their Lies* could be said to contain anti-Judaic elements, antisemitic elements, or both. We have seen here that clearly this infamous treatise contains both kinds of anti-Jewish rhetoric. Acceptance of the now-commonplace division of "theological anti-Judaism" and "racial antisemitism" has led many to the erroneous conclusions that Luther's vitriol is essentially theological in nature and that antisemitism during the Third Reich was a primarily racial affair.

Even if we construe the biblical-exegetical portions of Luther's *Judenschriften* as nonrational, we are still faced with the prospect that at the very least the motivations for the sociopolitical recommendations of the last section of *On the Jews and Their Lies* may be described as irrational, and thus antisemitic. The antisemitism of the treatise, however, is not limited to the seven-part political program, but is intertwined with anti-Judaic argumentation throughout. For Luther, the sixteenth-century Jew was in reality indistinguishable from the biblical-era Jew. In fact, he was worse. He blasphemed Christ and Mary and slandered Christians. Such charges were part of the reformer's nonrational anti-Judaic arsenal.

Yet, for Luther, the early modern German Jew was also lazy and obdurate, a thief, and a usurer. A small number of sixteenth-century German Jews were guilty of usury, a fact that exasperated Josel of Rosheim. Thus, there were also xenophobic aspects present in Luther's litany of anti-Jewish charges. Yet, even worse, he believed that Jews were capable of ritual murder and poisoning wells. These accusations do not accord with rational empirical thought, and thus they qualify as irrational antisemitism. He made all of these accusations in a context in which he had very few personal contacts with real Jews, a fact that underscores the largely irrational nature of the allegations.

This is not to say that the sole or even the primary impetus of Luther's antisemitism is "racial" in the modern sense of the term. Luther did not think in terms of biology when he criticized Jewish behavior. There is no doubt that a large portion of *On the Jews and Their Lies* is dedicated to theological/biblical argumentation. Yet, even these religious arguments are not free from characteristically irrational medieval defamation. To depict his vitriol as "theological" anti-Judaism is overly simplistic and does not suit all of the evidence.

What, then, of Luther's apparently declining health during the latter years of his life—the years in which he wrote his most antagonistic works on "the Jews?" Edwards has demonstrated that even if the frail physical condition and mental anxiety of the waning years of his life did not dictate

Luther's scathing anti-Jewish tone, they must have contributed something to this angry demeanor. Edwards's contention that Luther's social and theological worlds were inescapably intertwined is also correct. Luther's severe anti-Jewish social and political program was based both in his theology and his late medieval outlook upon this "outgroup."

Was Luther then "projecting" his own fear and self-loathing upon "the Jews?" Did this late medieval monk who grappled with deep spiritual anxieties (*Anfechtungen*) his entire life see "the Jew" in the mirror of his mind?[84] Did the *Judenspiegel* of his earlier, arguably philosemitic work give way to the *Judenspiegel* of *On the Jews and Their Lies* and *On the Ineffable Name*? Unfortunately, while such views are fascinating and may tell us something about the workings of the mind of an antisemite, they are in the end both speculative and an oversimplification of Luther's "early" and "late" picture of Jews.

Next, we should consider how influential was Luther's late medieval context in shaping the antisemitism of these later works. Luther saw the Jewish people as end-time enemies of God; in his mind, they were in league with the devil, the Turks, and the Roman Catholic church. There is no question, either, as to whether Margaritha's *The Whole Jewish Faith* exerted some influence on Luther's view of "the Jews." It is only a question of how much of this influence was at work in his writings about Jews and Judaism.

Oberman's portrayal of Luther in his late medieval context is generally accurate. Certainly, Luther did not rely solely upon Jewish ritual murder or usury to make his case against the Jewish people. Yet he did seek to bolster his nonrational anti-Judaic polemic with such irrational and xenophobic late medieval rhetoric. We should not attempt to diminish the force of such irrational language, interspersed as it is between much larger blocks of text that are essentially nonrational in nature, nor should we conclude that the impact of the irrational antisemitic defamation was somehow lost on his audience.

What, then, may be said of Maurer's approach? Maurer presents the "young Luther" as something of a hero for the Jewish people. The Church–Synagogue struggle is eased since it is now merely a microcosm of the Church–World struggle. While there is some truth to the picture of the "young Luther" as somewhat philosemitic, the artificiality of this "young Luther"–"old Luther" distinction hedges against such a sweeping statement.[85] This view of the Church–World struggle does concur, to a point, with Luther's apocalyptic view of the coalition of God's enemies, which included among others "papists," Jews, and Turks. Even so, I contend, contra Maurer, that the Jewish Question has not been replaced by the Humanity Question, but rather subsumed under the Enemies of God Question.

Is Luther's doctrine of justification central to his approach to the "Jewish Question?" In light of the cruciality of God's wrath to this foundational Lutheran concept, there is no question that it is at least as important as Luther's social outlook. For Luther, sinners without God need to be justified—declared righteous in God's sight on the basis of having received Christ's righteousness.[86] Yet, must we then jettison altogether discussion of philosemitism and antisemitism when we approach the question of "Luther and the Jews?"

Clearly this is not an appropriate solution. As we have seen, Luther's theological and social outlooks were deeply enmeshed with one another. If we grant that Luther's theology drove his seven-point social program in *On the Jews and Their Lies,* must we conclude that this harsh answer to the "Jewish Question" necessarily follows? The fact that Calvin proposed no such social program against Jews, despite espousing a doctrine of justification that differed very little from Luther's and who, like Luther, had a strongly critical view of contemporary Judaism, is reason enough to answer in the negative.[87]

How does the view of antisemitism that I have portrayed here affect our view of the nature of Luther's anti-Jewish diatribes? Clearly, if we accept the strict "theological anti-Judaism" vs. "racial antisemitism" rubric, then we are left with no choice but *either* to center our answer in his doctrine of justification because he was a theologian who lived prior to the advent of late nineteenth-century cultural and biological notions of race, *or* to project anachronistically modern notions about race onto his view of the Jews. Neither of these two answers deals with the question either historically or holistically. Luther's "theology of the Jews" included both nonrational anti-Judaic and irrational antisemitic components, and was supported by xenophobic elements.

What implications may be drawn from these conclusions? First, it seems that Luther's sociopolitical recommendations regarding the Jewish people largely went ignored by contemporary political leaders.[88] The violent internal struggle of Christianity turned the animus of the Lutheran Protestants away from Jews and onto Roman Catholics in the post-Luther Germany of the sixteenth century. Though a great deal more research needs to be done, it seems that the seventeenth through nineteenth centuries saw no significant employment of Luther's *Judenschriften* on the part of German Protestants in the service of anti-Judaic or antisemitic goals. Luther's influence on Protestant approaches to the Jewish Question appears to have been rather uncertain until at least the late nineteenth, or perhaps the early twentieth century.[89]

By the time these works began reappearing with growing frequency in Protestant literature after the First World War, and in Nazi propaganda beginning in the 1930s, the mixed reception that they received in sixteenth-century Germany became a distant memory. How were the vitriolic antisemitic recommendations of *On the Jews and Their Lies* interpreted by German Protestant clergy and theologians while Hitler and the Nazis directed the bloody, protracted mass murder we now call the Holocaust? It will become evident that these works, received by Protestants living in a society that was becoming increasingly hostile to Jews, and decontextualized and utilized by a regime with motives more nefarious than Luther's, were based nonetheless at least in part on an irrational hostility that was congruent with Nazi antisemitism.

3

CONFESSING CHURCH AND GERMAN CHRISTIAN ACADEMIC THEOLOGIANS

In 1937, Jena University theologian Wolf Meyer-Erlach, a member of the pro-Nazi German Christian wing of the Protestant church, published a book titled *Juden, Mönche und Luther* (Jews, Monks, and Luther) in which he refers to Jews as "an incessant army of demons." Jewish antagonism toward Christianity, Meyer-Erlach urges, represents a "deadly danger by which the Jews threatened the Reich." After centuries, he intones, National Socialism is now the "fulfillment" of Luther's designs against Jewry.

Meyer-Erlach used his influence to bring committed Nazis to the theological faculty at Jena University, promoting through his many publications a "de-Judaized" form of Christianity. He dedicated himself wholeheartedly to the pursuit of the goals of both National Socialism and the German Christians through his responsibilities at both Jena University and the Institute for Research into and Elimination of Jewish Influence in German Church Life, commonly called the "Eisenach Institute."[1] His personnel file at the Jena University archive, along with his written works, are littered with glowing references to National Socialism, to "the Führer," and to the goal of a "de-Judaized," "Nordic" Christianity. Meyer-Erlach was one Protestant academic theologian who summoned in often colorful fashion his limited academic skills in the service of the Nazi regime.

In chapter two, I demonstrated that Luther's writings specifically dedicated to the sixteenth-century "Jewish Question" are peppered with both anti-Judaic and antisemitic rhetoric, supported with xenophobic elements. Meyer-Erlach's realm—the world of academic theology in 1930s Germany—now becomes our focus. I will examine responses to Luther's writings about Jews and Judaism from four academic theologians who were members of the polarized Confessing Church and German Christian wings of the German Protestant Church. Did these theologians consult Luther when confronting the "Jewish Question," and if so, in what manner did they utilize his writings? While this survey of responses by these generally lesser-known individuals to Luther's writings will reveal significant shades of difference, their works will provide us with a window on conventional wisdom about Jews and Judaism within German Protestant academic theology during the Third Reich.[2] Before examining their biographies and some of their works, however, I will explore briefly both the academic context in which Protestant theologians operated and the role they played in German society.

The Political University

On April 7, 1933, the Nazi regime commenced its first wave of far-reaching repressive legislation, beginning with the Law for the Restoration of the Professional Civil Service. In the same month, the Law against the Overcrowding of German Schools and Universities was introduced. The latter law at first affected only Jewish students, as it effectively restricted the number of Jews to a maximum of 1.5 percent of the total number of students attending German schools and universities. Later amendments, however, would limit the total number of places made available in universities, and drastically reduce the number of young women who could receive a university education. The enforcement of subsequently introduced legislation meant that by December 1934, Jews could no longer work as teaching assistants or lecturers in German universities.[3]

Despite all of this, neither Hitler nor the Nazi leadership acted with the same enthusiasm in imposing Nazi views and values in the universities as they did in the schools. Perhaps predictably then, important decisions affecting institutions of higher education—including academic appointments and funding for research—became flashpoints for typical internecine competition between government agencies, including the Education and Interior ministries. Also involved in these sorts of disputes were powerful student organizations such as the Nationalsozialistischer Deutscher Studentenbund (National Socialist German Students' Federation; NSD-StB), as well as the Sturmabteilung (Storm Troopers; SA), and university professors and rectors. In April 1935, rectors were entrusted with new and sweeping authority by the Education Ministry. In reality that ministry's political weakness and the interference of the previously mentioned parties and organizations made this directive difficult to enforce.[4] As we will see shortly, however, in the case of one of the more "nazified" universities like Jena, a forceful persona like Wolf Meyer-Erlach could by the power of his office attempt somewhat successfully to push the institution's scholarship in the direction of the Führer.

The Role of Academic Theologians

One Nazi opponent, reporting in April 1937 to the Sozialdemokratische Partei Deutschlands (Social Democratic Party of Germany; Sopade), compared Nazism to a religion, arguing that a "Church-State" had emerged that demanded absolute loyalty, including the submission of the soul. Yet, this phenomenon emerged neither overnight nor entirely in plain sight. Instead, the observer likened it to the refurbishment of a railway bridge. Such bridges could not be destroyed altogether; this would make rail travel impossible. Instead, each day individual girders and rails were replaced "until the passengers, who had either not paid much attention, or imagined bits and pieces were being refurbished, realised that they were crossing an entirely new structure."[5] In a sense, Protestant academic theologians who were supportive of the regime filled the role of ideological railway bridge worker.

Yet, what general role did Protestant academic theologians play in their professional lives? First, we must recognize that, so to speak, they "served two masters." As professors in German universities, they were civil servants. As professors of Protestant theology, they also worked in conjunction with their confession and with their regional churches.[6]

During the Nazi regime, as a civil servant the university professor was not expected to serve typical higher education ideals such as unfettered intellectual inquiry and political objectivity. Instead, as Harvard sociologist E. Y. Hartshorne observed at the time, a professor was "politically bound." "He is committed to its [i.e., the State's] philosophy and must not only refrain from criticizing the government but must openly fend for it in word, deed, and attitude."[7]

Those who were supportive of the anti-Jewish policies of Hitler and the Nazis played a very clear role, providing a sort of respectable, "scholarly" tool for the regime. The scholars that the Nazis employed to advance their antisemitic program often were very highly regarded. Among them were university professors and members of the academy, some of whom were world famous authors—"the kind of people Allied scholars used to meet and fraternize with at international congresses."[8]

How, then, may the thought of such antisemitic scholars be characterized? Alan Steinweis surmises that there were three tiers of antisemitic discourse in Nazi Germany. The bottom tier included the more tactless forms of propaganda against Jews, intended to influence those in the German populace who were less astute intellectually. The second tier encompassed "middlebrow" speech, intended to ensure the social acceptability of antisemitism among more-educated Germans.[9] The third and highest tier comprised what he calls "the product of Nazi Jewish studies," which would have included Wilhelm Grau's *Forschungen zur Judenfrage* (Research on the Jewish Question), the scholarly journal of the Reichsinstitut für Geschichte des neuen Deutschlands (Reich Institute for the History of the New Germany).[10] The ideas from this tier in fact funneled down to the other two. Steinweis's schema provides a helpful means for discussing varying kinds of antisemitic discourse in the Third Reich.

The biographies of theologian Gerhard Kittel, philosopher Martin Heidegger, and political theorist Carl Schmitt demonstrate the wellspring of esteem for Hitler among highly educated Germans who had not supported the Nazi Party prior to 1933. Kittel, Professor of New Testament at Tübingen and an important figure in German Protestantism during the Nazi era, was both a member of the Nazi Party and an early member of the German Christians. These three men offered a "restrained alternative to the old [Nazi] fighters' rage against Jews . . . that neither Hitler nor his deputies could have provided."[11] The academic theologians who supported the Nazis thus provided them with respectability among academia both inside and outside Germany.[12]

The majority of academic theologians from the Confessing Church and the German Christian wings of the German Protestant Church did not appeal in the first place to Luther's writings about Jews and Judaism to support their anti-Judaism and antisemitism, but instead looked elsewhere.[13] Rather, there is a diverse, significant, and yet overlooked minority of theologians who published writings that dealt explicitly with Luther's view of the Jewish people. Such works were a means of both buttressing their own often antisemitic and anti-Judaic views and encouraging the church at large to view Jews in the same light as they and Luther did. Books and articles penned by four academic theologians—Erich Vogelsang, Wolf Meyer-Erlach, Hermann Steinlein, and Gerhard Schmidt—demonstrate such appropriation of Luther's *Judenschriften*.

Erich Vogelsang, Königsberg Luther Specialist

Erich Vogelsang was born in 1904 in Beverungen (west of Göttingen), the youngest of seven children, two of whom died while serving in the First World War. During his university studies at Berlin, he was influenced by such Protestant theological luminaries as Karl Holl and Reinhold Seeberg. As noted in chapter one, Vogelsang was, with Emanuel Hirsch, a central figure in the "Luther Renaissance" launched by Holl. It was Hirsch, as Vogelsang's Ph.D. advisor, who would have the strongest influence on the young theologian. After receiving his doctorate in 1928, in the autumn of 1929 he passed his Habilitation at Königsberg University, where he began serving as a lecturer. In 1937, he became full professor and chair of church history at Gießen.[14]

Vogelsang joined the Nazi Party in April 1933 and the SA in November of that year. He was regional chairman of the German Christians in East Prussia, and in the struggle concerning the appointment of a "Reich bishop" for the German Protestant Church, he supported Hitler's choice, Ludwig Müller. Yet, his view of Müller eventually soured. In January 1934, Vogelsang and a number of other professors of theology called for Müller's resignation because the Reich bishop had issued a decree that they regarded as a "muzzling" of free speech.

Having registered as a volunteer for military service back in 1935, Vogelsang was called up to the German army in 1939, at first as a writer for an infantry regiment. Later that year, he was promoted to sergeant. After a military mission along the Maginot Line in June 1940, he returned home. From 1941 to 1944, Vogelsang's division was deployed to Belgium, northern France, and finally to the Russian front. He was mortally wounded in Vitebsk (now part of Belarus) in June 1944. Vogelsang's brief but significant academic career focused on Luther scholarship, and his work on the "young Luther" stirred considerable academic debate among theologians.[15]

Here I will examine his engagement with the twin themes of Luther's German-ness and his struggle against Jews. In an essay titled "Das Deutsche in Luthers Christentum" (The German in Luther's Christianity), Vogelsang complains that Luther scholars have been derelict in their duty by not applying their skills of scholarship to "the German Luther" as they have to other topics. The topic, he complained, has either been dealt with by scholars in a cursory fashion or has been ceded to "popular" works.[16] Vogelsang hopes to begin to remedy this situation.

Yet, even he cannot resist a little hero worship:

> ... Luther is always Luther: this unique, unchanging, indivisible human being: German-born and raised as a Christian, from German peasant and miner's blood and at the same time at home in the monastery, a framer of the German language without equal ... a "prophet of the Germans" ... whose influence nevertheless extended far beyond Germany. ...

Despite this effusive praise, Vogelsang attempts to sketch a picture of Luther's German-ness that is integrally related to his Christianity. Luther, he believes, weaves together the religious and the political, particularly in his dealings with foes such as Roman Catholicism, Islam, and Jewry.[17]

His "political, national consciousness" is part of his *Deutschtum* (German-ness). And yet, this consciousness is not a uniquely *German* trait. In fact, Vogelsang even has difficulty saying that the sum of Luther's characteristics is particularly "German." Vogelsang believes that Luther's answer to the question of German existence lies in God's revelation in Jesus Christ.[18] Such primarily nonrational argumentation is characteristic of Vogelsang's work overall, and perhaps one reason why one historian regarded him as a "moderate" German Christian.[19]

Vogelsang's *Luthers Kampf Gegen die Juden* (Luther's Fight against the Jews; 1933) offers a much more subtle approach to the topic of "Luther and the Jews" than, for example, Nazi philologist Theodor Pauls's three-volume *Luther und die Juden* (Luther and the Jews; 1939).[20] Rather than merely highlighting the many negative things Luther declared about Jews as does Pauls, Vogelsang contextualizes the reformer's views toward them with a taste of the historical and theological development since the Protestant Reformation. From a more theologically driven symbolic point of view than Pauls, he nonetheless shares a dim view of the Jewish people.

He begins by lamenting the position of prewar Christian theologians for following the lead of "Lessing's Enlightenment" in "leveling the differences between Christianity and Judaism" and for having no appreciation for Luther's fight against the Jews. He also blames them for following liberal German theologians Schleiermacher and Ritschl in not recognizing categories such as the "wrath of God" and the "curse." In addition, Christians in Germany permitted the abuse of the sacrament of baptism as a means of assimilation for Jews. At the outset, he is signaling his intention to right these purported wrongs via Luther.[21]

Vogelsang rejects the picture, forwarded especially by Rabbi Reinhold Lewin's influential work *Luthers Stellung zu den Juden* (Luther's Position on the Jews; 1911), that Luther began as a philosemite and ended as an antisemite. Instead, he believes that the Jewish question is consistently for Luther "first and last a Christ-question"; for Luther, the cry of the Jews that "his blood come over us and our children" is the key to the "Jewish Question." Relating Luther's position on the Jewish people, the death of Christ and "the curse," he argues that Jesus Christ is the "turning point" in the history of Judaism. The crucifixion became a "perpetual" curse to Judaism.[22]

Vogelsang next discusses the various problems with Judaism. These include a supposed boasting about lineage, circumcision, the Law, the Temple, and the key point for Luther, which he deems to be the Jewish hope for a "fleshly Messiah." Again following Luther, he considers "a demonic power" to be the driving force behind Jewish "lying" and "blaspheming" about Jesus. Yet, Vogelsang also describes this "demonic power" as an "inexplicable power"; indeed, it is the same power that stands behind the "all-explaining" rationalism—it is the "power of the devil."[23] Here, the gifted young scholar intertwines the traditional Christian belief in demons with a direct attack on both rationalism and Judaism. The irrationalism of Vogelsang's position is not left implicit. In fact, he links Judaism and rationalism directly to the devil.

The work is by no means free, however, of the language of Germany in the 1930s. The "liberal man" cannot accept with Vogelsang that the "world-historical" Jewish question that was "masked for a hundred and fifty years" came to the fore once again in the "German revolution of 1933." The Enlightenment and liberal Christian theology have clouded the view of Christian Germans with regard to the "Jewish Question."

Luther did not fear reaching out beyond the realm of theological academia and thus draws the political consequences for the Volk from his most fundamental religious insights.[24] Theology must speak outside the halls of the university and to the Volk—something Vogelsang is trying to do himself, with support from the great German reformer. There is no doubt a message to fellow Protestant theologians here.

What, then, does he believe was the nature of Luther's answer to the so-called "problem?" Only if the "Christ question" is first solved "for the *whole* Jewish Volk *as a Volk*" would there be a "real and final clarification" of the question. Could the answer remain theological and be answered by conversion? Not so. Appealing to Luther's *On the Ineffable Name* (1543), he suggests a *"clean divorce of Jews and Christians."*[25]

Identifying one of the social, ethical, and political problems for the Volk which needs to be addressed by Luther's ideas and demands, Vogelsang notes Luther's struggle against usury—which the reformer viewed the same as theft—and draws a parallel between Jewish usury and "the curse" of capitalism. Clearly Germany should break free of the "slavery to interest." He also teases out a crass socioeconomic antisemitism present in Luther who fears that Jewish usury will lead to the impoverishment of the "boss and host" and the enrichment of the "servant and guest."[26] Knowing that the "Jewish Question" involves the concrete political notions of State and Volk, Luther recommends expulsion as the "only really fair solution."

Vogelsang later treats a highly enigmatic passage regarding Jewish blood in *On the Ineffable Name*. Because the Jews are purportedly so greedy, argues Luther, they attract and gather to themselves "loose, wayward, depraved Christians." They have done this for many years, and thus their blood has become "mixed, unclean, and watery." The Jews have learned from the defector Christians how both to hate and murder them. A sort of heinous symbiosis takes place between the two, and they become a "den of cutthroats and devil's dregs" because a "renegade Christian will be a bitter enemy of Christians."[27]

Although he admits that "racial mixing" (*Rassenmischung*) does not appear in Luther's "field of vision," Vogelsang nonetheless is not afraid to describe Jewish "degeneration" on the basis of this phenomenon and to base it on this very passage. He notes that Luther does not comment on the reverse danger that German blood might become tainted by Jewish "admixture" (*Beimischung*). Vogelsang anchors the reason for Luther's omission in the difference of historical situation. Luther knows no program of mission to Jews and, since the "Judaizing" of Christians is more his concern, he "hardly counts on conversion of Jews."[28]

Though Vogelsang is generally careful not to force Nazi conceptions of race onto Luther, he cannot resist here. He does so in a very qualified manner, lending his analysis an air of fair-mindedness. What results is a rather careful historical-theological analysis coupled with the highly charged language of "racial mixing" and Jewish "degeneration."

Vogelsang closes by noting that his readers have the responsibility to view Luther through the lens of a differentiated "Jewish Question" that has been affected by Jewish emancipation, assimilation, and an increase in Jewish Christianity. The question is relevant not just to Germany; it is "world-historical" in nature. It must be dealt with from a theological standpoint—"under the gaze of eternity" (*sub specie aeternitatis*)—and more specifically, "in the face of the cross of Christ."[29] Given what Vogelsang has said earlier about the cross of Christ, he is clearly not speaking of it as the fountain of grace and salvation, but as the place of cursing for the Jewish people.

For Vogelsang, Luther's theological reasoning leads to practical political and "social-ethical" conclusions and demands. He is keenly aware of the historical situation of his readers: the wake of the so-called "revolution" of 1933. Crucially, Vogelsang lambastes the espousal of both Enlightenment thinking and theological liberalism on the part of German Protestant theologians, revealing conservative and anti-modern currents in his thinking. Nonrational biblical-theological reasoning dominates Vogelsang's theological arsenal. Yet, his willingness to attribute supposed Jewish "degeneration" to "racial mixing" demonstrates that he, like Luther, was given to irrational antisemitic arguments as well. It is precisely because Vogelsang's analysis is much more careful and his scholarship more credible than many other German Christians that his analyses are lent an air of refinement, making the effect of his anti-Judaic and antisemitic sentiments more devastating than anything forwarded by more radical figures such as Wolf Meyer-Erlach.

Wolf Meyer-Erlach, Jena Professor of Practical Theology

Wolf Meyer-Erlach was born Wolf Meyer in 1891 in Kitzingen on the Main (near Würzburg). As noted, during the Nazi era, he mustered in often lively fashion his limited intellectual capabilities for the benefit of the regime. His writings, though stylistically enigmatic and colorful, are nevertheless fairly commonplace in their content, at least in German Christian circles.

Meyer-Erlach studied theology at Erlangen and Tübingen for the four years preceding the First World War. At the outset of the war, he volunteered for military service, and one year later, he suffered a serious brain injury caused by the explosion of a grenade. His physical condition deteriorated, and he was dismissed as unfit for service in 1916.[30] That year, he served briefly as dean of a parish orphanage in Windsbach (near Nuremberg). In 1918, he became pastor in a small village community called Fessenheim, where he remained until 1929.[31]

Meyer-Erlach's Fessenheim days were important to his formation as an "academic" theologian. Around 1920, he acquired a set of the Weimar edition of Luther's Works from the legacy materials of a deceased member of a Munich consistory, and said that he spent many nights working through the reformer's writings in the parsonage. Also in the 1920s, Meyer-Erlach began an extensive yet temporary career as an author of popular treatises on cultural-historical matters and radio plays with such titles as "Nordic Seers and Heroes" and "German Suffering."[32]

In 1929, he became pastor of a congregation in Würzburg-Heidingsfeld. In 1931–1932 he was a regular radio preacher in Bavaria, receiving an assignment from a radio station in Munich. Meyer-Erlach became a member of the Nazi Party on May 15, 1933, and was also the acting leader of the German Christians in Bavaria from June until October of that year.[33] Contrary to the wishes of the theological faculty, and despite not holding a doctorate, he was hired by Jena University as a full professor for practical theology (also in 1933). He served as dean of the theological faculty in 1934–1935.

Meyer-Erlach was instrumental in bringing both Walter Grundmann and Heinz Eisenhuth—both committed German Christians and Nazi

Wolf Meyer-Erlach. *Landeskirchliches Archiv der Evangelisch-Lutherischen Kirche in Bayern.*

Party members—to the theology faculty of the university, and was also a prominent member of the Eisenach Institute. He had been called Wolf Meyer, but on May 1, 1935 had his last name officially changed to Meyer-Erlach in an effort to avoid having it understood to be Jewish.[34] In 1935 he was appointed rector at Jena, this time against the vote of the university faculty, and he served in that capacity for more than two years. Athens University awarded him an honorary doctorate in 1937. On September 29, 1945 he received a certificate dismissing him from his teaching post at the university, for having joined the Nazi Party after April 1, 1933 and having "campaigned actively" for the goals of the party.[35]

After his dismissal, Meyer-Erlach worked various secular jobs until 1948, when he became theological clerk to a church official in Wittenberg. He fled the German Democratic Republic in 1950, serving at first as a theological clerk in Erlangen, and then—with the help of Martin Niemöller, at that time the head of the Protestant church in Hesse—for eleven years as pastor of a church in Wörsdorf (near Frankfurt am Main). In 1962, he received the Federal Cross of Merit from the Federal Republic of Germany in part for providing aid to families in East Germany. Meyer-Erlach died in nearby Idstein in 1982.[36]

When called upon after the war to give a defense of his activities on behalf of the Nazi Party and authorities, he did not merely demur, but rigorously attempted to portray his relationship to the party in an oppositional light, claiming that the Nazis had "persecuted" him. There is a small grain of truth to his protestations. He and other leading German Christian figures such as Grundmann did indeed come under SD (*Sicherheitsdienst*, or Security Service) surveillance on several occasions. He also came under Gestapo scrutiny on at least one occasion, though the reason for this unwanted attention is not clear.[37] Yet, as Susannah Heschel notes, the Eisenach Institute, of which Meyer-Erlach and Grundmann were key members, came under SD surveillance as a matter of course; all groups that sponsored public meetings were subject to such scrutiny in the Nazi state.[38]

In a postwar letter to the acting rector at Jena, Meyer-Erlach offers a periodic assessment of his attitude toward the Nazi Party. He claims that he fought *against* the party until 1933. Then, because Hitler promised to be the "German Cromwell," he fought *for* the Führer from 1933 until 1937. After 1937, when he recognized Hitler's "deceit" and the party's betrayal of its own program, he once again fought *against* the party.[39] In another letter of self-defense, he details what he describes as "persecution by the party," claiming that his removal from office and all of the "persecution measures" to which he was exposed were due to a long list of actions on his part. These include his multiple sermon series from the Old Testament in which Protestants, Catholics, and Jews took part, his retention of a Jewish convert as his family doctor during his employment as a minister, "participation in the inauguration of a Jewish Synagogue," discussion evenings in Würzburg on Luther's *That Jesus Christ Was Born a Jew* (which, he notes, were "forbidden by the party") and his "sharp repudiation of parental protests against my accentuated preferential treatment of the Old Testament in religious instruction."[40]

Although some of these claims are difficult to prove or disprove, many are rather easily refutable. His claim to have fought *against* the Nazi Party prior to 1933 is belied by his comment, made in 1935 or later, that he had fought for Hitler "since 1922."[41] If Meyer-Erlach fought *against* the Nazi Party after 1937, it would be more than a little difficult to explain his words in rejecting the doctoral thesis of Wilhelm Richter in 1940. Richter, he says, misses the "realization of National Socialism that the racial question is the basic question for everything."

Evaluating the successful 1942 dissertation of Fritz Schmidt-Clausing, Meyer-Erlach joyfully intones his pleasure that the Frankfurt-based Institute for Research on the Jewish Question, which he notes was "founded by Rosenberg," is interested in Schmidt-Clausing's work and that it, along with "other important offices of the party and of the state" have been made mindful of the efforts of the theology faculty at Jena.[42] Likewise, in his 1944 evaluation of Karl Peter Adams's dissertation, he notes that the "National Socialist worldview" finally brought race, "racial soul" (*Rassenseele*), and "racial character" (*Rassencharakter*) to Germany.[43]

His participation in the inauguration of a Jewish synagogue at Würzburg took place in 1929, and thus serves as a rather weak argument for persecution as the Nazis were not yet in power in Germany.[44] His supposed rejection of "parental protests" against his "accentuated preferential treatment of the Old Testament in religious instruction," he says, took place both before and right after the Nazis took power. The consistently harsh anti-Old Testament tenor of his writings during the entire Nazi era strains the credulousness of this argument. Finally, the purported Würzburg "discussion evenings" on Luther's *That Jesus Christ Was Born a Jew*, if they took place during Nazi rule, could hardly have been philosemitic in nature if they are consistent with his excoriating antisemitic rhetoric.[45] If they took place prior to 1933 (perhaps while he was pastor in Würzburg), they once again prove little with respect to his supposed persecution by the party.

Rhetorical examples of Meyer-Erlach's commitments abound. During his rectorate address in 1935, in his inimitable style, he calls students and faculty alike back to a time of the greatness of the "political University of Jena," where "political professors" and "political students" were "drunk on honor, liberty, and fatherland." Further, he warns "It is not good . . . if the faith of a Führer like Hitler is betrayed" by the most highly educated minds. And finally, he implores, "What we need today are not living encyclopedias, but workers, fighters, and warriors."[46]

Some passages from Meyer-Erlach's essay "Luther und Gustav Adolf" (Luther and Gustav Adolf; 1943) help to demonstrate his love for an idealized "Teutonic" Luther. The "spirit and soul of the Teutons" is found in this German miner's son. He urges further, "Luther's faith is not the humble, submissive believing of dogmas and theories, Luther's holiness is not the fully unfavorable kind of self-disavowal of the monk. . . . Luther's faith is the hard, unrelenting Teutonic defiance, the unshakable Teutonic loyalty."[47]

During the Second World War, Meyer-Erlach was sent to occupied Europe to lecture German troops about why they were fighting. Goebbels's Propaganda Ministry published the lectures, including *Der Einfluss der Juden auf das englische Christentum* (The Influence of the Jews on English Christianity; 1940) and *Ist Gott Engländer?* (Is God an Englishman?; 1940)[48] In the former work, Meyer-Erlach sought to tie England to Judaism, arguing that in fighting England, Germany was in fact battling "world Jewry." He colorfully and ardently sketched his attacks on the failure of an English Reformation that he viewed as having "nothing together in common with the German Reformation."

The English "'Reformation,'" which does not measure up to the idealized German Reformation, was led by the "religious-revolutionary Presbyterians and Puritans," of whom he regarded Cromwell as the greatest. Despite the attempts of English Christians such as *The Pilgrim's Progress*'s author John Bunyan and Baptist minister Charles Spurgeon to "strive for the right knowledge of Christ," English Christianity, which rejected Luther's "fight against the Old Testament" and warnings against the Jews, was "decisively shaped" by the Old Testament and the "spirit" of Judaism.

Meyer-Erlach charges (with unintended irony) that the English Volk are inclined to "fanatical nationalism." They embraced the god of Israel, who is the "national god of the Englishmen." "The god of Israel, not the God of Jesus Christ, became their god."[49] In his conclusion, he intones,

> The history of English Protestantism is an almost classical example of how Judaism [achieves] victories in English Christianity through the Old Testament, how a whole Volk is Judaized in spirit and soul and body, that is, politically, economically, culturally, and religiously. English Christianity, the English church, the empire-church actually became "the lengthened arm of Judaism."[50]

For Meyer-Erlach, the English Reformation is an example of an insidious Judaism that seeks to destroy Christianity.

In *Verrat an Luther* (Betrayal of Luther; 1936), he selectively utilizes quotations from Luther about the Hebrew Scriptures to reinforce his own anti-Old Testament bias. "With all harshness," he says, Luther "rejected the idolatrizing of the Old Testament." Moses was not given to the Germans, but rather "to the Jewish Volk alone. . . ." He does not, however, stress Luther's affirmation of and love for the Old Testament. "Luther separated the prophetic from the legal and historical in the OT [Old Testament]. *Only the prophetic, only the reference to Christ had worth for him.*"[51] Like many other German Christians, Meyer-Erlach utilized Luther's view of the Hebrew Bible not only to diminish its importance for the Christian, but also to associate it with the Jewish Volk, thus driving a wedge between the (German) Christian and the Jew.

Meyer-Erlach's engagement with Luther's writings about Jews and Judaism was both lengthy and thorough. He considered Luther studies his specialty. Among the courses he taught at Jena were "Luther and the Jews" and "The Revolutionary Luther." In an undated Eisenach Institute document, Meyer-Erlach's area of responsibility is listed as "Clarification of the Attitude of Great Religious Characters toward Judaism (Luther, Herder, Stöcker, etc.)."[52] His publications about Luther include *Betrayal of Luther* (1936), "Luther and Gustav Adolf" (1943), and *Jews, Monks, and Luther* (1937).

In *The Influence of the Jews on English Christianity*, Meyer-Erlach summarizes what he regards as Luther's drastic change in attitude toward the Jewish people. According to Meyer-Erlach, the Jewish people greeted Luther's beginnings around 1520 in the hope that with the collapse of medieval Christianity the collapse of anti-Jewish legislation and antisemitism in general might also occur. They even spread Luther's "little missions book," the "most Jew-friendly writing of many centuries," *That Jesus Christ Was Born a Jew,* throughout Europe.

Despite the fact that Luther "turned against antisemitism" in this early writing, he "very soon woke up from this aberration." On "religious, völkisch, and economic grounds," Luther went from "friend of Jews to the greatest antisemite of the entire West," from the "protector of the Jews against his own Volk to the protector and guard of the Christian West against the murderers of Christ, against the vampires and usurers, against the Jews. . . ." One cannot confuse Christ, "the Redeemer of the peoples," he says, with "the Jewish messiah, the murderer of all peoples, the incarnation of the eternal Jew." To this end, Luther could pen *On the Jews and Their Lies,* the writing that was his "most passionate, most antagonistic to Jews," leaving it as his "legacy to the Christian people in Germany." He approvingly cites here Luther's seven "severe recommendations" against the Jewish people.[53]

Meyer-Erlach also garners support for German Christian and Nazi positions from Luther in his short book *Jews, Monks, and Luther.* He does so most directly in a section titled "Luther, the Enemy of the Jews." Here Meyer-Erlach utilizes the strident, irrational language of fear and danger. In one passage, for example, he describes the antagonistic relationship between Judaism and Christianity as a "deadly danger by which the Jews threatened the Reich."[54] A bit later he describes Jews as an "incessant army of demons." Whether speaking of Luther's time or his own, he believes the Jewish people to be (and to have been) a dangerous threat to the Reich that German Christians should fear.

Secondly, Meyer-Erlach—unlike Luther, I think—believes the Jewish "rebellion against God" to be *unique*, for it "is the rebellion of a whole people against their Creator." Meyer-Erlach does not seem to have drawn this insight from Luther. Luther indeed believed that Jews were in rebellion against God. Yet, as I demonstrated in chapter two, he also viewed them as part of an apocalyptic unholy alliance with "papists" and Turks as enemies of God.

Thirdly, he sees in National Socialism the fulfillment of Luther's anti-semitic desires for the Jewish people. Luther, the "pioneer of the Reformation" and "torch-bearer of a new world epoch," drew up the severe recommendations in *On the Jews and Their Lies*. The Nuremberg Laws, he notes ironically, appear alongside Luther's demands as "scientifically cool, fair, and objective."[55] Later, he states more succinctly that after centuries, National Socialism is now the "fulfillment" of Luther's designs against Jewry.[56]

Meyer-Erlach's theology, like that of many other German Christians, was radically liberal. He embraced a faith that was anti-dogmatic and skeptical of anything Jewish, including many parts of the Bible. Yet, like other more conservative academic theologians such as Vogelsang, he was a politically conservative nationalist who viewed the Jewish people as a danger to German society. His views received fairly wide exposure due to his multiplicity of publications and his institutional roles at the "nazified" Jena University and the ostensibly academic Eisenach Institute. His antisemitic discourse might best fit in the second, "middlebrow" tier of Steinweis's schema. While much of it obviously lacks objectivity, it at least bears the appearance of scholarship. As such, it might have been persuasive to some university-educated German Protestants.

The language of fear dominates Meyer-Erlach's discussion of Luther's opposition to Judaism. He sometimes imposes 1930s German fears on Luther and at other times highlights Luther's fears, demonstrating what he regards as the reformer's prescience regarding the "Jewish Question." His

Hermann Steinlein
and family (Steinlein
is third from left).
*Landeskirchliches
Archiv der Evange-
lisch-Lutherischen
Kirche in Bayern.*

Teutonic, anti-Old Testament, anti-dogmatic, antisemitic Luther heralds a Christianity determined to defend against its enemies, whether Jews in general or "Judaized" foes such as England. In his writings, "the Jews" are merely objects of irrational fantasy. His work thus represents one example of a jarring minority Protestant view—a theologically-fashioned "Luther to Hitler" thesis.[57]

Hermann Steinlein, Ansbach Pastor

Hermann Steinlein was born in Löpsingen (Bavaria) in July 1865, the son of a pastor. He studied in Erlangen, Tübingen, and Leipzig from 1884 to 1888. After becoming vicar in Augsburg in 1888, he was ordained in Ansbach the next year. Three years later, he became pastor in Ehringen, then in Ansbach in 1900, where he served until he retired in October 1934.[58]

In 1916, Steinlein received his doctorate in theology. He was politically active as a pastor during the Weimar years, working on behalf of the candidacy of Protestant theologians in the Bavarian Middle party (1918–1919) and against an electoral alliance of nationalist parties (1924). In Bavaria, this electoral alliance called itself the Völkischer Block and included the Nazi Party. Steinlein even practiced his sharp criticism of the block when the theologians met at their favorite table at the local pub.[59] In 1934, he served on the consistory until his retirement later that year. He died in Ansbach in December 1947.

Steinlein had a long and lively engagement with the issue of Luther and Judaism. In an article in 1937 for *Luther*, the journal of the Luther Society, he mentions that he referred to Luther's "sharpest anti-Jewish writing 'On the Jews and Their Lies'" in a newspaper article approximately forty-five years earlier (i.e., ca. 1892).[60] In 1929, he wrote a brief apologetic work titled *Luthers Stellung zum Judentum* (Luther's Position on Judaism). Four years later, he penned a brief article about Luther's *Judenschriften*.[61]

Steinlein was the author of several polemical works against Mathilde Ludendorff. Mathilde was the second wife of Erich Ludendorff, who was a prominent military figure during the First World War and an early rival to Hitler in the Nazi Party. The couple led a fringe movement called the Tannenberg League that sought to infuse Nazism with their conspiratorial brand of antisemitic and anti-Christian religion. Steinlein's anti-Ludendorff literature dealt with her views on Luther and the Reformation.[62] The Ansbach pastor also engaged other popularizers of the view of a rabidly antisemitic Luther, including Theodor Pauls.[63] In 1935, Steinlein published an article titled "Luthers Stellung zur Frage der Judentaufe" (Luther's Position on the Question of Baptism of Jews) in the *Junge Kirche* journal. Two years later, he wrote a polemical article against Meyer-Erlach's portrayal of Luther's view of the Old Testament, which he titled "Luther und das Alte Testament" (Luther and the Old Testament).[64] I will consider these last two articles here.

In "Luther and the Old Testament," Steinlein critically engages Wolf Meyer-Erlach's portrayal of Luther's views about the Old Testament in the Jena theologian's *Betrayal of Luther*. He contends, first, that Meyer-Erlach's depiction is one-sided. Steinlein argues that Meyer-Erlach simply ignores Luther's "great respect" for the Old Testament. Yet, Meyer-Erlach himself includes a number of Luther citations that, avers Steinlein, should serve as proof that Luther rejects what Meyer-Erlach describes as the "idolatrizing" of the Old Testament. Steinlein complains further that Meyer-Erlach does not explain just what this "idolatrizing" encompasses.[65]

Combating the idea purported in "radical-völkisch circles" that Luther became more critical toward the Old Testament later in his life, Steinlein avers that this was "only a return (albeit in a still more aggravated way)" to the anti-Jewish hostility of Luther's earlier days. Steinlein points out that this conception is (falsely) tied together by those in these circles with his "anti-Jewish [*antijüdische*] attitude." The reality, he argues, is that in this later period, Luther cherished the Old Testament even more than before.

The most convincing proofs come from the "three anti-Jewish writings of 1542/43," which he says contain roughly 850 biblical quotations, 600 of which come from the Old Testament. By his count, 80 percent of Luther's biblical citations in *On the Jews and Their Lies* are from the Hebrew Scriptures. Luther's "very energetic fight against Judaism" relies primarily upon evidence summoned from the Old Testament, which the reformer regarded as "unshakable" truth.[66]

In his conclusion, Steinlein says he wants to illustrate "that Luther's position on the Old Testament is substantially more conservative than that of positive theology. . . . There is also . . . no positive Old Testament scholar, who for example still accepts the composition of the whole Pentateuch by Moses—quite different from Luther!" Further tying him to a theologically liberal position, Steinlein continues that Meyer-Erlach portrays the position of the representatives of "positive theology" toward the Old Testament as if it were, in comparison with Luther, a "hyper-conservative position." The direct opposite, he protests, is the case.[67]

Steinlein begins his 1935 article about Luther's position on baptism of Jews by mentioning a very controversial and current case. The recent baptism of a Magdeburg Jew who was later accused of having committed severe sexual crimes led those "radically" völkisch elements of the church to argue strenuously against baptism of Jews.[68] They argued from Luther's "very clear anti-Jewish" position that such baptisms were a "betrayal" of the great reformer. Thus, Steinlein asserts, he must examine the "purely religious" question of Jewish baptism in a scholarly way, based on historical sources.

He briefly traces the evolution of Luther's thought regarding Judaism in general, asserting, notably, that Luther's "unpleasant experiences" even with baptized Jews caused his later turn against them. Yet, even his "sharpest anti-Jewish writings" close with a prayer for Jews' conversion. He thus establishes an indirect argument for Jewish baptism in Luther's espousal of the possibility of Jewish conversion to Christianity.

Not only is Jewish conversion possible for Luther, but some "Caesar Jews" in fact have converted to Christianity despite being "scattered among the heathens." It is also important to Steinlein that Luther refers to the "pious Old Testament Israelites" (the "Mosaic Jews") as "church."[69] Steinlein is implying here that anyone who is part of the "church"—whether Jew or gentile—is worthy of baptism, the rite of membership, and the sealing of the faith of the Christian. Thus, withholding of baptism from Jews is out of the question.

He closes with five conclusions. In three of these, he refers to writings from Luther's later "anti-Jewish" period. Even in *On the Jews and Their Lies*, Luther affirms that the "'new Volk of God and Jerusalem is now the Christian church, gathered from Jews and heathens.'"[70] Another argument includes instructions for the performance of Jewish baptism from this "anti-Jewish" period. In his final point, he cites Luther's *Vermahnung wider die Juden* (Admonition against the Jews; 1546), where the reformer appeals to Christians to offer conversion and baptism to Jews who earnestly desire them.

Steinlein closes by arguing, first, that Luther was indeed very cautious about Jewish baptism and, second, that he was in no way fundamentally opposed to the practice. In fact, he supported it for "serious" converts. Steinlein's closing statement leaves no doubt as to his own view on the matter: "The statement that the baptism of Jews is in every case a betrayal of Luther, contradicts sharply the historical facts and is a strong distortion of Luther's actual opinions."[71]

We may draw several inferences from Steinlein's piece on baptism of Jews. The first pertains to methodology. He asserts that the question of Jewish baptism is a "purely religious" question to be addressed in a "scholarly" way based on historical sources. Having cited a particularly controversial case of the baptism of a Jew accused of criminality, he wants to interject some cool rationality into the discussion. The subject's current, topical nature is not lost on him. Yet, he does not want such concerns to determine the outcome of the investigation—and certainly not when based on such an extreme and exceptional case.

Clearly, Steinlein is also concerned with objectivity and dealing with evidences that run counter to his claims. He does not seek to hide Luther's negative views about Jews and Judaism, but presents instead a nuanced view of Luther's position that incorporates both the reformer's opposition to Judaism and his desire for individual Jews to convert to Christianity. In so doing, he demonstrates both the centrality of baptism for the Christian faith and, perhaps only by inference, a rejection of Nazi racialization of Jews—at least for those willing to convert to Christianity.

Lastly, the very real nature of the issue at stake for Steinlein illustrates that it was no esoteric debate. The article illustrates the intertwining of the political, the social, and the theological—for acceptance of baptized Jews into the membership of a state-recognized Christian church would demonstrate a form of opposition to the Nazi state, a counter-cultural impulse, and an affirmation of human dignity rooted in the universal image of God. Steinlein's introductory discussion of the Magdeburg baptism serves to underscore this important reality. Ironically, he is able to garner such support for what is albeit a small population of Jews from the very source that also recommends their complete ostracism from society.

In his journal articles about Luther's views on the Old Testament and Jewish baptism, we encounter conservative theological defenses of both. In both articles, Steinlein uses the term *anti-Jewish* exclusively to describe Luther's writings.[72] He also takes positions on both issues that would have put him at odds with both the German Christians and—especially with regard to baptism of Jews—Nazi authorities. By and large, he seems to support Luther's generally dim view of Jews and Judaism, but true to his conservative theological sensibilities, he upholds what he believes to be Luther's fundamental support for the Old Testament—rightly interpreted—and for the Christian sacrament of baptism, even for (genuinely converted) Jews. Steinlein's commitment to conservative Lutheran theological principles, together with his rather strict abstention from both irrational argumentation and xenophobic stereotyping, demonstrate his espousal of an almost exclusively nonrational anti-Judaic posture toward the Jewish people.

Gerhard Schmidt, Nuremberg Seminary Rector

The son of a church councilor, Gerhard Schmidt was born in Untermagerbein (Bavaria) in 1899. He studied at Erlangen, Leipzig, and Tübingen, and then attended seminary at Munich for his practical theological instruction while serving as vicar in Munich and Burghausen. In 1928, he became a lecturer at the academy for female teachers in Erlangen. From 1935 to the outbreak of the Second World War in September 1939, he was rector at the seminary in Nuremberg. He served in the military for four years before becoming dean at Regensburg, a position he held until 1945. Though Schmidt was a member of the Confessing Church, neither of these seminaries was run by that wing of the German Protestant Church.[73] After a brief postwar sojourn as a clerical member of the high church council in Munich, he became full professor for practical theology at Erlangen in September 1946. He died in a traffic accident in Erlangen in September 1950.[74]

Schmidt wrote an article on Luther's position concerning the Old Testament for the journal *Junge Kirche* in 1937.[75] In it, he holds together as consistent Luther's high regard for the Old Testament and his rejection of

modern Judaism. Anticipating the possible objection that the two arguments are incompatible, he surmises that Luther knew the difference between the "old Volk Israel and later Judaism" or "the Jews of Moses" and
"the Jews of the Caesar."

He contends from Luther that while the "Caesar Jews" are "deserted"
by God and have been under a "gruesome curse" for fifteen hundred years,
the "Volk of the Old Testament" were blessed by God in a special way. He
argues further that Luther loved the Old Testament and regarded it as
Holy Scripture. Schmidt sums up cogently, "He does not reject the O.T.
because of the Jews, but rather the opposite: because of the O.T. he rejects
the Jews!"[76] This summary is indicative not only of Schmidt's position toward the Jewish people, but also of his affirmation of the Old Testament
as Word of God, both positions being in accordance with Luther's views.
Such support of the Hebrew Scriptures can also be interpreted as both an
ironic jab at the German Christians, many of whom rejected the Old Testament as inspired Scripture because of its Jewish content, and an attempt on
Schmidt's part to reconcile his anti-Judaic views with the antisemitic views
of Hitler and the Nazi regime.[77] In his article, Schmidt quotes approvingly
portions of On the Jews and Their Lies and On the Ineffable Name, which
he describes as the reformer's "famous anti-Jewish writings," in order to
demonstrate Luther's views both toward the Old Testament and the Jewish
people.[78]

Schmidt details how Luther levels accusations at Judaism from the Old
Testament itself. The Jews of Luther's time are thus, as noted earlier, under
a "gruesome curse" and can be God's people no more. They are cursed,
Schmidt believes, because they have rejected Jesus, who is the true Messiah. Schmidt believes that Luther turned against the "impertinence and
insolence" of these contemporary Jews who refused to believe in Jesus. The
Volk of the Old Testament (the "Jews of Moses"), however, were especially
blessed by God. Thus, this Confessing Church figure indeed "sacrificed the
Jews in order to save the Old Testament."[79]

Yet, there is a restraint to Schmidt's criticism of Judaism that differentiates his work from the more excoriating treatment expounded by Meyer-
Erlach. Schmidt condemns as an "aberration" any "fusion of the Jewish
question with the things of the O.T." Luther, he says, saw things more
clearly. The reformer renounced present-day Judaism solely from the Old
Testament Scriptures.[80]

The tack taken by Schmidt is representative of a characteristically conservative Confessing Church approach that affirmed the authority of the Old Testament while demeaning the present-day Jew, defining him by the curse brought on by his rejection of Jesus as the Messiah. It is unclear what Schmidt would recommend regarding the plight of Jews in Nazi Germany. It seems that he is attempting to preserve the theological tradition of Christian anti-Judaism without speaking a clear word as to how that tradition should be implemented socially or politically.

What we do know from Schmidt is that the Jewish people should turn to Christ. We do not know which anti-Jewish measures of the Reich—if any—Christians should oppose. While he uses predominantly nonrational anti-Judaic reasoning, Schmidt's sole reliance upon Luther's most antisemitic literature and his jab at the "impertinence and insolence" of the "Caesar Jews" of Luther's day (and his own?) point toward an underlying attitude of general disdain that may have been antisemitic, or at least xenophobic.

Conclusions

At the start of this chapter, I asked whether German Christian and Confessing Church academic theologians appealed explicitly to Luther's works in support of their own views on Jews and Judaism. We have seen that a small but significant cross-section of these theologians indeed did so. The works of these relatively minor figures help us to comprehend one crucial part of the conventional wisdom about Jews and Judaism among German Protestants during the Nazi era.

The types of arguments that they employed, however, differed in important ways. As noted, German Christian theologians usually adopted Luther's irrational antisemitic rhetoric as their own, often coupling it with notions that included idealized portraits of "Teutonic" or "German" greatness and anti-Enlightenment sentiment. Confessing Church theologians utilized Luther's nonrational anti-Judaic arguments against Jews primarily, but often tacitly approved of state involvement in line with Luther's antisemitic social program.

The writings we have encountered here also vary widely in scope, in approach, and in the party persuasion of the authors. As to scope, only Steinlein and Vogelsang wrote works exclusively about "Luther and the Jews."

Both Schmidt and Meyer-Erlach touched on the theme while addressing broader issues.

In approach, the authors exhibit both commonality and dissonance. Meyer-Erlach's theology of Judaism is dominated by shrill, irrational antisemitic language, but is combined with a lesser degree of nonrational anti-Judaic argumentation. Erich Vogelsang's argumentation is primarily nonrational, but contains occasional glimpses of irrationality. Though he champions the "German" Luther, Vogelsang's Luther—even in his "German-ness"—is first and foremost the *Christian* Luther. He approaches Luther in a much more sophisticated manner than does fellow German Christian Meyer-Erlach. To an audience of Protestants in the Germany of the 1930s, his cautious brand of anti-Judaism and antisemitism would have appeared to be the stuff of refined propriety.

Schmidt's brief article illustrates the issue of selectivity. He ignores altogether Luther's arguably philosemitic literature, choosing to highlight Luther's position toward the Old Testament primarily from *On the Jews and Their Lies.* Luther wrote so many volumes and commentaries on the Old Testament that the choice of works concerned primarily with the "Jewish Question" could seem rather odd for a theological writing on this particular subject. Given that his audience was comprised of Christians in the Germany of 1937, the choice seems less peculiar. In the case of Hermann Steinlein, we see a theologically conservative scholar engaging a theological topic with great skill and care, taking an anti-Judaic posture that is nonetheless almost completely free of irrational antisemitism.

Wolf Meyer-Erlach and Erich Vogelsang were German Christian theologians in German universities. Hermann Steinlein was a Confessing Church pastor and fellow Confessing Christian Gerhard Schmidt a seminary rector. How do their differences in vocational and theological commitments affect our understanding of their responses to Luther's writings about Jews and Judaism?

As demonstrated in chapter one, support for Luther cut across the spectrum in the Church Struggle. Members of the German Christians, the Confessing Church, and those in the Protestant middle all appealed to Luther to support their views on various issues. For many, this was also true with respect to Luther's views on Jews and Judaism. We have seen here that a Confessing Church pastor, a Confessing Church theologian, and two German Christian theologians all agree that Luther was "correct" to be antisemitic, or at least "anti-Jewish."

The nature of Protestant antisemitism and anti-Judaism in Nazi Germany was multifaceted. Degrees of antisemitism and levels of discomfort with Nazi policies certainly existed. Schmidt's article, for example, leaves one with the ambiguous impression that support for Nazism may be wrong, but that the Jewish people are nevertheless cursed by God. No heroic actions on behalf of Jews are recommended, and the implications of his affirmative appeal to Luther's harshest antisemitic treatises—which recommend severe measures against them—is evidence enough that he probably would not have supported such resistance. Similarly, Steinlein offers no hope for Jews, except in conversion to Christianity. Both rely heavily on nonrational argumentation in their valuation of Jews and Judaism. Clearly Meyer-Erlach and Vogelsang, despite their differences in scope and approach, support at least the irrational antisemitism of the Nazis, and perhaps the anti-Jewish policies of the regime.

Not only did Confessing Church and German Christian academic theologians vary in the degree of their antisemitism, but they had different approaches to Luther as well. Most did appeal to Luther in one way or another—to his German-ness, to his view of baptism, or to his position on the Old Testament. Some, like Meyer-Erlach, Steinlein, and Schmidt, highlighted Luther's position toward the Old Testament. Though the three took varied positions on its authority for the Christian, they each used Luther's stance on it to denigrate contemporary Judaism to varying degrees. Some were theologically conservative. Others were radically liberal in their religious outlook. Regardless, the majority of German Christian theologians, some employing Luther and others not, sought to move their readers' views of Jews closer to that of Hitler and the Nazis. Most theologians from the Confessing Church camp sought to rescue Luther and Christianity—but not their Jewish neighbors—from the Nazis.

4

CONFESSING
CHURCH PASTORS

Luther's way is a way
of internal tension
between love and anger
toward the Jews. It is
"Christian antisemitism,"
which loves the enemy,
whom it must fight.

—Walter Gabriel,
Dr. Martin Luther on the Jews:
Luther's Christian Antisemitism
according to His Writings (1936)

The baptism of Jewish subjects was not solely a religious act during the Third Reich; it carried serious political undertones as it signified the inclusion of Jews in a state-supported social institution. When the subject was an adult, the act of baptism was connected especially closely to conversion. As such, it went to the heart of an integral feature of Protestant Christianity. Since conversion was part of Luther's answer to the "Jewish Question" of the sixteenth century, the act of publicly sealing that conversion through baptism garnered his attention as well. It is thus very important here to examine German Protestant responses to Luther's view on the matter. In one instance, a Confessing Church minister baptized a purportedly morally suspect Jewish man, an act that mushroomed into an explosive case that garnered a great deal of press coverage, putting local Confessing Church officials on the defensive.

In 1935, the Württemberg Confession Community published a series of newsletters covering the situation in the German Protestant Church, the Confessing Church's struggle with the German Christians, and their debate with the National Socialist worldview.[1] The October 16, 1935 issue contains two articles concerning baptism of Jews. The temporal proximity to the passage of the Nuremberg Race Laws highlights the existential importance of the subject. The first of the two pieces discusses the baptism of a Jewish subject, Albert Hirschland, which was carried out by Confessing Church pastor Oskar Zuckschwerdt of Magdeburg in March of the same year.

Because the case was splashed across the pages of *Der Stürmer*, it also attracted responses from the Confessing Church journal *Junge Kirche* and the newsletter of Zuckschwerdt's local Confessing Church council, the Provincial Council of Brethren (Provinzialbruderrat) of Saxony.[2] The case involved a scandalous matter dealing with the reputation of a pastor and his movement and the legitimacy of the practice of Christian baptism of Jews.[3] The affair also reveals some decidedly antisemitic tendencies in the baptizing pastor's thinking.

According to the Council of Brethren in Saxony, it was Hirschland's doggedness that led to Zuckschwerdt's agreement to perform the baptism. The pastor had only recently rebuffed another Jew who "had desired baptism apparently only from external grounds," and he initially rejected Hirschland's request as well. Hirschland persisted that he was at variance with the Jewish faith and wanted to have a Christian marriage with his Polish fiancée, who had been born into a Jewish family but baptized into the Christian faith as a child. Zuckschwerdt sought advice from members of the Consistory, who answered that the baptism of Jews was still "permissible in principle" and the decision of whether to baptize a particular Jew was left to the individual pastor.[4]

Now free of doubts about Hirschland's sincerity, and given the tacit approval of his church superiors to proceed, Zuckschwerdt intensively catechized his baptismal subject. He baptized Hirschland, who was director of a private commercial school, in mid-March. Their catechetical sessions continued until Holy Week, however, since Hirschland wanted to participate in Holy Communion at that time. The picture is painted of an eager

Front page of a special issue of *Der Stürmer* (August 1935). The
headline reads: "Albert Hirschland: The Magdeburg Race Defiler."
United States Holocaust Memorial Museum.

convert to Christianity who sincerely wanted to join the church and have a Christian household.[5]

Yet, the pastor and the public were "deceived" by Hirschland. He had purportedly been carrying on illicit affairs with an unspecified number of schoolgirls since the previous year. The Council of Brethren in Saxony put it this way: "Even in his house and among his acquaintances nobody suspected that his relationship to schoolgirls was different from that between teacher and pupil. How it was possible that Hirschland could deceive the public about it is incomprehensible. . . . Nobody can look into the deepest soul of a human being." Clearly the Council of Brethren believed the charges against Hirschland, but there is no record that they investigated the matter.

Zuckschwerdt was on a protracted sabbatical when the trial against Hirschland took place, during which time Zuckschwerdt's parish church council unanimously passed a resolution declaring their "unshaken confidence" in him. In a June 27 communication, they expressed their "regret that Hirschland, condemned as a sexual criminal, was admitted into the Christian congregation by baptism." Yet, counter to unspecified accusations made by one newspaper, their pastor had complied with "existing church law regulations" in granting Hirschland's baptism. Upon his return to active ministry, Zuckschwerdt declared (as had his parish church council) that he had complied with the "generally applicable church-legal regulations" and that "during the whole duration of instruction" he "had known nothing of the moral lapses of the baptismal candidate."[6]

On August 23, Zuckschwerdt's attorney, himself a member of the Council of Brethren in Saxony, sent an official letter to the editorship of *Der Stürmer* on behalf of his client.[7] He requests that *Der Stürmer* "incorporate in the next issue of [their] weekly paper" corrections to three specified untruths. First, "It is *untrue*," he says, that a "proper amount of Jewish blood" flows through Zuckschwerdt's veins. "It is *true* that Pastor Zuckschwerdt is of purely Aryan descent." Second, it is "*untrue* that Pastor Zuckschwerdt thinks differently about the Jews than do Christ and Dr. Martin Luther." It is "*true* that Pastor Zuckschwerdt's religious reasoning and ecclesiastical action are grounded in the gospel of the Lord Jesus Christ and the reformational principles of Dr. Martin Luther."[8]

Third, he argues, it is "*untrue* that on March 17, 1935, Pastor Zuckschwerdt baptized 'the more than hundredfold race defiler, the dangerous habitual criminal Albert Hirschland' and admitted him into the Protestant church. It is *true* that Pastor Zuckschwerdt did not have the faintest idea of Hirschland's crimes, which first became public 3 months later through the trial against Hirschland." He requests that *Der Stürmer* send "without delay" documentary evidence of rectification to him—in the form of the issue containing the corrections—and closes with a very thinly veiled threat of further legal action. He sent a copy of the letter to the Council of the Protestant Church of the Old Prussian Union in Berlin.[9] *Der Stürmer* never printed the requested retractions.

Zuckschwerdt's antisemitic tendencies are revealed in both his religious instruction and his public comments. As part of his catechizing of Hirschland, Zuckschwerdt discusses Paul's Epistle to the Romans "in connection" with these "present questions," "for example the *fatal role* of the Jews in public life, in politics, art, and the press."[10] Further, he mentions the "special task" the baptized Jew has toward *his Volk* and the "obligations toward *our Volk* which he must fulfill," by which he meant service to the nation in wartime. While the Württemberg article in toto is a defense of Christian baptism of Jews, the author includes without comment the pastor's antisemitic reasoning as part of the catechetical process. In context, it is quite clear that "his Volk" refers to the Jewish people as a whole, while "our Volk" seems to refer not to the Confessing Church, nor even to the German Protestant Church, but to the German Volk.[11]

Zuckschwerdt also resorts to a defense of his "Aryan" heritage in response to a public attack of his baptism of Hirschland. The Württemberg newsletter reports that in August *Der Stürmer* published a photograph of Zuckschwerdt, derisively implying that he looked nearly as Jewish as the Jew he had baptized. He responds with vigor, saying the attacks are "based on malicious defamation." He in fact can verify his family tree from 1604 on his father's side, and from 1501 on his mother's side. It is easy, he says, to prove his "pure Aryan descent" far beyond what the state requires.[12]

The use of such language may be understood in part by the climate of Nazi Germany in 1935—hundreds of Confessing Church leaders and many others were being arrested and imprisoned for their beliefs.[13] Yet, he strikes two distinctly dissonant notes when he appears to affirm the logic of the Aryan Paragraph with respect to pastors, while denying its application to baptized church members. At the very least, he seems more concerned with defending himself than the Jew he has baptized, even if that act had demonstrated at least a modicum of courage. Zuckschwerdt baldly embraces racial-biological antisemitic ideology, and garners no editorial comment from the writers of either the Württemberg or Saxony articles.

In this chapter and the next, I will address the utilization of Luther's anti-Jewish writings among Confessing Church and German Christian pastors and bishops amid the backdrop of the unfolding Nazi terror against the Jewish people. While this theme was somewhat less prevalent among unaffiliated Protestant pastors, it became an ideological battleground between some Confessing Church and German Christian clergy.[14]

There were approximately eighteen thousand Protestant pastors serving in Germany during the Third Reich.[15] As leaders of both individual congregations (consisting of dozens or hundreds of members) as well as regional and national church councils, pastors and bishops were influential on account of both their positions of authority within the churches and their relationships with their members. The reach of those who had their theological works published was further still. The Protestant church was an ingrained social and cultural institution recognized by the state, but was nonetheless in a condition of long-term decline by the time the Nazis came to power. Even so, it still "received tax revenue collected for it by the state from every baptized member."[16]

Confessing Church pastors numbered just over 5,200 in 1934, but this figure dipped to less than five thousand by 1937 and probably remained near that level until 1945.[17] As such, they constituted a bit less than 30 percent of all German Protestant pastors. Despite varying degrees of protestation against Nazi encroachments on church sovereignty, including the maintenance of illegal seminaries for pastoral training, the Confessing Church remained a state church, part of the German Protestant Church. The Confessing Church "was unable to conceive seriously of becoming a 'free' church, that is, one dependent entirely on the contributions of a voluntary membership. The close relationship that traditionally existed between church and state . . . continued to inform the Confessing outlook."[18]

Before considering writings by several Confessing Church pastors, I will address a few important matters. First, I will examine briefly the issue of general popular opinion toward Jews in late Weimar and Nazi Germany. Next, the general tenor of the relationship between pastor and parishioner is worth exploring here, if but briefly, to demonstrate the currency of the ideas that were being expounded from German Protestant pulpits. A brief discussion of Confessing Church responses to Luther's views on Jewish baptism follows.

Then, I will consider some works by Heimsheim pastor Heinrich Fausel in the context of his family's rescue of a Jewish family, after which I will address the very direct confrontation of Luther's views on Jews and Judaism in the works of Berlin apologist Hansgeorg Schroth and Halle pastor and Confessing Church leader Walter Gabriel. My examination of the works of Schroth and Gabriel will demonstrate that Confessing Church clergy could be "anti-Nazi" and "antisemitic" at the same time. Finally, I will explore an intriguing unsigned manuscript titled "Luther on the Jewish Question." Taken together, these writings demonstrate the limits and inconsistencies of the narrowly conceived nonrational Confessing Church theology in its confrontation of the "Jewish Question."

Popular Opinion about Jews

Despite the "cover of totalitarian uniformity" of German society during the Third Reich, the "social, political and religious structures of the previous period were preserved," revealing "the public's heterogeneous view of the government's ideology and policy."[19] Popular opinion about Jews between the years just prior to the Nazi ascent to power and the end of the Second World War may be divided along the lines of two distinct periods. The first ran from the 1930s until the beginning of the war, a period in which public reactions centered upon "racist legislation and the exclusion of Jews from various spheres of life" in German society. The second lasted for the duration of the war, the period which saw their mass deportation and extermination, what became known as the "Final Solution."

During the first period, reactions to the exclusion of Jews from German life fell into at least four lines. Some "viewed the racial legislation as a possible permanent solution of social, cultural and biological segregation and isolation" that should nonetheless be predicated upon "the preservation of public law and order." A second group, which included many members of the SA, believed the government's policy toward the Jewish community to be not extreme enough and "launched a series of violent anti-Jewish initiatives" aimed at "accelerating and radicalizing 'the solution' of the Jewish Question 'from below.'" The reaction of the third group, which included many religious people, the Marxist left, and liberal intellectuals, consisted of "overt criticism in the opposite direction, based on religious, social or economic grounds." The final group apparently took no position on the issue of antisemitic regime policy.[20]

During the war years, in contrast to this differentiated picture, the most pronounced response was "almost total silence" and passivity toward the plight of Jews. This was the case even though many expressed diverse opinions on religion, foreign policy, the economy, and so on. Despite a few notable exceptions of objection to the mass deportations and extermina- tions in the east, and a successful campaign of protest against euthanasia, most were deafeningly silent. Just why this was so can be attributed in part to extensive Nazi regime propaganda campaigns against "Bolshevistic," "world" Jewry and a depersonalized attitude toward Jews brought on by their "gradual disappearance from the German social landscape." Juxta- posed against this general passivity is the stark reality that the mass mur- der of Jews beginning with the invasion of the Soviet Union in June 1941 was general public knowledge among the German population by 1943.

Laity–Pastor Solidarity

A brief survey of church periodicals across the divides in the Church Struggle demonstrates the general solidarity of church parishioners with their pastors and vice versa. Many of these periodicals contained adver- tisements for events that included laity as part of their target audience. One such ad, which appeared in the weekly German Christian publication *Evangelium im Dritten Reich* (Gospel in the Third Reich), was for an "Aca- demic Conference of 'German Christians'" in Berlin. The conference was to include lectures by professors and German Christian leaders. Students, pastors, and "interested laity" were among the invitees.[21] Another issue promoted a "Conference of the German-Christian Young Theologians" in Berlin with the bolded title "Attention, Theologians, Laity."[22] In November 1937, a report on the German Christian "Eisenach 1937" conference, writ- ten by an "enthusiastic participant," appeared in the German Christian weekly *Deutscher Sonntag* (German Sunday).[23]

In another issue, a "C. Pfaff, Bad Cannstatt" writes a letter to pastors and "fellow public speakers," encouraging pastors by telling them of the joy, strength, and courage people have received through their lectures and sermons. Pfaff further expresses thanks to their wives and children for making sacrifices for the mission of the church.[24]

Confessing Church laypersons also demonstrated such solidarity with their pastors. The June 21, 1935 issue of the Oeynhausen Provincial Coun- cil of Brethren's newsletter contains an article on "Declarations of the Non-

Theological *Synodalen* [synod members]." The non-theological members of the synod pledge to stand with their pastors in their struggle for the sole validity of the Scriptures and the Confession in the German Protestant Church, declaring that pastors and parishioners alike share "joint responsibility" for their church.[25]

The snippets presented here simply serve to demonstrate general lay support for the positions taken by pastors in the Church Struggle. What pastors had to say often had a "decisive influence" on their congregants' points of view.[26] Thus, these clippings demonstrate that they would have been likely to support their pastors' stance regarding Luther and the "Jewish Question."[27]

Confessing Church Pastors

Luther and the Baptism of Jews

An article titled "Luther and the Baptism of the Jews" appeared directly after the item about the scandalous Hirschland–Zuckschwerdt affair in the Württemberg newsletter of October 1935. The author is again unnamed. As its introduction indicates, the occasion for the piece is the uneasiness among church members caused by *Der Stürmer's* publication about Luther's treatise *On the Jews and Their Lies.*[28] The disquiet is due, first, to the fact that the editor of *Der Stürmer*—and not the church—supposedly had made people aware of Luther's attitude toward the Jewish people and second, that in spite of the reformer's animus toward them, the Protestant church still carries out baptism of Jews.

The writer defends the position of the church in the matter. "The church never made an attempt to cover up the attitude of Luther." In 1931, the *Landesverein für Innere Mission* in Dresden published the treatise so that its content would be made public.[29] Further, Luther's judgment about Jewish character, as reflected in writings toward the end of his life, should not be misunderstood. After many attempts to "win them for the Gospel," very often he had been disappointed by Jews' refusal to convert.

Next, he points to two passages that prove—contra *Der Stürmer*—that Luther never rejected baptism of Jews. The first passage, from *On the Jews and Their Lies,* shows that it is possible for Jews to convert to Christianity and receive the grace of God. The second is from his *Admonition against the Jews,* a sermon preached three days before his death; in it, he holds out the possibility of both conversion and baptism to Jews who accept Christ as their Messiah.

The author concludes that to be truthful to Luther's position, one cannot simply pass over these affirmations. "The portrayal of *Der Stürmer* remains one-sided." He caps his argument by citing John 3:16, which describes God's love for the world, offering eternal life to all who believe in Christ.[30] The unnamed author's line of reasoning delivers a clear implication. Salvation, publicly affirmed and sealed in the act of baptism, is thus promised to *all,* including Jews.

In this second article, the writer simply seeks to counter, in the first instance, the biased portrayal of Luther's position on Jewish baptism offered in *Der Stürmer.* He also attempts to defend the church against a supposed suppression of the reformer's attitudes toward Jews and Judaism. Its proximity to the article on Pastor Zuckschwerdt provides a sober reminder—that antisemitic attitudes prevailed among even those who were willing to defend the rights of baptized Jews.

The Württemberg newsletter articles serve as a defense of Pastor Zuckschwerdt's innocence in the Hirschland affair and of the practice of baptism of Jews in general, which they root in the words of both Christ and Martin Luther. The language is purely that of faith; it is essentially nonrational. The same can be said for the very similar Saxony newsletter article.

The Council of Brethren in Saxony also sought to affirm their institutional support for their local pastor in light of the fact that Magdeburg's German Christian bishop Friedrich Peter had recommended that Protestant pastors in Magdeburg distance themselves from Zuckschwerdt.[31] In his legal letter to *Der Stürmer,* Zuckschwerdt's attorney seeks to defend his client against the "untrue" allegations of his supposedly Jewish bloodline, his purported disagreement with Christ and Luther about "the Jews," and the invidious charge that he had known of Hirschland's offenses before he baptized him. As such, it is primarily a defense of this upstanding "Aryan" pastor. It only addresses implicitly the issue of the rights of baptized Jews.

Taken together, these documents paint a picture of the Confessing Church's belief in conversion and baptism of Jews, an avowal whose primary purpose was the protection of church sovereignty. They nonetheless advanced the unintended consequence of asserting the rights of the few Jews who would be willing to convert to Christianity.

Heinrich Fausel, Heimsheim Pastor

Heinrich Fausel was born in 1900 in Reutlingen, near Stuttgart. After passing his *Abitur* (a college entrance exam required in the German educational system), he served in the military in the waning months of the First World War. From 1919 to 1922, he studied Protestant theology and philosophy at Tübingen and Marburg. Fausel would later marry his friend Hermann Diem's sister Helene. After serving as vicar in several churches in the early 1920s, in 1927 Fausel became pastor in Heimsheim, where he remained until 1946.[32]

Heimsheim was located in the largely agricultural district of Leonberg in Württemberg (southwest Germany) and had approximately 1,150 inhabitants in 1939. Enthusiasm for Nazism was relatively low in Leonberg, as traditional regional and family ties superseded the need for identification with a political party. Nevertheless, many did join the party in spring 1933, due in large part to opportunism.[33]

From 1934 to 1936, Fausel was part of the regional Council of Brethren and a delegate to the national Confessing Church synods. He served briefly as mayor of Heimsheim after the war. In 1946, he became the part-time director of a secondary school that prepared students for Protestant seminary, a post which became full time in 1952. In 1956, he received his doctorate in theology from Tübingen, and began teaching there in the following year. Tübingen bestowed an honorary professorship upon him in 1963. Fausel died in 1967.[34]

Fausel's theology generally steered clear of political statements, but also bore marks of the "orders of creation" theology associated with Althaus. In a district-wide liturgical festival of song that took place in Heimsheim in May 1933, Fausel urged parishioners that if they wanted to see a resurrection of the Volk, they must hear the Word of God anew and honor God in their heart "who at all times leads and guides us, not only in times of upswing, but also in times of judgment and downfall." The "Volk lives," he proclaims, "if it affirms itself as *order of creation*, ordered in the world [by God]. . . ."[35]

There is a sense in this short homily that, yes, Germany can undergo a "resurrection" after bad times, but in order for it to happen they must honor God and serve each other. There is no sense of triumphalism, and the means for this resurrection are explicitly scriptural and spiritual—and in no way political.

In several of his wartime and early postwar sermons, he mentions the suffering of the German people, particularly with respect to loved ones dying in battle. However, there are only occasional references to the suffering of neighbors. In a sermon preached in Heimsheim on New Year's Day, 1945, Fausel describes how the name of Jesus

> signifies for us the blessedness, the salvation, the rescue for us in the midst of a lost world. In this name sins are forgiven and dead ones raised up, devils driven out and sick ones healed. . . . Where this name is, is the victory. This applies also to us, to our present. Where this name of Jesus is proclaimed, there is nothing lost, even if we lose belongings and many are taken from us, to whom our heart belongs.[36]

The sermon makes no mention, however, of the sufferings of millions of Jews and others, who had already died at the hands of the Nazi regime by the beginning of 1945. Similarly, his farewell address to his Heimsheim congregation two years later, to which I will return later, focuses almost exclusively on German suffering.

As part of a week-long series of lectures in January 1934 in Leonberg titled "Christianity in the Third Reich," Heinrich Fausel delivered his lecture on "The Jewish Question." A short report on the lecture that appeared the next day in the Leonberg Daily notes that the town hall where it was held was "completely filled."[37]

Fausel begins by limiting his portrayal of the Jewish Question to the realm of the church. He says, "In the realm of the church, it [the Jewish Question] does not concern the question of the designated race [the Jewish race]" or "the psychological-bodily characteristic of a Volk" but rather Christ, who is the center of the world. In Christ, so argues Fausel, the fate of the Church, the fate of the peoples of the world, and also the fate of the Jews are decided. "That is the premise from which we proceed. . . ."[38] With this nonrational argument, Fausel, like many others in the Confessing Church, seeks to distance his portrayal of the Jewish people from the notions of biology and race current in Nazi circles both inside and outside of the church.

He next explores several images of Jews selectively drawn from the Hebrew Scriptures. He appeals first to Isaiah 5, which contains a parable about God the divine grower of the vine and the people of Israel, caretakers of a beautiful vineyard. Fausel likens the vineyard to the law of God. Israel, the Volk of God, is called to produce the fruits of justice and righteousness through the Law of God. But they do not heed this call, and instead desire to be lords rather than servants, owners instead of tenants and caretakers of the vineyard.[39] Fausel offers here a typically one-sided presentation of Jewish disobedience and obduracy. Here is an example of nonrational language being used to denigrate Jews and Judaism. The Christian Scriptures have many positive things to say about Israel and the Jewish people as well, in both the Old Testament and the New. Yet, Fausel's examples from the Hebrew Scriptures emphasize all of the negatives, and none of the positives about Israel's existence.

In a rather clumsy but revealing introduction of his discussion of Israel's fate according to the New Testament, Fausel, describing the "Jewish Question" as a "besetting" problem, maintains that it is the "awakening of modern racial consciousness" that makes it "impossible" to answer solely from the Bible. Since the mid-nineteenth century there has been a "terrifying foreign invasion," which threatens the very existence of the German nationality, and against which the German Volk must defend itself. Fausel here explicitly regards the granting of equal rights to European Jews as a tragic consequence of the implementation of the thinking of the French Revolution.[40]

He further maintains that "there is no racial question in our sense [of the word] in the world of the New Testament." Here he implies without explanation that there is a "racial question" upon which he and his audience can agree. The opposition between Jews and gentiles in the New Testament is not about race, he says—it is about Christ. Yet, Israel's rejection of Christ was, he argues, a *"unanimous rejection by an entire Volk, its leaders included. . . ."*[41] There is no mistaking here how completely Fausel views Jewish rejection of Jesus as Messiah. He nevertheless affirms elsewhere that God sent his Son as part of "this Volk," that is the Volk of Israel.[42]

He spends the second half of the address discussing Luther's writings about Jews and Judaism. Fausel begins here by stressing his desire to correct the "half-truths" prevalent about Luther's position toward "the Jews." He recounts in rather brief detail Luther's progression from a fairly positive position toward them to the unleashing of his "full wrath" on them. He situates this evolution in the social and political context of sixteenth-century Germany.

Luther, Fausel avers, started with a relatively positive attitude toward Jews. Then, however, he had some negative experiences with individual Jews after a Judaizing sect had gained influence in Moravia by 1532. Luther responded in 1538 with the treatise *Against the Sabbatarians,* in which he "completely dissociates himself from the Jews."[43] A Jewish rebuttal to this treatise was then published, while authorities permitted a large number of Jews to settle in the city of Luther's birth, Eisleben, provoking his anger further.

Then Luther's "full wrath" broke loose. He wrote three treatises against the Jews between 1542 and 1543. Two of these—*On the Jews and Their Lies* and *On the Ineffable Name*—deal not only with theological, but also social and political matters.

Fausel cites three primary concerns of these treatises. First, he says, "Luther sees in the Jews the enemies of Christ." The "Christ Question" is central. Second, "Luther suggests a set of tremendously sharp measures against the deniers of Christ, which he commended to the authorities." Third, "Luther lost hope for conversion of the Jewish Volk, but held fast to the hope of individual conversions."[44] Crucially, I think, Fausel recounts not only the reformer's nonrational arguments—for example, the supposed Jewish boasts about lineage and chosen-ness. He also references Luther's antisemitic sociopolitical arguments, which are drawn neither from the Bible nor from theological tradition.

He quotes Luther, who opines, "It is a lie whenever they state that they are kept imprisoned . . . they hold the Christians captive in their own land, sit behind the oven, lounge around and roast pears, gorge themselves like animals, drink alcohol . . . blaspheme our Lord Christ as a magician. . . ."[45] Here a nonrational anti-Judaic charge—their supposed blasphemy of Christ as a magician—is mingled together with xenophobic images of lazy, gluttonous Jews. In chapter two, we noted how Luther accepted irrational medieval tales about purported ritual murder and host defamation. This example serves to demonstrate the almost seamless interweaving of nonrational, irrational, and xenophobic charges against Jews prevalent especially in these later writings of Luther, and by extension, in Fausel's appropriation of them.

Fausel later elucidates Luther's infamous seven severe recommendations against Jews. Attempting to dissociate the reformer's approach from more vulgar forms of antisemitism, Fausel differentiates between Luther's recommendations and typical medieval argumentation. He twice notes, for example, that it is the "authorities"—not the "excited masses" or an "unrestrained mass [of people]"—that have the right to punish Jews for their supposed crimes. Fausel also contextualizes Luther's polemics, noting that

in the last half-year of his life, the reformer spent much more time denigrating Catholicism than he did Judaism.[46]

Fausel then applies Luther's anti-Jewish writings to the current situation. Luther's position, he argues, should lead his fellow Protestants to
affirm "the national efforts for the protection of (our) own Volk" and to
reject "all attempts to introduce the Aryan Paragraph into the area of the
church legally."[47] The introduction into the church of the Aryan Paragraph—which was not mandated by the Nazi regime—was supported by
the German Christian faction, while the Confessing Church remained divided over the issue. Many in the Protestant "middle," including Paul Althaus, supported its implementation.

Fausel calls the adoption of the Aryan Paragraph "senseless," in part
because this "foreign invasion" did not occur among the German Protestant clergy. ". . . Of the 18,000 German pastors," it would apply for "approximately 6," he says. His numbers are wrong—there were more likely
between 33 and 90—but his argument underscores the prevailing Confessing Church view that the issue was "minor" because it involved so few
ministers.[48]

Fausel explicitly supports the prohibition of mixed marriages between
Jews and non-Jews and placing restrictions on the number of Jewish civil
servants in Germany. "An absolutely valid reason" for these, he says, "is
present in the menacing foreign infiltration of [our] own Volk by a decadent Judaism, which is uprooted from its own faith and its *Volkstum.* . . ."

He also opposes the creation of separate Jewish-Christian congregations on biblical and reformational (i.e., nonrational) grounds. In matters
regarding Jewish Christians, of which Luther speaks, "the freedom of the
Gospel is greater than the connection by Volk to race. . . ."[49] Fausel thus
circumscribes his nationalistic and racial views with the Gospel. Utilizing
in rather sophisticated fashion Luther's writings, passages from the Old
and New Testaments, as well as xenophobic and antisemitic stereotypes,
he presents both his view of Jews and his remedy for the present situation
as he sees it.

What, then, may we conclude from this? First, Fausel's lecture "The
Jewish Question" contains xenophobic, nonrational anti-Judaic, and irrational antisemitic elements. To be sure, Fausel's apolitical theology dictated that most of the argumentation would be biblical and confessional,
that is, primarily nonrational. In this, Fausel was certainly not alone, especially among his Confessing Church brethren. Yet, at crucial junctures

in his argument, he utilized the irrational antisemitic language of fear and endangerment to describe the perceived Jewish threat to the German Volk.

Still, the fact that nine years later, under the threat of being thrown into a concentration camp themselves, Fausel and his wife would shelter a Jewish woman in their home seems, on the surface of it, something of a startling turnabout. Yet, a few factors militate against, or at the very least mitigate, this view. First is the lack of a personal confession on his part that the words that he, as a respected religious leader, spoke to a completely filled parish hall in Leonberg in 1934, could have contributed to anti-Judaic and antisemitic suspicion and hatred in his local community. Nowhere does Fausel seem to have countered or even qualified the views he presented there. As mentioned, several of his wartime sermons make reference to the suffering of German compatriots and sons who had fallen on foreign soil. And there is an occasional reference to the suffering of neighbors. His farewell address to his Heimsheim congregation focuses almost exclusively on their own suffering, which was certainly very real.

We cannot assume that Fausel's participation in the rescue of Herta Pineas was motivated completely by love of neighbor or a sense of personal guilt for his anti-Jewish attitudes. Perhaps his friendship with the more outspoken Württemberg Ecclesiastical-Theological Society compatriot Hermann Diem and, more broadly, with the chain of Protestant Württemberg rescuers, might reveal some positive peer pressure for such a course of action. Perhaps Heinrich's wife Helene, who is mentioned by name in Hermann Pineas's recollection of the events two years later, exerted some influence.[50] Even more likely, and more importantly, Fausel's words and actions demonstrate that people, religious and nonreligious alike, often do not act in ways that are consistent with their worldview. The participation in Herta Pineas's rescue, however, and his signature on the Society's 1946 Declaration on the Jewish Question (to which I will return in the Conclusion) reveal at the very least a more general sense of collective guilt for the awful fate that had been visited on millions of Europe's Jews.[51]

Walter Gabriel, Halle Pastor

Walter Gabriel was born in October 1887 in Oberschmon (near Halle on the Saale). After completing his university studies at Halle, he was ordained as a minister in 1912. From that time until 1918, he served in several churches, first as assistant pastor and then as pastor. For the next four years, he held the posts of pastor and chaplain (in Magdeburg), and finally naval pastor (in Cuxhaven, north of Bremen). From 1923 until 1943, he was the pastor of the St. Laurentius church in Halle on the Saale.[52]

Gabriel would become part of the province of Saxony's Council of Brethren of the Pastors' Emergency League, representing the constituency of Halle.[53] He also represented Saxony at the momentous Barmen Synod (May 29–31, 1934) which produced a declaration opposing both the German Christians and Nazi intrusion in the church, but failed to address the more divisive issue of the implementation of the Aryan Paragraph in the church.[54] On November 11–12, 1934, the churches of Saxony held their first formal synod at Halle, signifying their official formation as the Confessing Church of the province of Saxony.[55]

In 1936, Gabriel spent six weeks in custody and in 1938 was granted amnesty after a special court complaint was lodged against him because of a purported offense against the law concerning treachery. On January 9, 1941, Gabriel, now district chairman (*Bezirksobmann*) of the Confessing Church in Halle, was arrested and later interned at Dachau. Released from internment in December 1942, he nonetheless had to cease pastoral activity. Despite some protests from ministerial allies, Gabriel's place in the provincial Council of Brethren was given to another pastor. The unity of the provincial church leadership was shattered. He was reinstated into his ministerial office in 1945, once again serving St. Laurentius in Halle, a post he held until he was granted emeritus status in 1962. Gabriel died in Halle in August 1983.[56]

In 1936, the pastor and Confessing Church leader from Saxony published a short book titled *D. Martin Luther Von den Juden: Luthers christlicher Antisemitismus nach seinen Schriften* (Dr. Martin Luther on the Jews: Luther's Christian Antisemitism according to His Writings).[57] Gabriel's work here—at least in terms of methodology—resembles that of Vogelsang more than it does Pauls.[58] His conclusions, however, though not completely unique, differ with these interpretations of Luther and the "Jewish Question."

Gabriel begins with a description of the current historical context as he sees it, recognizing that the "Jewish Question" is currently being discussed widely. Like Vogelsang, Gabriel laments that Germans are living more in the shadow of Lessing, Moses Mendelssohn, and the Enlightenment than in Luther's shadow. Yet, the surrounding events are giving "renewed attention" to Luther's writings about the Jewish people. Luther is "hardly well-known" and his "struggle for the Lord Christ alone is nearly forgotten." Yet, he is remembered as "the German," "the fighter against political Catholicism," and "the creator of the unified German language."[59]

He laments how it is "only" with reference to the Jewish question that Luther is now quoted, making reference to a *Der Stürmer* portrayal of Luther as a Jew-hater and rejecter of Jewish baptism and to the espousal of a separate "Jewish Christian" church, which appeared in the German Christian paper *Positives Christentum* (Positive Christianity). It is from Luther, contends Gabriel, that we need an answer to the "Jewish Question."[60] He attempts to formulate such an answer by beginning with Luther's historical context.

As Gabriel sees it, the "Jewish Question" is for Luther a completely *religious* and *missionary* issue. Luther never changed his (positive) "fundamental position" that Jews were "blood brothers" of Jesus, "bearers of the revealing God," and the "chosen people." After these summary statements, Gabriel comprehensively traces Luther's position vis-à-vis the Jewish people throughout his career. He even covers Luther's encounters with Josel of Rosheim.[61]

Gabriel then spends the longest portion of the treatise discussing *On the Jews and Their Lies,* quoting Luther extensively. In one very intriguing passage, Gabriel says that the reformer now "recommends the *method* of a 'sharp mercy' instead of the initial friendliness."[62] He seems to be implying that rather than undergoing a change of heart, Luther instead undertook a change of method. This reading of Gabriel is consistent with his claim that Luther's fundamental position toward the Jewish people did not change.

In keeping with the idea of a religious and missionary answer to the "Jewish Question," Gabriel states that Luther's introduction to *On the Jews and Their Lies* would have strengthened the "theological apologetics" of the beleaguered Christians of Luther's day who were endangered in their faith by proselytizing Jews.[63] Next, he follows the reformer's condemnation of supposed Jewish blasphemies and disobedience, again with copious quotations. Then, he focuses on the seven severe recommendations.[64] He later pauses to admit that while Luther did not talk so gravely about Jews in a glib manner (but rather, "Christianly," "religiously"), nonetheless others of his time still spoke more moderately than he. Furthermore, on more than one occasion he refers to Luther's speech as "crude."[65] This is an important admission, showing a nuanced approach to the infamous treatise that acknowledges its paradoxical combination of excoriation and mercy.

Gabriel's conclusions are thus rather well developed and calibrated. Nevertheless, he calls Luther's approach to the Jewish people "Christian antisemitism," which Gabriel attempts to portray as consistent with Saint Paul's view in the Epistle to the Romans. He positions this concept between a crude or vulgar antisemitism and overt philosemitism: "Luther's way is a way of internal tension between love and anger toward the Jews. It is 'Christian antisemitism,' *which loves the enemy, whom it must fight.*"[66] He next proceeds to discuss twelve bases of this attitude.

The first such basis is quite revealing. "The Jews *are* the chosen Volk of God. . . ." he says. He cites only *past* achievements to show this chosenness to be true; their history, the message of the Prophets, the Old Testament, and even their status as "blood-brothers" of Jesus.[67] The second basis juxtaposes these achievements with their post–New Testament-era performance, underscoring this "way of internal tension."

Despite their chosen-ness, "The Jews as an entire Volk have always fought against God," have "crucified Christ on the cross," and "still today as a Volk do not accept Christ." What, then, is the bottom line of this second conclusion? "*They are rejected as a Volk.*" The third conclusion is that pious Jews who convert to Christ are regarded as "beloved brothers." Fourthly, Christians must not argue with Jews, for this has no purpose. They have been scattered and are homeless in the whole world. Their own prophets testify that Jesus is the rescuer from sin and death.[68]

While the first four bases are essentially theological in nature, the next four are basically sociopolitical. Not only should the church carry out a mission to the Jews, but the state should be extremely wary of these enemies of Christ and Christians who are "devoted to money." Next, the state should carry out Luther's sociopolitical recommendations. Another basis reaffirms that the sociopolitical recommendations are part of the "sharp mercy" that Luther espouses. Thus, Gabriel integrates Luther's theological method with sociopolitical understanding.

Yet another basis speaks to the issue of eschatology—whether or not at the end of days, but before the Second Coming (*Parousia*) of Jesus, the Jews would convert to Christ.[69] Luther leaves this question undecided. Luther also did not recommend a separate "Jewish Christian" (or "non-Aryan") church, as some of Gabriel's contemporaries were recommending.[70] Finally, Gabriel does not believe the "racial-biological view of the

Jewish question" to be the solution, and it "hardly came into Luther's field of vision." Instead, *"For Luther the Jewish Question is a purely religious and moral, social affair."*[71]

Gabriel concludes with a multifaceted approach to the Jewish question. He argues that if German Protestants are to "remain a Christian Volk," they must reject both the Enlightenment view of Judaism as only a religion and not a nation and "an unchristian antisemitism" that sees in the Jews "only a devilish, inhuman nation." The solution is not force, but Jewish mission.

Yet, there is also a place for the state in Gabriel's solution. Church and state must work together for a solution to the Jewish question. Tellingly, Gabriel says that it will "certainly" be "good and wise" if the church leaves the "racial and social details" to the "wisdom of the state."[72] Here he appears inconsistent. Shortly before, he had argued that for Luther the "Jewish Question" is "a purely religious and moral, *social* affair." Yet, the church is supposed to leave the "racial and *social* details" to the state.

Either Gabriel is simply articulating his concept of "social" affairs poorly, or he is unwilling to recommend that the state follow Luther's seven-point plan. He is willing to attack "unchristian antisemitism," which clearly would include racial-biological Nazi antisemitism. Yet, he is also willing to leave the consequences of "unchristian antisemitism" in the hands of the Nazi authorities. It is worth remembering here that this work, like the Württemberg newsletter, appeared shortly after the Nuremberg Laws were enacted.

In closing, Gabriel posits a conception of "Judaism" that is developed more fully in the writings of Hansgeorg Schroth. According to Gabriel, Luther sees "Judaism" in any religion or intellectual ideal (including the Enlightenment) that rejects Christ as Son of God and Redeemer. There are thus living in Germany both a good number of "Jews" from a religious standpoint and "Jews" from Luther's point of view.[73]

Hansgeorg Schroth, Berlin Apologist

Hansgeorg Schroth was born in Stuttgart in April 1904. From 1934 to 1938 he served as a scholarly advisor in the Apologetische Centrale (Apologetics Center; AC) in Berlin. The AC came into being in 1921 as a department of the Central Committee for Inner Mission. Its primary function was to serve as the "material collecting point for all religious, ideological, sectarian movements" as well as an "information and exchange center" for organizations and individuals working in apologetics. This task was particularly salient in light of the growing number of new religious groups and ideological movements in early Weimar. In cooperation with the Protestant Press Association, the AC informed not only Protestant congregations but also the general public about such movements. Equipped with its own library and press archive, it produced and printed thousands of copies of apologetic leaflets, pamphlets, and books.[74]

Part of a group of twelve colleagues, Schroth's official area of responsibility was "völkisch-worldview questions and documentation service." His job description included "the observation of the cumulative völkisch currents, their explanations and manifestations, as well as theological treatment of the questions raised thereby." During his tenure with the AC, he wrote numerous short tracts about theological and topical matters.[75] After the Gestapo closed the AC in late 1937, Schroth became employed as a *Volksmissionar* (evangelical missionary) in Berlin-Steglitz.[76] Beginning in June 1938, Schroth served as a "lay assistant to the rectory who was equipped with theological education. . . ." Thus, at this point, Schroth was not an ordained minister.[77]

Schroth resigned from this position in August 1939, intending to shift focus in his ministry. Yet, with the outbreak of the war, he was sent out to an Inner Mission post in the former border province of Posen-West Prussia, to fill a spot vacated by an army conscript. Sometime later, he served for an indeterminate amount of time at a reserve military hospital in Döberitz-Elsgrund. After the war, he resumed work as an evangelical missionary and belonged to a working group of the German Protestant Church Congress (Deutsche Evangelische Kirchentag) called "Jews and Christians."[78] He was ordained as a minister in September 1951, and in 1958 was involved in discussions to reconstitute the AC with a new name and mission. He retired from the ministry in 1968.[79]

I will examine two works written by Schroth in 1937, published just months apart. I will address them out of their chronological order, as the arguments of the later work help us to understand Schroth's general view of Jews and Judaism. The first is an article titled "Christentum und Judentum" (Christianity and Judaism).[80] Here, Schroth makes six assertions about the relationship between Christianity and Judaism. It slowly becomes evident that he is deeply suspicious of Judaism. Ever since the emergence of Christianity, there has been a "deadly opposition" between Judaism and "non-Judaism," particularly between Judaism and Christianity. In contrast to the likes of Althaus and Elert, however, he rejects a "völkisch Reformation" to rescue Christians from what he describes as the "Jewish-Bolshevistic" enemy. The bases of such attempts are not in accordance with those on which the Christian church stands.[81]

With his second assertion, Schroth gives further reason to rebuff the völkisch Reformation. Racial-thinking (*Rassegedanken*) views history—including the history of Judaism—through the lens of the unchangeable racial-soul (*Rassenseele*). Schroth rejects such an approach. Yet, the antipathy toward Judaism becomes more evident in this third point. Here he states baldly, "The nature and activity of Judaism today culminate in Bolshevism." In discovering the relationship between Judaism and Christianity, it is crucial for him that Bolshevism is viewed as a "system of the most conscious atheism and anti-Christianity." Further, "The Jewish–Bolshevistic struggle for annihilation against religion and church shows the true face of the Jew."[82]

Hence, while the basis of Schroth's suspicion of Judaism may be different from that of either Meyer-Erlach or Vogelsang, the outcome is the same. The Jew is the enemy of the Christian not because of his race, but because of his alliance with anti-Christian Bolshevism. Since Roman times, and right to the present day, the Jew has not only opposed Christianity, but has desired a "world revolution."

Point four highlights further Schroth's rejection of the völkisch version of the faith, including an Aryan Jesus. It is not because the Jew is anti-völkisch that he is ungodly; it is his "political-world-revolutionary messianic dream." Behind these claims and goals is none other than Satan himself.[83]

His fifth argument demonstrates his desire to fight the fight along biblical-theological rather than political-historical lines. It is again not a völkisch worldview but a separation of the Christian from the anti-Christian Jew that is needed. We can infer that there is no third category of Jew for Schroth. The Jew *as a Jew* is clearly to be targeted with the "Christian antisemitism" of Luther.

With his final argument, Schroth rejects the centrality of the Volk, as he asks whence salvation comes—from Christ or from the Volk?[84] For Schroth, salvation is not linked with the created order of the Volk, but with redemption through Christ. Luther's "Christian antisemitism"—an attempt at a purely religious solution to the Jewish Question that I will consider shortly—is also recommended. The sum total of Schroth's six points is a concoction consisting of a nonrational embrace of traditional Christology and an irrational espousal of Jewish–Bolshevistic world-domination conspiracy thinking.

Having established Schroth's basic view of Jews and Judaism, we now have a framework for understanding his earlier treatise, *Luthers christlicher Antisemitismus Heute* (Luther's Christian Antisemitism Today).[85] He notes very early in this work that the German church needs specific answers to questions regarding the racial idea of the Nazi worldview. The Protestant churches that aligned themselves with the Nazis became campaigners for Aryan legislation in the church. When the Protestant church has a debate about "antisemitism," he implores, it must do so on the basis of its own "self-understanding" and not with a political or church-political aim.[86] Schroth, in true Confessing Church fashion, seeks for the church to be the church.

He proceeds to describe the basis of Luther's attitude toward Jews, his "Christian antisemitism." With Gabriel, he contends that Luther's fundamental attitude did not undergo a radical change late in his life. Rather, his position was "unshakable" and justified "salvation-historically." Schroth defines this concept of "salvation-history," prevalent among German theologians of the nineteenth and twentieth centuries, as the "history of God with us, revealed in Jesus, the Christ, testified and found in the Scriptures."[87]

Next, Schroth places Luther's antisemitism in its historical context. On the whole, he argues, the reformer proceeded from an essentially medieval mindset that regarded the Jew as holding a "completely foreign nature" and thus deserved isolation from the Volk. Not only this, but the Jew purportedly played a prominent role in Luther's Germany as merchant, banker, and capitalist. Government was strongly influenced by Jewish advice. This ubiquitous figure "constituted a political factor" and thus the "Jewish Question is already at Luther's time a political question." Schroth's historical analysis here leaves much to be desired, as he greatly overestimates the influence of medieval Jews.[88] His view of Jews seems to be at least mildly paranoid, as he sees their influence everywhere. He has thus already established reasons for his Protestant audience to be anxious about them. He moves next to explicate Luther's "Christian antisemitism."

Schroth argues that Luther's antisemitism, which Schroth places in direct opposition to politically based antisemitism, is grounded in salvation-history. The political essence of the Jew is not at the center of Luther's *Judenschriften*; it is not the Jews as a Volk that form a danger, but the Jews as a religious community (*Religionsgemeinschaft*). He spends several pages citing Luther, emphasizing passages that describe the religious nature of Jewish opposition to Christianity.

Schroth turns later to "Luther's Measures against the Jews." These measures are not rooted in "mere historical, political, völkisch, or racial facts"; these realities are no more than a consequence of their rejection by God. The Jews, the devil, and opponents of Christianity are all reliant on a *"parasite existence."*[89]

This last description is extremely problematic, for Schroth immediately launches into several statements from Luther about the spiritual condition of Jews. He provides no further explanation for this highly incendiary racial-biological language. Nothing in this work indicates directly his support for a racialized version of antisemitism, yet his acceptance of a supposedly pervasive Jewish–Bolshevistic world conspiracy against Christianity coupled with his unqualified use of such an expression must have left the Protestant reader with the impression of a "world" Jewry that was highly dangerous.

Luther did not call for "human, völkisch, or political vengefulness and brutality." Rather, what was required was a Christian "office of the sword."[90] Yet, it was not the church but the authorities who were to exercise this office. Schroth proceeds to enumerate the seven well-known recommendations. He discusses Luther's view of Jewish baptism, concluding that Luther affirmed it, but did not envision it happening except in a few cases. In applying this view of Christian baptism of Jews to the present situation, Schroth argues for baptism of genuine converts, not those who convert due to the political conditions.[91]

Schroth's next move is in reality the core of the whole book. To the church, the Jews represent a symbol of God's anger. The "Jewish Question" is really a threat to the church's very existence, not because "the Jews" are a physical threat to the church. The threat comes rather from the insidious influence of anti-Christianity, which "Judaism" represents. For Luther, Judaism really "means" (read *symbolizes*) "anti-Christianity." Thus, the Jewish Question is no longer "Jew or German?" but "German without Christ?" or "German with Christ?"[92]

Later, in a section subtitled "Salvation-history and Modern Antisemitism," he posits a three-point approach to antisemitism. First, the church must do its work of preaching the Gospel and the Law. In so doing, it cannot become the "Jew." Nevertheless, the church should reject political, "anti-Christian" antisemitism. Second, he reasserts that the word of the church is a "theological and salvation-historical word" (i.e., a word from God). Third, he suggests "concrete" measures that Lutheran churches should take. He includes here a strong defense of mission to Jews and Jewish baptism, a denunciation of the *Gleichschaltung* of the church via "ecclesiastical Aryan legislation," along with a rejection of the formation of a separate Jewish church.[93]

His conclusion simmers with intensity. First, he asks, "World, do you belong in obedience to the God of Jesus Christ or to the gods of your National Socialism?" These are startling words, given the context in which they are written. Here he directly confronts the religious nature of Nazism. Christians have to choose whom they will serve. His interrogative infers a complete lack of compatibility between Christianity and Nazism. However, he targets not only Nazism in this rousing conclusion. The Jewish people do not escape his gaze. He asserts that for Luther the one who rejects Christ has a part with the Jews in his crucifixion. For Schroth, this raises the question of how to respond to the "*fundamental atheism of Jewish Bolshevism.*"[94] For the Christian it is a question of whether one will surrender "anti-Bolshevistic" and "antisemitic" acts to the obedience of Jesus Christ. Here he once again distinguishes between Christian and anti-Christian antisemitism, and Christian and anti-Christian anti-Bolshevism. The Christian should oppose both "Judaism" and Bolshevism—but from a proper spiritual motivation. In the end, Schroth calls for resistance to all things anti-Christian—including völkisch national Christianity—just as Luther opposed the Jews.[95]

Schroth does not make the case for his symbolic view of "the Jew." There is no question that Luther believed the Jewish people to be cursed and that other such enemies of God sought to destroy Christianity. It is not at all clear, however, that Luther regarded Jews and Judaism as special symbols of such scorn and anger, at least not to the degree that Schroth wants to press the issue. If the "Jew" or "Judaism" was symbolic of anti-Christianity, then what did Luther's other apocalyptic enemies of Christianity—Catholicism, Islam—represent? Schroth's assertion is unconvincing, especially given the narrow focus of this brief work.

His view of antisemitism is fairly nuanced, if decidedly unheroic. He does not posit an untamed antisemitism that views all Jews as racially or biologically inferior, as do the Nazis and many of the German Christians. What he does call for is a "Christian antisemitism" that is somewhat convincingly drawn from Luther's thinking. His "salvation-historical" basis is consistent with Luther's primarily theological outlook, even if this point is overstated.

Yet, I argued in chapter two that Luther's anti-Jewish treatises contained both antisemitic and anti-Judaic rhetoric. It is fascinating that though Schroth is willing to call his position "antisemitism," he insists that he is doing so from a purely religious or theological basis (in other words, a nonrational basis). Yet, his rather paranoid view of a supposed Jewish–Bolshevistic world conspiracy falls outside of the realm of rationality and entails instead an irrational hostility. Significantly, *he* viewed his wariness of contemporary Jews and Judaism in terms of a *religiously* based fear of Jewish atheism and anti-Christianity. Nevertheless, since this fear was unfounded in reality—Jews did not seek to dominate Christians and indeed the world through atheistic Bolshevism—we may rightly categorize this particular aspect of his thinking as irrational antisemitism.

In the end, Schroth supported baptism of Jewish converts, rejected implementation of the Aryan Paragraph in the church, and urged a theological confrontation with the "gods of National Socialism." Christian Wiese describes Schroth's offerings as "courageous" in their historical context. He qualifies this by calling his salvation-historical antisemitism "dangerous and counter-productive," leaving Jewry as the "eternal symbol" of anti-Christianity.[96] I would not disagree with Wiese.

Nevertheless, Schroth's courage clearly did not extend to the unconverted Jew. The unbaptized Jew is for him in fact just as dangerous to Christianity as the Nazis believe that *all* Jews are to Germany. In the end, Schroth's view of Jews and Judaism would leave the dichotomous prospect of hope for the baptized Jew, but only fear for the unconverted Jew, who would be left in the wary gaze of the Christian.

"Luther on the Jewish Question"

In the Protestant Central Archive (Evangelisches Zentralarchiv; EZA) in Berlin exists a collection of documents titled "Archiv für die Geschichte des Kirchenkampfes: VKL zur Judenfrage 1936–1943" (Archive for the History of the Church Struggle: VKL on the Jewish Question 1936–1943).[97] Included in the collection is a four-page typewritten manuscript titled "Luther zur Judenfrage" (Luther on the Jewish Question). Though the document's date and authorship are unknown, the measured tone and embarrassment with Luther's excesses, the provenance of the collection, and oblique sarcastic references to German Christian arguments all point to a Confessing Church author (or at least someone sympathetic to the Confessing Church) and to a date somewhere between 1936 and 1943. As such, it provides another window into Confessing Church discussion of Luther's views about Jews and Judaism in the Third Reich.

The author begins by noting the Luther literature pertinent to the discussion. His list includes *Magnificat* (1521), *That Jesus Christ Was Born a Jew, Against the Sabbatarians, On the Jews and Their Lies,* and *On the Ineffable Name and on the Lineage of Christ.* He neatly presents his argumentation in outline form, with four principle points, three of which I will examine here: "Luther's Demands," "Fundamental to the Demands of Luther," and "Luther's Theological Struggle about the Issue."[98]

He begins the section on "Luther's Demands" by listing the seven demands from *On the Jews and Their Lies* in two columns, with three on the left and four on the right. The three on the left-hand side are said to be "religious" in nature; the four on the right, "social." The religious demands include the burning of synagogues and schools, the confiscation of Talmuds and prayer books, and the prohibition against rabbinic teaching. The social strictures encompass the destruction of houses, the denial of safe passage on the highways, the economic prohibitions (including the proscription against usury), and (failing the efficacy of the other recommendations) their expulsion from the land.[99]

The author explains the necessity of Luther's religious demands on the basis of purported Jewish propagation of anti-Christian propaganda via "polemical pamphlets." The Jews of Luther's Germany were supposed to have tried in "scholarly form" to "reinterpret messianic prophecies," to "link the work of Jesus" with magical tales in the style of Hellenistic legends, and to "make blasphemous statements about his person and ancestry."

He demonstrates the religious nature of each of Luther's demands by examining purpose clauses from *On the Jews and Their Lies* that pertain to each one. For example, the purpose of the suppression of the above polemical pamphlets is that God and Christianity might be honored, and that the German Christians of Luther's day be the kind of Christians who do not permit "public denial of his [God's] son." Thus, the discussion of the "religious side of the matter" is argued in nonrational fashion.[100]

What, then, of the "social side of the matter"? Recognizing the harshness of Luther's sociopolitical recommendations, he admits that they seem "brutal." Yet, they are clearly necessary, for they serve the church and the gospel, "allow certain provisos and caution against hyperbole and hate," and deal thoroughly with social issues.[101] He again demonstrates his point through direct and effective appeal to Luther's *On the Jews and Their Lies.* In the end, the author believes that for Luther the social issues are subsumed under a theological rubric.

He next explicates five concerns that are fundamental to Luther's demands. The items are quite significant, and demonstrate a keen sense of biblical and historical–theological awareness. First, he advances Luther's now-familiar disappointment with the lack of Jewish conversions to Christianity, which are due to their "obstinacy." Yet, Luther's attitude, he says, "is not determined race-legally," but by the New Testament and Christian pedagogy. Second, the reformer's demands are meant to be put into practice by the church and "not actually directed to the 'State' in the modern sense." "The Volk among which the Jews lived was a Christian community, the territorial lords, servants of God" who had a Christian mission.[102]

In making this second "fundamental" statement about Luther's demands, the author is stressing that there are important differences between sixteenth-century Germany and Nazi Germany, implying rather provocatively that the Nazi authorities have no real sense of Christian mission. His claim that Luther's demands are meant to be carried out by the church and not the state may be shaped more by his reticence to support anti-Jewish Nazi policy than by what Luther had to say.

Third, he attributes Luther's knowledge of some of the crimes of which Jews were accused—including well-poisoning and ritual murder—directly to Margaritha's *The Whole Jewish Faith.* The passing on of such "horror stories" in the form of "verified facts" is "not credible."[103] The reference to Margaritha is not entirely unique, but the language is surprisingly critical of Luther. In a manner that was anything but common in German Protestant circles, he explicitly rejects irrational antisemitic medieval slander, anchoring his rejoinder in the language of rationality.

Fourth, the author contends that some of Luther's judgments about Jews (for example, when he calls them "Jewish vermin") "betray the irritability of the older Luther." Similar judgments are also expressed in his later writings against the pope. Fifth, he offers some brief words of caution, warning first against a "false canonization" of Luther—a notion that he ties to judgments about Jews in Germany which are "torn out of context," and which is clearly a swipe at German Christian notions about the reformer—and admonishes his readers to "accept that which drives one to Christ and to reject what breathes a foreign spirit."[104]

The author later addresses "Luther's Theological Struggle about the Issue." The "discrepancy" between Luther's early statements about the matter and his "late polemic pamphlets" can only be bridged, he says, when one observes that the reformer's "concern [about] the Jewish question" is not "political, sociological, [or] racial-legal," but "theological, ecclesiastical." Significantly, he notes that Luther's debates with Jews come in the "same breath" with struggles against "Turks," the pope, and sectarians. These debates were "severe," but the "means of his age," while "often overwhelmingly crude," were "spiritual." Luther, like Saint Paul, was fighting about "the validity of the gospel."[105]

The final section of the manuscript deals with "Antisemitism in Luther," and delivers a concluding salvo that is quite provocative. "For Luther the Jewish question is thus a question of the church, and about Christianity, and only in a derivative sense about the Volk." It is Luther's "theological education" that takes up the "preponderant space," and not the "police measures proposed to the territorial rulers." Luther calls for strictures against those Jews who deny Christ ("and only these!"): "If it must be," they may be expelled from the land—but only because "Jesus is the Christ" and should "remain" so.

Taken as a whole, the passage is illustrative of the kind of dichotomy that commonly existed in the thinking of many Confessing Church pastors and theologians. The author rejects völkisch notions out of hand, but seems to support implicitly anti-Jewish measures against Jews who deny Christ. Despite some veiled criticism of the Nazi authorities, the author leaves the impression that Jews in Nazi Germany have two choices: convert or be expelled.[106] It is not scrupulous, he concludes, to cite Luther out of his intellectual context. "Even Luther's most aggressive writing on the Jewish Question closes with the prayer for Israel's conversion."[107] Despite such an apologia, the manuscript represents, for its era, one of the more nuanced treatments of the issue of "Luther on the Jewish Question."

Conclusions

I have examined some representative cases that demonstrate the various Confessing Church approaches to Luther's *Judenschriften* in Nazi Germany. Two traits of the chief figures studied in this chapter—the scope of their writings and their approaches to Luther—are characterized by both commonality and difference. Many Confessing Church pastors were writing about "Luther and the Jews," or at least about the "Jewish Question." In most cases, the writers were keen to defend against a one-sided Luther who gives German Protestants permission to follow the Nazis in their anti-semitic program. None of those whose works are examined here, however, explicitly recommended any special protections for unconverted Jews. This serves to underscore Wolfgang Gerlach's assertion that the witnesses within the Confessing Church were indeed silent, at least to the plight of Jews who remained as Jews.[108]

The Württemberg Confessing Church's article on Luther and Jewish baptism was written in October 1935, on the heels of the introduction of the Nuremberg Race Laws. The writer seeks simply to counter, in the first instance, the one-sided portrayal of Luther's position on Jewish baptism offered in *Der Stürmer;* he also seeks to defend the church against a supposed suppression of the reformer's attitudes toward Jews and Judaism. Its proximity to the article on Pastor Zuckschwerdt, who defended his "Aryan" heritage when publicly ridiculed by *Der Stürmer,* serves as a sober and ironic reminder that antisemitic attitudes prevailed among even those who were willing to defend the rights of Jews who converted to Christianity.

Walter Gabriel's *Dr. Martin Luther on the Jews: Luther's Christian Antisemitism according to His Writings* attempts to demonstrate Luther's position toward the Jewish people throughout the reformer's career. Gabriel intentionally addresses his own historical context in order to tackle the present needs of the church. In much the same way, Schroth's *Luther's Christian Antisemitism Today* is a topical examination of "Luther and the Jews," with a good deal of modern application. His "Christianity and Judaism" is a broader work that attempts to describe the nature of the relationship between the two religions.

Heinrich Fausel's lecture "The Jewish Question" was delivered in 1934 in a parish hall in Leonberg in Württemberg. In it, the Heimsheim pastor sought to address the thorny issue of how Christians should deal with the Jewish citizens of Hitler's Germany. After stressing the topic's importance and surveying the history of the issue in modern Germany in the first half of the lecture, Fausel spends the second half addressing Luther's approach to Jews and Judaism. Fausel seamlessly blends history and theology throughout the lecture.

How may we characterize the various approaches to Luther's treatises? Gabriel's methodology is fairly nuanced, avoiding the simplistic and misleading caricature of Luther's position toward the Jewish people found in the writings of many figures in the German Christian movement. He approves of Luther's opposition to Judaism, but attempts to take the sting out of such opposition by redefining *Jew* and *Judaism* in symbolic terms. This move is unconvincing because it is not supported sufficiently in Luther's writings.

His attempt to define Luther's position as both "*purely* religious" and "social" also fails to persuade. Ultimately, what Gabriel regards as "Christian antisemitism" is essentially nonrational (in his words, "religious") and his "unchristian antisemitism" is fundamentally irrational ("racial-biological"). Yet, he cannot resist the xenophobic generalization that Jews are "devoted to money." In addition, his umbrella definition of "Judaism" includes the intellectual ideals of the Enlightenment. Thus, Gabriel opposes both Judaism as a religious entity and, by extension, rationality in general. That is, at least those forms of rationality that deny Christ's role as Redeemer and Son of God. His version of anti-Jewish rhetoric is driven by nonrational anti-Judaism, but is reinforced with such irrational antisemitic arguments.

Like most other Confessing Church figures, Schroth places priority on the religious, theological nature of the "Jewish Question." Unlike most, however, he injects a great deal of inflammatory language, language that is more consistent with Nazi and völkisch portrayals of Jews and Judaism. Like Gabriel, he attempts to redefine *Jews* and *Judaism* as symbols of rejection of Christ and Christianity. He is even less successful in his attempt than Gabriel, as he does so at greater length, with the irrational specter of the atheistic, Bolshevistic Jew lurking in the background. Heightening the dissonance is his curious coupling of such Nazi-esque language with excoriation of Nazi and völkisch ideology.

Fausel's 1934 lecture "The Jewish Question" includes xenophobic, nonrational anti-Judaic, and irrational antisemitic components. As with most of his Confessing Church fellow travelers, the majority of the argumentation is nonrational. At pivotal points, Fausel nevertheless employs the irrational prose of fear and imperilment to describe the perceived Jewish "invasion" of the German Volk. Elsewhere, he also reflects "orders of creation" theology in close connection with the life of the German Volk.

Despite sheltering Herta Pineas in his home some nine years after the Leonberg lecture, demonstrating both sympathy for a Jewish woman and courage in the face of potential recriminations from the Nazi authorities, Fausel appears to have never confessed publicly the anti-Judaism and anti-semitism that he advocated to a completely filled parish hall in Leonberg in 1934. His wartime sermons and his farewell address in Heimsheim focus almost exclusively on the suffering of his congregants and that of fellow Germans; there is absolutely no mention of Jewish suffering. The complexity of Fausel's character lays bare in microcosm the internal conflicts between indifference, empathy, and even antagonism felt by many so-called "bystanders" in Hitler's Germany.[109]

Common to all of the writings here is the idea that Luther's position on the Jewish people is essentially religious, theological, or salvation-historical. All affirm Jewish baptism and/or the possibility of Jewish conversion to Christianity via Christian mission. Most, to one degree or another, reject racial–biological notions of antisemitism. (Schroth's citation of Luther's sixteenth-century usage of the term *parasite* to describe Jews serves as an exception.)

Tellingly, only one, Fausel, speaks directly to the issue of what the state should do with unbaptized Jews (though the author of the unsigned article about "Luther and the Jewish Question" implies at least that unbelieving Jews in Luther's day could justifiably be expelled from Germany). Fausel affirms unambiguously the prohibition of mixed marriages between Jews and non-Jews and placing restrictions on the number of Jewish civil servants in Germany. Both of these views were consonant with the Nuremberg Race Laws, which were enacted beginning in September 1935, more than a year and a half after Fausel's lecture. Only the Württemberg Confessing Church's article on Zuckschwerdt's baptism of Albert Hirschland exhibits an embrace of antisemitic ideology that is based at least in part on racial–biological argumentation.

It seems that among these Confessing Church writers, Schroth is the most wary of Jews. He alone fears an atheistic Jewish–Bolshevistic plan for world domination. Paradoxically, he also rejects explicitly both the Aryan Paragraph in the church and the formation of a separate "Jewish Christian" church. He also confronts most directly the Nazi worldview, challenging not only Germany but the world to choose between the God of Jesus Christ and the gods of National Socialism. All in all, Schroth's work is the most confrontational and the most enigmatic.

Despite its relative brevity and outline form, the unsigned article on Luther and the "Jewish Question" is in fact one of the most balanced encountered here thus far. The author admits to Luther's crudeness, rejects the idea of taking the reformer's word as gospel, recognizes the corrupting influence of Margaritha's antisemitic medieval slander on Luther, and argues against an irrational acceptance of such "horror stories," which are "not credible." He even implies that Nazi authorities are unjustified in applying anti-Jewish measures against converted Jews. While he does not rail against Jewish unbelief, neither does he provide Jews with any hope of *earthly* rescue.

The thread that ties together all of these works is the tendency of Confessing Church writers to rely very heavily on nonrational modes of thinking. All of the authors here explicitly urge the importance of viewing the "Jewish Question" and its related implications in a "theological" or "religious" manner. This generally means viewing the issue through the lenses of Scripture, Luther, or both. Yet, crucially, most are inconsistent in this regard, as they reach too easily for irrational and/or xenophobic reasoning in their writings and lectures. Despite this general agreement in starting point, the conclusions reached are modestly diverse.

The incremental but rapid marginalization and oppression of the Jewish people in German society following the Nazi ascent to power led the Protestant churches to reassess how they viewed this increasingly endangered minority. The Church Struggle ensued, splintering the tenuous union of Protestant churches into smaller and smaller subgroups. Despite this fracturing, and despite the vastly disparate tenor of their writings, a degree of unanimity about whether to help the Jewish people existed even between the diametrically opposed Confessing Church and German Christian wings. This general accord is unsurprising, given that it mirrors overall German public opinion about the Jewish minority, especially during the war years.

The range of views among Confessing Church clergy seems to indicate some degree of sympathy for the plight of Jewish Christians. A small number, including those involved in the "Grüber Office," actively helped them. Dietrich Bonhoeffer supported both converted and unconverted Jews by vigorously agitating against the implementation of the Aryan Paragraph in the German Protestant Church, by actively participating in resistance against Hitler and the state, and by limited rescue efforts on the behalf of unconverted Jews.

But, the narrow focus of the nonrational theology of most Confessing Church pastors—its constricted emphasis on conversion to Christ—neglected other biblical themes (justice for oppressed peoples, love of neighbor, for example) that might have applied to their precarious position as a state-supported institution with a tiny minority of Jewish members and living in communities with threatened and persecuted unbaptized Jews. Contributory factors in this general reticence to help included Luther's irrational antisemitism, nonrational anti-Judaism, a long-standing cultural antipathy toward Jews, and a real fear of recriminations by the Reich. Further, a selective appropriation of Christian Scripture—emphasizing all of Israel's failures and none of its accomplishments—reveals a degree of tendentiousness in their thinking.

When Confessing Church pastors and theologians wrote about "Luther and the Jews," it was often from a rather defensive posture. Keen to uphold Luther's reputation as a great German reformer, they had a very difficult task. Many of the reformer's seven severe suggestions in *On the Jews and Their Lies*—whether motivated by "sharp mercy" or not—really did seem to presage the Nuremberg Laws and even in parts Kristallnacht. Other passages contained late medieval antisemitic slurs. Some of these men appear to have undertaken their scholarly task with great earnestness. Yet, ultimately their serious efforts served more to explain Luther's motivations than to recognize that the reformer had, in the case of Jews at any rate, both failed to love his neighbors as himself and spoken falsely against them. Most were convinced that Luther was divinely (i.e., nonrationally) justified in his harsh opposition to Jews. Some even urged a "Christian" antisemitism as the answer to the so-called "Jewish Question." Nearly all failed or refused to recognize the irrational support for hatred of Jews that the reformer had built upon his nonrational anti-Judaic foundation. The German Christian clergy, as we will see next, openly supported the Nazi anti-Jewish measures, and were not shy in employing Luther to bolster their argument.

5

GERMAN CHRISTIAN PASTORS AND BISHOPS

On 10 November 1938,
Luther's birthday, the
synagogues in Germany
are burning.

—Martin Sasse,
*Martin Luther on the Jews:
Away with Them!* (1938)

In his work on Berlin's Protestant social milieu in the Third Reich, Manfred Gailus has shown that in Berlin at least, Confessing Church pastors "more often than their DC [*Deutsche Christen*; German Christian] colleagues" came from "academically educated upper-middle-class families" and were more likely to have come from families with a theological tradition. The correlation was even stronger for those where such a tradition was long running and where a parent was a member of the "theological and ecclesiastical élite."[1] The reflection of this relative lack of theological tradition and academic education in the German Christian movement, borne out statistically by Gailus, we will observe here textually and thematically. German Christian pastors, "in comparison to their BK [*Beken-nende Kirche*; Confessing Church] opponents," he shows, "came relatively often from lower social classes" and "more frequently came from Prussia's eastern provinces." This latter fact leads him to conclude that "a family history on Germany's ethnic boundary in the east apparently made them more receptive to völkisch ideology. . . ." The Protestant social milieu in Berlin was split "almost down the middle into two sharply opposed camps, the German Christians or völkisch Protestantism versus the Confessing Church as the more traditional, national conservative faction." While some correlation may exist between living in the east and being receptive to völkisch ideology, the effect of völkisch penetration of the Protestant intellectual–theological milieu even outside the German Christian movement should not be underestimated.[2]

Despite the fierce debates and church–political struggles within the Protestant church, the German Christians, like the Confessing Church, were loath to the idea of forming a breakaway movement, and remained part of the German Protestant Church, attempting to transform it from within.[3] As a result of the Church Struggle, in only three of the regional churches (Hanover, Bavaria, and Württemberg) did the Confessing Church operate with relative freedom.[4] With as many as 6,000 pastors, 600,000 laity and considerable church–political influence in the majority of the provincial churches, the German Christians constituted a very significant minority in German Protestantism.

Unlike many of their counterparts in the Confessing Church, German Christian pastors were unabashed in speaking out about current events in Germany, including the deteriorating situation for Jews in the Reich, which they generally applauded. The language in German Christian church publications and pronouncements often included irrational conceptualizations that echoed leading Nazis, including Hitler, as well as prominent nineteenth- and twentieth-century racial ideologists and German cultural apologists. A thin veneer of theological reasoning would generally appear alongside antisemitic language that could otherwise have appeared in the Nazi Party newspaper *Völkischer Beobachter*. Doris Bergen has referred to the German Christians as "antidoctrinal," at least partly on the basis of this intentionally "destructive" approach to doctrine.[5] We will see here that the German Christians, consistent with this approach, often uncritically employed decontextualized passages from Luther with aplomb in their quest to "de-Judaize" the German church.

In this chapter, we will observe first the mixed reactions of Protestants to pivotal events such as the enacting of the Nuremberg Race Laws and Kristallnacht. Next, we examine the biography of a key German Christian bishop, along with his notorious work on Luther's views about Jews and Judaism. We then tackle a lengthy article, written by a pastor and editor of German Christian publications, in which Luther's anti-Judaic and antisemitic arsenal is mined to combat the threat of "world Bolshevism." Lastly, we will encounter the approach to Luther's *Judenschriften* in the writings of the Reich-wide leader of the German Christian press.

Pastors on Luther, Jews, and Current Events

Though both the boycott of Jewish businesses (1933) and the Nuremberg Laws (1935) caused great hardship and signaled very difficult times ahead for Jews in the Third Reich, it was the public violence of Kristallnacht on November 9–10, 1938 and its immediate aftermath that brought home most vividly the brutal reality of anti-Jewish fervor extant among both the regime and the general populace in Nazi Germany.[6] It presaged, as well, the awful horror awaiting Jews at the hands of the Order Police (*Ordnungspolizei*) and the so-called "special task forces of the Security Police" (*Einsatzgruppen der Sicherheitspolizei*) under cover of war in Poland and Russia from 1941 to 1943 and the implementation of the Final Solution in the death camps.[7] Any significant recounting of the numerous and varied documented accounts of the oppression and violence against European Jews would lie outside the scope of this book.[8] Yet, how did German Protestant Christians—clergy in particular—respond to the momentous events that preceded the war and the Holocaust?

The Nuremberg Race Laws

The Nazi regime enacted its first wave of antisemitic legislation beginning in April 1933, in the immediate wake of the boycott of Jewish businesses. The second wave of legislation against German Jews occurred in 1935, with the most significant measures being the "Nuremberg Race Laws," hastily passed after the party rally in September in Nuremberg, and culminating in the First Supplementary Decree of the Reich Citizenship Law in November, which clarified the issue of who was a full or part Jew. Michael Burleigh and Wolfgang Wippermann rightly note the irony that "these criteria were based upon a religious, rather than a scientific, definition of race."[9]

Like Wolf Meyer-Erlach, many German Christian pastors recognized the similarities between the Nuremberg Laws and the sociopolitical recommendations of Luther's *On the Jews and Their Lies*.[10] The German Christians in Hanover greeted the laws with euphoria, seeing them as a "way to the liberation of the German Volk from the Jews" which complied with a "central demand of the reformer Martin Luther." Every Christian, they believed, should therefore agree with the legislation.[11] Speaking at a meeting in Emden, East Friesland German Christian leader Heinrich Meyer expressed the opinion that as with the Reformation, God had once again chosen Germany—this time to solve the "Jewish Question." In doing so, he referenced *On the Jews and Their Lies*, highlighting in particular the seventh of Luther's sociopolitical recommendations.[12]

In the immediate wake of the passage of the Nuremberg Laws in September 1935, Günter Niemack, a German Christian vicar in Grabow, penned an article titled "Gibt es ein Auserwähltes Volk Gottes?" (Is There a Chosen Volk of God?)[13] In this two-page piece, Niemack denigrates Jews and their German Protestant sympathizers. He wraps his condemnations in appeals to *On the Jews and Their Lies*.

To frame the invective against his contemporaries, he begins by patching together two quotations. In the first citation, Luther rails that it is a "desperate thing" that "the Jews" are and have been for fourteen hundred years "our plague, pestilence, and every misfortune." The second statement, Luther tells of their "bloodthirsty, vengeful, murderous" hopes, which are supposedly part of the message of the biblical book of Esther. The reformer speculates sarcastically that the reason they were chosen as "God's Volk" was to strangle and murder the pagans.

Niemack then targets a statement by the writer of an article in the August 1935 edition of the *Berliner Stadtmission* (Berlin City Mission). This "brave theologian," thinking that he is watching over the "allegedly endangered confession of Lutheran faith" in the National Socialist state, said that God "saves this Volk [the Jewish people] for his ultimate world-historically great deed. Refined in the furnace of suffering—and who knows into which bloody torments of antisemitism . . . it becomes ripe for conversion." Niemack observes that this "disgraceful confession of a 'confession-faithful' contemporary" was already exposed in an article in the *Völkischer Beobachter* and protested by the acting Protestant bishop of Berlin, who argued that "whoever occupies himself in the era of National Socialism with glorification of Jews excludes himself from the number of those who, under Adolf Hitler in spiritual agreement with Adolf Stöcker (the founder of the Berlin City Mission), want to remove [the] Jewish demon from Germany."[14]

Niemack angrily contends that such "so-called confession-faithful ministers" may no longer teach young people in German schools, but suggests that they apply to give their "Jewish religious instruction" in schools designed for Jews, if they are "finally erected," as in accordance with the "Reich Law." "For us Germans," cries Niemack, "the Jews are no chosen Volk of God." Luther "clearly and lucidly instructed us" in *On the Jews and Their Lies* that they are "liars and blood hounds" who have "falsified" the Scriptures with their "glosses." "God chose us," Niemack intones, "that we might live and work hard on holy German soil. . . ."[15]

One month later, *Gospel in the Third Reich* carried a brief article titled "Rassengesetze und christlicher Glaube" (Race Laws and Christian Faith). It summarizes a piece in the *Positive Christianity* periodical by Wilhelm Rehm, at that time the Reich leader of the German Christians. Rehm argues that the fact that the German Protestant Church did not communicate to its people the position of Luther toward the "Jewish Question" in his still current writings was a serious guilt-by-omission (*Unterlassungsschuld*). If it wants to be a *Volkskirche,* he contends, it will only include members with German blood. The elimination of Jews from the Protestant churches and pulpits is not a violation of "principles of Christian faith."[16]

Kristallnacht

On November 7, 1938, a seventeen-year-old Polish Jew named Herschel Grynszpan sought an audience with the German ambassador in Paris. He was refused, and was instead referred to a junior official named Ernst vom Rath. A stateless person, Grynszpan had just learned that his parents and two sisters had been deported from Germany to Poland. The troubled teen had come armed with a revolver, with which he shot vom Rath five times. Vom Rath was seriously wounded, taken to a hospital, and died two days later on November 9, which just happened to mark the anniversary of both the failed Hitler putsch in Munich and the founding of the Weimar Republic. On the day of the shooting, Goebbels's Propaganda Ministry instructed the press to give prominent place to the event and to describe it as an at-

tack by "world Jewry" on the Reich which would incur the "heaviest consequences" for the Jews of Germany.[17]

The consequences were grave indeed. Hundreds of Jewish synagogues—
perhaps as many as one thousand—were destroyed. At least 7,500 of their
businesses were destroyed, their goods looted. Between November 9 and
16, some thirty thousand Jewish men were arrested and taken to Dachau,
Buchenwald, and Sachsenhausen.[18] Though the official Nazi report on the
pogrom estimated only ninety-one deaths, the death toll was certainly
much higher—probably hundreds, and perhaps more than one thousand.
There were at least three hundred suicides in Germany as a result of the
despair brought on by the pogrom.[19] While hundreds of thousands of Jews
had left Germany during the first five years of the Third Reich, tens of
thousands of fearful Jews now began to emigrate with heightened urgency
to other places, including America, Palestine, and the United Kingdom.[20]

German Christian pastors and bishops responded to these events in
fairly uniform fashion. On November 20, 1938 an article in this vein appeared in *Deutscher Sonntag*. The piece is characterized both by strident
language and direct appeal to Luther. The author, Stuttgart pastor Immanuel Schairer, gloats, "The German Volk have done a deed, which the mil-
lennia will witness! A deed full of significance and serious consequences. It
has destroyed the sites of the Jewish religion!"[21]

After hurling accusations at Jews regarding their purported blasphemies from *On the Jews and Their Lies,* he asks how one can still have com-
passion on such a person. If cursing of the Savior is not enough to inflame
the reader's soul, then he is adjured to listen to what Martin Luther had to
say near the end of his life in recognizing the "world-Satan." He follows
with a lengthy quotation drawn from the section containing the seven sociopolitical recommendations in *On the Jews and Their Lies.*[22] For Schairer,
the answer to Luther's question—"What shall we Christians do now with
this rejected, cursed people, the Jews?"—was beginning to be carried out in
the streets of Germany on November 9–10.

Support for the events of November 9–10, however, was not unanimous
in the German Protestant Church. Pastor Hans-Martin Rotermund of
Dorfmark directly opposed the excessive anti-Jewish violence of Kristallnacht, declaring in a sermon that these crimes were incompatible with
the Christian conscience. As a result, the local chapter leader of the Nazi
Party and his deputy attacked him in a political meeting. On two Sunday
evenings following these events, the local chapter of the Nazi Party staged

Newly arrived prisoners, with shaven heads, stand at attention in their civilian clothes during a roll call in the Buchenwald concentration camp. Some still have their valises and other luggage with them. These prisoners were among the more than 10,000 German Jews who were arrested during the Kristallnacht pogrom (November 9–10, 1938) and sent to Buchenwald. Another 20,000 German Jews arrested at the same time were imprisoned in Dachau and Sachsenhausen. *United States Holocaust Memorial Museum, courtesy of Robert A. Schmuhl.*

readings from *On the Jews and Their Lies* in the village cinema hall.[23] Ironically, here it is the Nazis quoting Luther to refute the pastor.

Similarly, in December 1938, Protestant pastor Erich Klapproth, a member of the Confessing Church and a seminary pupil of Bonhoeffer, protested the events of the pogrom in a letter to Hitler, Goebbels, and Göring, saying "not only will I on no account justify the numerous excesses against Jewry that took place on or after Nov. 9 of this year . . . but I reject them, deeply ashamed, as they are a blot on the good name of the Germans. . . . I have spoken out of the ardent concern of a Christian who prays to his God every day for his people and their rulers."[24] Unlike Rotermund and Klapproth, however, a Pastor Dünsing received from his colleague Dornblüth information that a "Pastor K. from Hanover reacted with satisfaction in his sermon to the events in the *Pogromnacht* [Kristallnacht]." Pastor K. lamented that *On the Jews and Their Lies* was "hardly well-known in the parishes" and that a Protestant clergyman had "the obligation to refer to this writing."[25]

In the weeks following Kristallnacht, a local ecclesiastical controversy concerning Luther's *Judenschriften* erupted in Prussia. On November 19, 1938, the *Preußische Zeitung* (Prussian Newspaper; PZ) printed the "drastic proposals of the reformer for the solution of the Jewish question under the heading 'Martin Luther's Prescription.'" Just over two weeks later, they printed a follow-up article by an "H. H." titled "Pastors do not want to believe it. But, Luther really wrote against the Jews in such a way."[26] According to the PZ, they had "rendered these demands of Luther word-for-word (in quotation marks)" and had added none of their own comments.

To their "astonishment," however, the Protestant Consistory of the province of East Prussia telephoned the editorship of the PZ "and communicated that several ministers had inquired whether the Luther citations quoted by the 'P.Z.'" were really correct.

> We would have understood every other doubter because the pronouncements of Luther on the Jewish Question really are so radical and seemingly so modern and National Socialist that someone who does not know the writings of the reformer can hardly imagine that Luther spoke in such a way. If there are however called men [in the sense of being called to be a minister], who must know it exactly, then that should really be the Protestant ministers. If they do not read Luther in the original text, of whom should it otherwise be required?

The writer proceeds to chide the Protestant ministers, noting that this "regrettable ignorance" of Luther's "world of thought" might be "one of the causes of the painful confusion within the Protestant church."[27]

He provides the exact source of their quotation of Luther's demands (the Weimar edition), noting that the Königsberg State- and University Library was also in possession of "one of the few still extant copies of the 1543 edition" of *On the Jews and Their Lies*. In closing, he expresses his hope that Protestant clergymen reread "these passages" and in fact "the entire writing," and pass it on to "believers." Luther had required that the preachers "make no bones with the truth about the Jews." "Today the authorities and Volk are far ahead of the clergy in the fight against Judaism. How the times have changed!"[28]

As might be expected, the article caused quite a stir among the leadership of the Protestant church in Prussia. Two days later, on December 6, the superintendent of the board of directors of the district synod in Marienwerder, West Prussia, Pastor G. Feix, wrote a memo about the matter to the Protestant Consistory of the province of East Prussia.[29] In it, he notes that he was charged by colleagues in his church district primarily to address to the Consistory the issue of whether the claims of the December 4 article "conform to the facts." Also in question was the substance of the PZ article's charges about Luther's attitude toward the "Jewish Question."

Feix attached to his memo a self-published training course letter "for congregational and confirmand instruction." In the letter, he says, "a straightforward position was taken on the Jewish Question and my attitude was shared by the majority of my colleagues in the church district." The contents of the section titled "Jewry!" reveal the adjective "straightforward" to be a profound understatement.[30]

Despite the fact that the "Jewish press of the whole world" attempts to deny it, Feix opines, the Talmud is "absolutely binding for every Jew." He calls "this Talmud" the "most misanthropic invention of a subhuman spirit" and says that it "shows the fanatical hate and will for destruction with which Jewry fights everything non-Jewish and above all Christianity." His portrait of a fanatically hateful Jewry allows him to prod his readers (presumably teachers) to join the fight against them. "When we therefore ask ourselves today, whether we as Christians can take responsibility for the fight of the Third Reich against this Jewry, so we may answer confidently: 'Yes!' because we know that since the crucifixion of Christ Jewry sinned against and still sins against all Christian and non-Christian peoples in the most noxious way."[31]

Feix promotes the idea of rejecting baptism of Jews until the creation of a "national Jewish Christian church." To support this argument, he suggests that the reader consult "Jesus' attitude toward spiritual Judaism" as depicted in John 8:42–44 and "especially also the Sermon on the Mount."[32] He turns next to Luther's writings to champion his singularly deprecating view of Judaism.

In *On the Jews and Their Lies,* says Feix, Luther "expresses his total disappointment about this 'chosen Volk'" and gives seven suggestions concerning the approach that Christian authorities should take to the "Jewish Question." Reiterating a popular German Christian refrain, he laments, "unfortunately this wake-up call of Dr. Martin Luther has been forgotten for a long time." He cites the seven recommendations in full.[33] Relying exclusively on condemnatory passages from Jesus and Luther, the district synod superintendent paints a dire portrait of Judaism for his audience of teachers. In light of a disparaging report in a local newspaper, he forwards this portrait as supporting evidence of a proper view of the "Jewish Question."

Taken together, these responses to Kristallnacht serve to underscore the divided nature of German Protestantism under the Nazi regime, Luther's significance in Germany nearly four hundred years after his death, and the resonating power of his anti-Judaic and antisemitic words, especially among the clergy of the German Christian movement.[34]

German Christian Pastors and Bishops

Martin Sasse, Bishop of Thuringia

Bishop Martin Sasse is probably the most notorious and oft-cited example of a Protestant church leader lending direct support to the antisemitic program of the Nazis.[35] The fact that he did so most famously by quoting Luther as justification for the violence against Jews on Kristallnacht is of course highly relevant here. Before discussing this infamous work, however, some biographical perspective would be helpful.

Born in Silesia in 1890, Sasse rose to prominence in the Protestant church early in the Nazi regime. By September 1933 he was a full-time clergy member of the *Landeskirchenrat* in Eisenach, and from March 1934 he was regional bishop of Thuringia.[36] His selection was not without controversy, as the vote for Sasse was preceded by "heated debate." Nonetheless, he was eventually selected by the Thuringian body, a fully committed German Christian council.[37]

Sasse's tenure as bishop was filled with controversy and church leadership struggles. These conditions characterized not only the Thuringian church, but the German Christians as a whole in the years 1933–1937.[38] Many of the skirmishes involved how the German Christian church would relate to the new Nazi state. On this important issue, Sasse in February 1937 told church leaders that the order and administration of the church could be "handed over to the state for safekeeping. "We will even then still go with the Führer" if the state will lend a religious basis to its *Staatsethik* (ethics of the state).[39] Thus, four years into the Nazi regime, after the implementation of the Nuremberg Laws, Sasse was openly supportive of Hitler.

Sasse, who had joined the Nazi Party in 1930, was also a signatory of the "Godesberg Declaration." This declaration, among other things, described Christianity as the "unbridgeable religious contradiction to Judaism" and called for the "establishment of an institute for research and removal of the Jewish influence on the church life of the German people." The Institute, of course, became a reality at Eisenach. As with other German Christian bishops, Sasse participated regularly in the Institute's annual conferences.[40]

Sasse died of renal disease in August 1942. Former Reich bishop Ludwig Müller gave a highly charged speech at the funeral, which was held in Eisenach. In it, he decried the fact that while at Sasse's installation as bishop (over which Müller had presided) brown uniforms were everywhere, "today I do not see a single one here." He proceeded to call Sasse a martyr, and hoped that the Führer would be able to accomplish the party program—including point twenty-four, which contained the call for a so-called "positive Christianity"—after the war was over.[41]

On November 12, 1938—just days after Kristallnacht, indeed while Jewish men were still being arrested—Sasse issued a decree on behalf of the Thuringian church council regarding the tumultuous events of the week, which was to be read in all church services on the upcoming day of repentance.[42] Tellingly, the decree condemns explicitly the "cowardly murder" of embassy council member Ernst vom Rath in Paris "by a Jew," but does not mention or condemn the antisemitic violence that had been raging in the streets of Germany. In fact, the decree is a call for Christians to fight against Jews on behalf of the Volk.

The crime against vom Rath illuminates, Sasse says, the "world-historical fight against the Volk-disintegrating spirit of Judaism." "National Socialism," the bishop intones, "has most clearly recognized this danger in our time and in responsible struggle for the German Volksgemeinschaft announced the most aggressive fight [against] Jewish-Bolshevistic godlessness." Explicitly exhorting the faithful to "stand faithfully on the side of the Führer," Sasse stresses that the "leadership of the Thuringian Protestant Church. . . . led the fight against the disintegrating spirit of Judaism and fought any kind of glorification of the Jewish Volk in the sharpest terms." This fight has entered a "crucial stage" in the "eventful year" of 1938.[43] He was certainly correct to view these events as a turning point in the complex but steady path to the Final Solution.

Sasse's notorious work *Martin Luther on the Jews: Away with Them!* was published in two versions—one in German and one in English. The demand for the German version was very strong. Heinz Dungs reported that fourteen days after it first appeared, thirty-seven thousand copies had to be delivered.[44] Though essentially the same text, there are a few differences between the English and German versions. Two in particular are well worth noting.

In the preface to the German version, Sasse says, "On November 10, 1938, Luther's birthday, the synagogues in Germany are burning."[45] This sentence is absent from the English version. From the context, it is clear that Sasse is exulting over what he sees as the apparently appropriate reality of Kristallnacht. Nonetheless, the absence of this sentence probably implies some reticence to applaud such violence explicitly in front of his English-speaking readership. The titles are slightly different as well. The German version can be translated *Martin Luther on the Jews: Away with Them!* while the English version is simply *Martin Luther and the Jews.*

This should not, however, paint a portrait of a complete watering down of Sasse's message. Take the following example, drawn from the English version:

> Only absolute misapprehension as to Luther's aims and ideas can permit Christians to take the part of and intercede for Jews. . . . As Protestant Christians we fully recognize the great debt of gratitude we owe to Luther and we feel it our duty to warn all Protestant Christians in the whole world against the Jews and their protectors with Luther's very own words.[46]

He regards the "measures adopted by National Socialist Germany" as "defensive provisions undertaken to protect the German nation against the Jewish race."[47] These words of warning presage the coming torrent of anti-Jewish rhetoric, which he lifts selectively from Luther's works.

Similar to Theodor Pauls, Sasse simply places selected quotations from Luther under bald anti-Jewish headings such as "The Synagogue, the Lair of Satan," "Jewish Lies," and "Scum of Mankind." There are literally dozens of quotations from Luther, with many taken from *On the Jews and Their Lies* and *On the Ineffable Name.* In the case of Jewish baptism, he cites only two cases from Luther, one of which entails a rejection of the practice, another of which merely demonstrates supposed Jewish animosity toward Christians.[48]

The target audience could not have been the highly educated or church elites. There is very little theological or biblical argumentation in the chosen passages, which indicates that contra fellow German Christian Vogelsang, but like Meyer-Erlach and others, Sasse was anything but conservative in his theological outlook. In any case, his main argument is clear: the Jews are a menace, and should be eliminated from German society.

Immanuel Schairer, Stuttgart Pastor and Publisher of *Deutscher Sonntag*

Immanuel Berthold Johannes Schairer was born in 1885 in Pfeffingen (south of Stuttgart), and descended from an "old Württemberg theologians' family"; his father and grandfather were pastors.[49] In 1903, he enrolled in the seminary at Tübingen University, completing his studies in Protestant theology there with a "brilliant exam." His path seemed set for a stellar career in the Württemberg regional church. His years of ministerial training were spent in several places, but the longest of these sojourns, two years, was in Stuttgart.[50]

His religious outlook comprised an especially unique combination of components for a German Protestant minister of this period. He was fascinated with the psychology of religion—which was not a terribly well-developed field in the early 1900s—and committed to a pietistic-revivalist view of Christianity. This theological approach contrasted sharply with that of his younger Stuttgart German Christian compatriot Georg Schneider, with whom he nonetheless shared a penchant for a more radically völkisch version of Christianity.[51]

In 1914, he completed his doctorate at Tübingen. During the First World War, he served as a pastoral caregiver at military hospitals. In 1925, he became pastor in Stuttgart-Hedelfingen, a post he would hold for more than a dozen years. Schairer joined the Nazi Party in 1932.[52]

The first issue of the German Christian gazette *Deutscher Sonntag*, of which Schairer was publisher and editor in chief, appeared in July 1933. It had a circulation of around ten thousand and was characterized by radical German Christian rhetoric, including attacks on the Confessing Church, virulent antisemitism, and ardent völkisch sentiment. Schairer's publishing prowess was not limited, however, to the weekly gazette. He also published several books, many with common German Christian themes.[53]

During the early years of the Nazi regime, Schairer was a leading figure among the Württemberg German Christians. Yet, because of his more
radically völkisch views, he and other such radical figures were ousted
from the Reich Movement of German Christians in 1936.[54] Indeed, beginning in 1934, the church council of Schairer's congregation began to raise
complaints with the Stuttgart church leadership. The accusations were
wide-ranging, including missed appointments, cancellation of religious
instruction, lack of sermon preparation, and the hiring of church space to
Nazi organizations such as the League of German Girls (Bund Deutsche
Mädel; BDM) and National Socialist Women's Organization (NS-Frauenschaft) groups. Finally, in summer 1937, he was suspended from his pastoral office.[55]

Yet, it was not only Schairer's conduct that earned him this suspension.
His writings included favorable Luther–Hitler comparisons, assertions of
a worldwide Jewish–Bolshevist conspiracy, and of international powers,
including "world Protestantism," cowed by Judaism. The dean responsible
for explaining to Schairer's congregation the decision of the high church
council to suspend their pastor stressed that the church "has the obligation
'that . . . Christ is really preached and not a German redeemer, not a Nordic
hero, not a martyr in the fight against Judaism, but rather Jesus Christ.'"
By October 1938, Schairer was forced to retire. He later took work in the
city of Stuttgart's public relief office.[56]

After the end of the Second World War, Schairer attempted to win back
his position as a minister in the Württemberg Protestant church. Yet, this
was not to be. In 1947, he was called before the denazification court. The
list of charges was supported by copious quotations from his writings,
mustered as evidence of his propagandistic engagement on behalf of the
Nazi dictatorship. Included among this evidence were quotations from the
Deutscher Sonntag article (cited above) in which he gloated over the burning of Jewish synagogues during Kristallnacht.

He received a sentence of twenty-eight months in a labor camp, which
was transmuted by the court due to his frail health. He was released from
the camp at Christmas 1947, but a ten-year employment ban imposed by
the court was still in effect. Five years later, after expressing regret for his
agitation in the pages of *Deutscher Sonntag*, he was allowed to receive his
full pension from the regional Protestant church, a pension that had earlier
been suspended. He died in February 1963.[57]

The October 10, 1937 issue of *Deutscher Sonntag* contains an article by Schairer titled "Weltbolschewismus und Weltkirche" (World Bolshevism and World Church). This four-page piece illustrates a characteristic German Christian association of Judaism and Bolshevism with immorality and apostasy. This connection was also present in wider Nazi circles.[58] In his article, Schairer weaves Luther's anti-Judaic and antisemitic argumentation into the fabric of his rather intricate but nonetheless paranoid screed against the supposed Jewish–Bolshevist international threat.

Schairer notes early in the piece that in Germany "it is unnecessary to address the particulars of the sinister activity of the world-Satan, of Jewish Bolshevism." In strident fashion, he thus ties Bolshevism and Judaism together with the arch-enemy of the Christian, Satan himself. Next, he takes issue with both the Dean of Canterbury and a favorite target of the German Christians, Karl Barth; the former for his supposedly sympathetic comments about communism in "red Spain" and the latter for his caution to his Swiss listeners not to "always strive against Bolshevism" for fear of helping fascism. If "'Bolshevism and church' can be named in the same breath," Schairer intones, "then we are initially astonished at this perverse relationship." This leads him to probe further as to "which circumstances make something so grotesque" possible. He gives two reasons.

First, "world Bolshevism" and "world church" are both "so-called international things, supranational powers, and thus already related in root and goal." Second, rather than being enlightened about this state of affairs, "our Christian circles" are seemingly "careless and unsuspecting." He portends to solve this purportedly sad state of affairs with a lesson on *Völker*, states, nations, races, and tribes.[59]

Each of these entities lives in a "well-ordered" manner and resides on its home soil. Yet, there are other entities "which have no designated domicile, are native in no country and whir around everywhere. We call these the supranational or international forces." He names five of these.

Unsurprisingly, the "oldest and mother of all five" is "world Jewry." Next follow "world Freemasonry," "world Catholicism," "world Bolshevism," and "world Protestantism," which he calls the "youngest child in the supranational family." Yet, the word "international" is "not at all widely understood" or is understood in a "completely false" manner in "our Christian circles." To the German, the word "appears as something beautiful, at least as something harmless." This is because it is simply taken to mean "present everywhere."[60]

Such "internationality," he argues, would indeed be "harmless." Yet, "the internationality of supranational powers contains a much, much sharper sting: the attack on everything national, the anti-national." He intones anxiously, "the basic law of all internationals means: extermination of national human beings, *Völker*, cultures, states. . . . Extermination to the root. . . ." This idea of "supranational powers" seeking to "exterminate" human beings, *Völker*, and so forth resonates with Nazi propaganda, especially, as argued by Jeffrey Herf, beginning in 1939.[61] Schairer thus instills a deep fear of an encroaching enemy, internationalism, the leader of which is "world Jewry."

"World Bolshevism" and "world church" both "descend from the same root: the religion of the Jews." Schairer, in direct contrast to Schroth, and in starker terms than Hirsch, contends that Bolshevism entails a religious entity.[62] In German Protestant circles, he certainly was not alone in assigning a (Jewish) religious quality to Bolshevism. Through Bolshevism, "an ancient faith of the Jews" finds its fulfillment, which entails in part destruction and subjugation of the "*Völker* of the world (*Goyim*) by the 'chosen Volk,' by the Israel of Jehovah." Bolshevism is "absolutely not a 'godless' entity, but the expression of a completely fanatical religiosity, a real religion, the real religion of the Jews. . . . Bolshevism is Jewish piety."[63]

In more concrete terms, Schairer states flatly, "the majority of and the most important leaders and string-pullers of Bolshevism" are "circumcised." "Even without this visible proof [circumcision], one understands the secret jubilation of world Jewry, its triumph over the hated peoples of the earth now finally arises. . . ." Schairer's connection of Jewish–Bolshevist religiosity with international conspiracy thinking illustrates clearly the seamless weaving together of the irrational with the nonrational.[64]

Pastor Schairer next discusses the relationship between Judaism and Christianity, lamenting the fact that Christian teaching included the notion that it was an offshoot of "pious Judaism" for centuries "until today." Christianity "until a few years ago" taught "the same anciently anchored conception," that it was built on the "Mosaic Old Testament," that it was the "true Israel," that the status of Christians is a "fulfillment of Jewish hope and promise"—without a recognition of its "malicious" nature. Thus, Christianity contributed "glory" to the "chosen Volk," doing itself harm in the process. He employs Luther as a corrective:

> We read today foremost from the long-misappropriated writing of Martin Luther from the year 1543 *On the Jews and Their Lies* the imploringly cautionary and pleading sentence:

"And you, my dear lords and friends, as are ministers and preachers, I want to have reminded completely faithfully of your duty with these words that also you warn your parishioners as before their eternal harm: that they beware of the Jew and avoid him, where they can!"[65]

Rather than continuing to spare "world enemy number 1" on the basis of "false Christianity," Schairer wants his readers to act as Luther's successors.[66]

But, what of the duality between Bolshevism and Christianity? Despite coming from the same "mother," these are two quite different "children." This conundrum is "simple" to solve, he says. "Judaism, the god of the Jews, the piety of the Jews, always possesses . . . as the Mosaic Testament demonstrates exactly, two sides which completely contradict each other."[67] In great and luridly graphic detail, he particularizes this purported contradiction.

In the pages of the Old Testament can be heard dissonant tones—one is "egregiously cruel, vengeful, and downright murderous," the other "extraordinarily lovely, gentle, kind-hearted, and noble." On the one hand, there are "wonderful promises . . . good living; paradise on earth." On the other, "the hound of hell released, the butcher's knife sharpened, a stream of blood spraying up to the mountains, a sword covered with human fat, a monstrosity raging over the earth, which does not rest, until it is a field of corpses; briefly: hell on earth!"[68] What can explain this shockingly contradictory state of affairs?

The "horrific threats and gory pictures" apply to the Goyim, "to the Völker of the world, to us!" The promises of "wonderful blessedness" and "heaven on earth" apply to "the servant Jacob . . . to God's chosen Volk, the favorites of Jehovah; to them alone!" He finally makes his argument explicit:

Religious Judaism thus (and the Jew is always religious!) gave birth to both: at one time sentimental, mild, and kind-hearted (toward itself). . . . The other time hard-hearted, cruel, bloodthirsty, and destructive—against the entire remaining Völker of the world (Goyim)—it directly spawns the murderous Jewish plague, the red terror.[69]

"Two essential demands," which he aims at "every clerical figure in Germany," are said to ensue from the "Völker-biological reality" that he has demonstrated. First, all "international entanglements" are to be disentangled. Second, the entirety of ecclesiastical existence, including its legal, constitutional, and organizational, as well as its theological, religious, and moral relations, should rid itself of any "trace of Jewish influence," whether of the personal or substantial kind. Even investigation of Jewish literature and scholarship should be limited to the goal of "learning to avoid it."[70] Schairer thus calls for the most thorough de-Judaization of German clerical life, a goal that would be concretely pursued beginning just a year and a half later in the work of the Eisenach Institute.

He closes by discussing the relation of German Protestantism's two most important figures (Jesus and Martin Luther) to Judaism, and what impact their examples should have on the German Protestant Church. He calls German Christians to ally with Jesus, "who opened the central attack on the entire Jewish system of life and faith. . . . Whether he wanted it or not—he nevertheless actually 'dissolved' and did not 'fulfill' Judaism."[71] In Jesus, the Jewish temple, priesthood, sacrifice, purification, food, circumcision, and law—its very essence—"experienced its collapse." Yet, soon again, Judaism "crept into" the world of ideas in early Christianity. "By then Martin Luther, too late and indeed too externally, unmasked again 'the Jews and their lies'" and gave to his German Protestant successors "the mission to complete his work."[72]

In toto, Schairer's work is a call to action for the Protestant church against a pervasive and encroaching "world enemy," "world Bolshevism," which was vivified by Judaism. One can hardly miss the echoes of Hitler in Schairer's work. Hitler, too, spoke in terms of "'world' or 'international Jewry' as an actually existing political subject with vast power that was hostile to Germany."[73] Further, Schairer paints a portrait of an international power that desires the "extermination" of the German Volk and nation. He frames this fearful portrait in a bloody and gory "red terror," supposedly spawned by the "religious Judaism" of the Old Testament. Without citing the Führer or other leading Nazis, Schairer could appropriate such irrational and publicly resonant concepts, while explicitly appealing in dubious fashion to Jesus and Luther for nonrational anti-Judaic support.

Heinz Dungs, German Christian Press Superintendent

Born in 1898, Heinz Dungs studied theology in Greifwald, Halle, Heidelberg, and Bonn. He was ordained as a minister in September 1923, and became a member of the Nazi Party on May 1, 1933. His younger brother Karl, a pastor in Essen-Kupferdreh, was given to polemical ways of thinking and exerted an important influence on Heinz. Heinz Dungs became pastor first in Kleinich (near Wiesbaden), then in Krefeld (1933), and later in Mühlheim-Ruhr (near Düsseldorf). He was an active member of the Protestant League.[74]

At Krefeld, Dungs edited the local gazette *Der Weckruf* (The Wake-Up Call). From there, this highly skilled individual quickly became regional press superintendent and editor of the Rhine region's *Der Weckruf* (1934). By 1937, Siegfried Leffler had appointed him press superintendent of the National Church Movement of German Christians, a radical German Christian group that strove to include Catholics in their movement. Before publication of church periodicals was halted in 1941, Dungs could still verify a total circulation of more than 100,000. He even managed to send German Christian propaganda in the form of newsletters and reports on Eisenach Institute work to soldiers serving on the front during the war.[75]

Dungs served as director of the Verlag Deutsche Christen (German Christian Press) in Weimar, which published "de-Judaized" Bibles and hymnals, along with the works of such German Christian protagonists as Leffler, Hirsch, and Meyer-Erlach. He was an active member of the Eisenach Institute and sat on its Scholarly Advisory Council by virtue of his position as leader of the German Christian publishing house. Though the Institute's publications were self-supporting, they were printed by Dungs.[76]

In the middle of 1935, the regional *Weckruf* began to exhibit a dual sharpening in tone that held positive affinities with the Nazi Party and was viscerally negative toward the Confessing Church. At this point, Heinz's brother Karl became a driving force and a regular contributor of articles. The paper's articles also demonstrated antisemitic attitudes in much the same way as did the Nazi Party, peppered by references to the later Luther. These attitudes can also be found with regularity in other publications edited by Dungs, including *Kommende Kirche* (Coming Church; 1936–1937) and *Nationalkirche—Briefe an Deutsche Christen* (National Church—Letters to the German Christians; 1937–1941).[77]

Holger Weitenhagen, in his incisive work on Dungs, incorporates a document that sheds light on the approach of the German Christian press to the "Jewish Question." One of three "Press Planning" documents in an appendix titled "Documents," it is based on "practical suggestions" in relation to the Jewish Question made by a "Kd. [*Kamerad*, or comrade] Oberlies" of Veitsberg and is dated October 7, 1938. Recipients included "Schneider-Stuttgart" (probably Georg Schneider) and (Heinz's brother Karl) "Dungs-Essen/Kupferdreh."

Some suggestions for subject areas to include in their gazettes and papers are "the connection of race and religion in Judaism," "Jesus and Judaism," and "[The] Bible and [the] Jewish Question." Another suggested area titled "The Attitude of Church-Historically Important Men of a Positive Kind to the Jewish Question" includes Luther, Stöcker, and others. This reflects a tendency among German Christian pastors and theologians to parade before their readers in hagiographical fashion influential völkisch and antisemitic Germans (including Stöcker and H. S. Chamberlain) as proof of historical and current support for their positions.[78]

Still another subject area in Dungs's Press Planning document entails the inclusion of "suitable print" from *Der Stürmer* or from Luther. There are nine areas of material relevant to the Jewish Question.[79] Luther's name appears in two of these, explicitly demonstrating that Luther's views regarding the so-called Jewish Question were to be part of the multifaceted intellectual arsenal of the German Christian press, at least from late 1938.

Dungs consistently tied the anti-Jewish legacy of Luther to current events in National Socialist Germany. As early as late 1934, he wrote that Luther, *"the most outrageous fighter which the world has ever seen,"* along with another great fighter, Hitler, belong "together for all times." In autumn 1935, he castigated two Protestant church officials for not grasping the "Jewish Question" well enough. In contrast to the "necessary *Kampf* [struggle] and enlightenment" of Julius Streicher, they apparently did not yet appreciate the threat of the "Jewish murderers" and their "devilish-Jewish greed." "They did not take hold of the blazing Luther anger about the sworn enemy of Christianity, the Jew."[80]

Dungs also contributed to other German Christian periodicals. Two such pieces appeared in *Deutscher Sonntag,* the first in the December 12, 1937 edition.[81] His first mention of Luther in the article is a plug for the book *Jews, Monks, and Luther* by "comrade Prof. Dr. Wolf Meyer-Erlach."[82] Here, the reader can compare the attitude of the present-day Protestant church (toward the "Jewish Question") with the work of the man "from whose life's work it [the church] grew up, Dr. Martin Luther." He bemoans the fact that the picture of Luther as "the great antisemitic pioneer" has in past years been withheld from the German people. Further, "seminal writings" about the "Jewish Question"—like *On the Jews and Their Lies*—got dusty in great scholarly libraries while theology students were unfamiliar with them.[83]

These writings have only become widely known to the public because of the "National Socialist revolution" and the struggle of Julius Streicher in *Der Stürmer*. Again from Meyer-Erlach, he decries the church of Luther's betrayal of their role as the "fighter against the pernicious power of Judaism." Following a now-familiar line, he describes how Luther first appeared as a protector of Jews, but "in a short time" became their "most resolute enemy." This latter period is characterized by *On the Jews and Their Lies*, whose social recommendations he compares to the Nuremberg Laws. Paraphrasing Meyer-Erlach, he notes with irony that the latter appear almost "scientifically cool" in comparison with the former.[84]

Dungs sums up Meyer-Erlach's views by way of three "keys": Luther's "religious knowledge, his völkisch insight, and his sense of social responsibility." He will only stress the most emphatic material from Meyer-Erlach in this article, which includes the exhortation that Luther's admonition to the preachers to warn the princes and masters about Jews, who are Germany's plague and misfortune, must be heard again. He even warns that Luther's Volk will "brush aside" those who call themselves Lutheran preachers if they do not listen to the reformer. "We, however, also want to fulfill our obligation on this point and render our contribution to the fight for Germany and the will of God."[85] Thus, Dungs believes that it is the social responsibility that is paramount for Meyer-Erlach, and no doubt for German Protestants.

The second article appeared early in 1939, just two months after Kristallnacht, and bears both the title and the cover art of Bishop Martin Sasse's book *Martin Luther on the Jews: Away with Them!* Here, Dungs says that Luther was a historical "religious freedom fighter" and "one of the greatest völkisch pioneers and the most prominent antisemite of his time." Yet, as in the first article, he states emphatically that the significance of his many anti-Jewish writings for the present is compelling, and remains "for the greatest part unknown." This time, Dungs makes reference not only to *On the Jews and Their Lies*, but also to *On the Ineffable Name*.[86]

The bulk of the article praises various books about "Luther and the Jews." He mentions one current collection of Luther's *Judenschriften*, Walther Linden's *Luthers Kampfschriften gegen das Judentum* (Luther's Polemics against Judaism, 1936). Yet, he reserves special praise once again for "our comrade" Professor Wolf Meyer-Erlach's *Jews, Monks, and Luther* and *Betrayal of Luther*. Finally, he introduces the focal point of the remainder of the article, Sasse's "16-page, tastefully bound" writing containing the "key elements" of Luther's commentary about the Jews. Dungs finds Sasse's decision to publish this work at this time a "particularly serendipitous thought." Not only is it "cheap" and attractive, but it comes at a pivotal time when the German people are "struggling with the solution to the Jewish Question." He also wishes that Luther's views be carried not only to Germans, but to foreigners as well.[87]

Dungs finds the up-to-date nature of Luther's suggestions "all the more astounding" as they are currently realized. He again emphasizes the importance of Luther's warning to preachers about the "Jewish danger." He believes that there may be "symbolic significance" in the fact that Luther's last sermon only days before his death was an "admonition against the Jews."

Finally, he drives home what he regards as special about Luther's position. As a "child of his time" he could not see the "racial question" as clearly as present-day Germans, who benefit from the crystal-clear view of the issue imparted by National Socialism. Yet, he gives his sharp position a religious explanation out of a "Christian responsibility before God for the . . . victory of his holy and good will over the powers of darkness."[88] Dungs is happy here to intermingle Luther's sixteenth-century nonrationality with National Socialist irrationality.

It is clear that Dungs sees the "Jewish Question" as a highly religious dilemma that nonetheless has very real social and political consequences. He utilizes Luther's *Judenschriften*, particularly as they are explicated by Sasse, as historical support for the position that Germans living in the Nazi Reich should take in 1939. Of particular importance in this piece is the significance he places upon Kristallnacht.[89] As he did in the 1937 article when he emphasized Meyer-Erlach's correlation of Luther's social recommendations with the Nuremberg Laws, here he joyfully proclaims the providential nature of Sasse's publication of a shorter and simpler linkage of these same recommendations with Kristallnacht. As their press superintendent, he glowingly reviewed and recommended the antisemitic and anti-Judaic literature of his German Christian compatriots.

Conclusions

In the past two chapters we have examined writings from two wings of the German Protestant Church who were diametrically opposed to each other. As with the Confessing Church in the last chapter, we have observed here some representative cases of German Christian writings that demonstrate the various approaches to Luther's *Judenschriften* in late Weimar and Nazi Germany. While the scope and context of the writings of the figures studied in this chapter varied with surrounding events, most approached Luther's writings in much the same manner.

A committed Nazi and German Christian, Bishop Martin Sasse wrote a short book about Luther and "the Jews" and issued a church decree urging Thuringian Protestant support for the Führer in his (and the Volksgemeinschaft's) fight against "Jewish–Bolshevistic godlessness" in the immediate aftermath of Kristallnacht. The decree exclusively addressed the event that took place in Paris on November 7 rather than the happenings in the streets of Germany on November 9–10. His dedication to the removal of the supposedly pernicious Jewish influence from German society was clear from his short book. His dedication to the elimination of Jewish influence from the Protestant church was later sealed with his signing of the Godesberg Declaration in April 1939, and affirmed by his regular participation in Eisenach Institute conferences.

The context for each of the Heinz Dungs articles that we have considered is illuminating. Both pieces were written for the German Christian publication *Deutscher Sonntag* and refer to crucial events in the development of regime oppression of German Jews. The first, written in late 1937, contains a favorable reference to the Nuremberg Laws and stresses Protestant responsibility toward the Volk. The second, written in early 1939, just two months after Kristallnacht, alludes to the events of November 9–10 and refers to the appearance of Sasse's book as "serendipitous." These pivotal events seem to have resonated strongly with the German Christian press superintendent.[90] Dungs's latter article represents part of the execution of the strategy called for in his "Press Planning" memorandum about the "Jewish Question." Consistently throughout his career, he followed the "later" Luther's view of the Jewish people, as is evidenced by his earlier statements about the "völkisch protagonist" and by these two articles.

How, then, should we characterize the various approaches to Luther's anti-Jewish treatises? Sasse's line of attack is anything but balanced. He does not consider evidence that runs counter to his view of Jews as a danger to the German people. Sasse seized on surrounding events to show them as positive fulfillment of Luther's wishes for the Jewish people. The scope thus involves not a full-scale defense or exposition of Luther's position regarding the Jewish people, but rather simply a biased sampling of the most strident and topically relevant proof texts that appear to support the recent antisemitic pogrom. The consistently irrational tenor of his work is starkly different from that of the Confessing Church works examined in the last chapter. His may be the least sophisticated of the works considered here, even if the conclusions are similar. Put simply, his approach was more propagandistic than theological. Stuttgart pastor Immanuel Schairer calls upon dubious nonrational anti-Judaic arguments replete with violent images and dire threats about Judaism ostensibly drawn from Luther and Jesus to buttress irrational Hitlerian arguments about an insidious and impinging "world Bolshevism."

I find it noteworthy for two reasons that Sasse and Dungs (here), along with Pauls, Vogelsang, Schmidt, and Steinlein (chapter three) all explicitly reference *On the Ineffable Name*. First, as noted here in chapter two, this work contains late medieval anti-Jewish paranoia and (perhaps even for its time) exceptionally harsh and crude language. None of these six men, despite their willingness to use the treatise to support their views, finds it necessary to discuss its harshness and vulgarity. Even Steinlein, whose analysis of Luther's views on Jews and Judaism is rather balanced, does not do so. Second, the fact that these figures cite this work—which is described as "known" by some German Protestants—suggests that, while it may not have contained a clear sociopolitical program as did *On the Jews and Their Lies,* it was part of the discussion of the "Jewish Question" in Nazi Germany.

What, then, can we ascertain from all of this? The gradual but intentional marginalization and oppression of Jews by the Nazi regime following the seizure of power led the Protestant churches to reassess how they viewed this increasingly endangered minority. Though the Church Struggle was certainly no valiant fight against Nazism, the pressure resulting from attempts by the Nazis to "aryanize" the churches and to consolidate them into one Reich church caused in part the ensuing Church Struggle, leading to the splintering of the tenuous union of Protestant churches into smaller and smaller subgroups. This context certainly must be considered when discussing ideas bearing on events that affected those outside of the ranks of their church.

This realization serves only to situate the often anti-Judaic and at times antisemitic tenor of the writings of some Confessing Church pastors. Yet, clearly the venom of the German Christian writings is not present to the same degree in the Confessing Church literature. As I have suggested, some Confessing Church pastors, by virtue of their opposition to state intrusion in church affairs, were fighting battles that most German Christian clergy were not. The danger of arrest by the authorities simply did not exist for most German Christian pastors. Still, from the standpoint of an ever decreasing and terrorized German Jewish population, the concrete effects of nonrationally driven apathy or ambivalence toward their plight (as in the Confessing Church) would have been hard to distinguish from the consequences of irrationally guided hatred and excoriation (as with the German Christians).

How, then, can typical German Christian views of the Jewish people be characterized in comparison to representative Confessing Church approaches to the same? First, the distinction between antisemitic and anti-Judaic discourse is nowhere more evident than in the writings of these generally polarized wings of German Protestantism. The German Christian literature is overwhelmingly laden with strident attacks on Jews based on irrational conceptions about them. They are said to possess "fanatical hatred" and "pernicious power." They are the "scum of mankind." The imagined threat of the Jewish people—alternately described as "Jewish Bolshevism," "international" or "world" Jewry—is touted as reason enough to follow the Führer and the state in fighting a "defensive struggle" against its supposedly "Volk-disintegrating" power. Much of this terminology, of course, merely mimicked Nazi racist discourses prevalent at the time. Ultimately, many in the German Christian movement believed it was a matter of annihilate or be annihilated.

In late Weimar and Nazi Germany, Protestant theologians and clergy who were so inclined could *legitimately* mine Luther's *Judenschriften* for both anti-Judaic and antisemitic material. This, despite the fact that Luther's pronouncements about Jews and Judaism were not entirely uniform. In the case of many German Christians, this endeavor was frequently undertaken with incautious aplomb. Most of these writings are characterized by selectivity and tendentiousness. Serious historical and theological investigation were either jettisoned entirely or practiced with extreme subjectivity. Even some of those who were willing to criticize Luther were perturbed that he had not been consistently antisemitic. Irrational rhetoric drawn from the reformer's early modern treatises was utilized with little or no embarrassment. Passages in which Luther called for Christians to deal lovingly with Jews often were simply ignored.

The German Christian writings also exhibit in general a decided lack of nuance with respect to the person and work of Luther. He is often paraded before his readers in hagiographic fashion along with other German "heroes" like Chamberlain, Stöcker, and Hitler. There is very little mention of his earlier, relatively philosemitic works. Countervailing evidence from Luther's later *Judenschriften* is also generally lacking.

There are two things that are especially noteworthy in the writings of these German Christian and Confessing Church pastors and bishops. First, the utilization of irrational, antisemitic argumentation, while certainly more prevalent and crass in the German Christian literature, is present to a lesser degree in the generally anti-Nazi Confessing Church writings as well. Neither party had a monopoly on hatred of unconverted Jews. In the case of the German Christians, however, even converted Jews could expect no help, but at best could be forced into separate congregations for Jewish Christians. Second, despite varying degrees of tolerance and intolerance of baptized Jews, both the German Christian and the Confessing Church figures tended to speak with one voice to unbaptized Jews. Very few of these Protestant Christians would speak out on their behalf. This general silence spoke volumes to a people who would face further dehumanization, violence, and death by the millions.

6

PASTORS AND THEOLOGIANS FROM THE UNAFFILIATED PROTESTANT "MIDDLE"

Bolshevism is the menace
of the stateless. It is
therefore no wonder that
it gets its main leaders
from stateless Judaism.

—Heinrich Bornkamm,
*What Do We Expect from the
German Protestant Church
of the Future?* (1939)

Over the course of the twelve-year Nazi rule, roughly 35–40 percent of Protestant clergymen were not affiliated with either the Confessing Church or the German Christians.[1] In 1936, the largest church-political group among professors of Protestant theology consisted of those aligned with neither of these two polarized wings of the German Protestant Church, comprising just over half of the total number.[2] Thus, the number of Protestant pastors and theologians who did not choose sides formally in the Church Struggle was very substantial. In this chapter, I examine the writings of two academic theologians and one pastor who addressed Luther's outlook on Jews and Judaism either directly or indirectly. Despite the fact that some exhibited sympathies with either the Confessing Church or the German Christians, all three were officially associated only with the German Protestant Church for the overwhelming majority of the Nazi period. Yet, they approached the Jewish Question in fairly unique ways.

From the turn of the twentieth century there was a "crisis of modernity" in German Protestant theology that was especially pronounced for academics, including theologians. For the theologians, the crisis had much to do with how to relate theology to Enlightenment modernity.[3] Political upheaval, rational and scientific challenges to religious faith, cultural affronts to traditional morality (especially in larger cities like Berlin), and the challenges to any belief in human progress facilitated by the brutality and irrationality of the First World War characterized the crisis. The predicament created great anxiety and distress. While artists, philosophers, and writers such as Thomas Mann, Bertolt Brecht, and Martin Heidegger grappled with the dizzying changes brought on by Weimar modernity, Protestant theologians also faced an existential predicament that needed to be addressed.[4] For many Protestants, Hitler's ascent to power seemed like a heaven-sent answer.

There were seventeen Protestant theology faculties in Germany during the late Weimar and early Nazi periods. With Germany's annexation of Austria in March 1938 (the "*Anschluß*") and the resultant addition of Vienna University to the Reich, the count rose to eighteen. Tübingen, Berlin, and Erlangen ranked as the three largest. From 1927 to 1932, the number of Protestant theology students nearly tripled to just over seven thousand. This growth, unprecedented in the history of German Protestantism, took place in the context of a huge surge in overall university attendance, due in part to large birth-cohorts in the years leading up to 1914.[5]

In stark contrast to the meteoric rise in the waning years of the Weimar Republic, the number of students studying Protestant theology fell by more than 80 percent from 1933 to 1939, to just over 1,300. This precipitous decline even surpassed the 60 percent decrease in the number of students studying in German universities overall. The general decrease in university attendance can be explained by the low birth-cohorts of the First World War years, the justifiably low expectation of employment after graduation, and the anti-university policies of the Nazi regime.[6] The numbers dropped drastically with the onset of the war, as young men were called up to service in the Wehrmacht.

During the Nazi era, Protestant academic theologians suddenly had fewer students to train for careers in pastoral ministry and academic theology than they did in the late Weimar years. Yet their work continued unabated during the Third Reich. Protestant theologians and pastors of varying church-political groupings, geographic regions, ages, and political affiliations worked on topical issues, including Christian approaches to Jews and Judaism. Luther's *Judenschriften* often were consulted to address this issue.

The three unaffiliated Protestant theologians and pastors examined here engaged with Luther's *Judenschriften* in a variety of ways. Some wrote primarily for other theologians, while the efforts of others were intended more for the Protestant rank and file. Even the more academic works, however, had some effect on overall Protestant opinion, as the influence of their ideas was filtered and passed on to wider audiences through sermons and lectures. The works of two of these individuals consistently provided anti-Judaic and antisemitic ammunition to the so-called Protestant "middle" and beyond. Their writings furthered nonrational anti-Judaic notions of Jews as a people separate from the Christian Volk and chief deniers of Christ, as well as irrational and xenophobic images of Jews as usurers and purveyors of anti-Christian Bolshevism. In the third case, we will witness the exercise of muted theological opposition to politically and culturally accepted hatred of Jews.

Heinrich Bornkamm, Gießen/Leipzig Church Historian

Heinrich Bornkamm was born the son of a pastor in 1901 in Wuitz, a village near Leipzig. The younger Bornkamm studied theology with some of the most prominent names in the field of church history of his time, including Hans Lietzmann at Jena, and Adolf von Harnack and Karl Holl at Berlin. He received his doctorate in theology under Holl in 1924, in Berlin. The next year, he completed his *Habilitation* in church history at Tübingen.

By 1927, at the age of twenty-six, Bornkamm was already full professor of church history at Gießen University.[7] We might be tempted to view him as something of a Wunderkind because of this seemingly meteoric ascent up the career ladder. Yet, the state of affairs in the field of academic theology in mid-1920s Germany must be taken into account. The First World War had depleted the country of many potential candidates for such posts. Thus, young church historians like Bornkamm, Hirsch (Göttingen,

1921, age thirty-three), Hanns Rückert (Leipzig, 1928, age twenty-seven), and others like them were able to achieve full professor status while still in their twenties and early thirties. This is not to minimize Bornkamm's intellectual prowess, which was recognized even by those who were otherwise critical of him.[8]

Bornkamm served as rector at Gießen in 1933 and 1934. From 1935 to 1945 he was full professor and chair of church history at Leipzig University. As a result of his membership in Nazi organizations, he was dismissed from Leipzig after the war. He joined the faculty at Heidelberg University in 1948, where he achieved professor emeritus status in 1966. In 1973, he received the Grand Order of Merit of the Federal Republic of Germany. Bornkamm died in Heidelberg in 1977.[9]

Beginning in 1935, through the Nazi years, and in the postwar period until 1963, he served as president of the Protestant League.[10] This organization, along with other cultural associations such as the Gustav Adolf Society and the Martin Luther Society, attempted rather successfully—at least during the early years of the Third Reich—to keep itself neutral with reference to the Church Struggle while at the same time maintaining loyalty to the Nazi state. Indeed, during his tenure as president, Bornkamm tried to steer a path of unification in the German Protestant Church. The League's membership stood at 260,000 in 1934. Despite clear affinities with the German Christians, open conflict with them over their inclusion of Catholics in the so-called "National Church" led to the departure of a large number of members from the Protestant League.[11]

Bornkamm joined the right-wing Christian-German Movement around 1930 and the more radical German Christians in 1933. In either late 1933 or early 1934, he joined the SA, exiting the organization either in December 1934 or shortly thereafter. He was also a member of the National Socialist Professors' League (NSLB) during the last seven years of the Nazi regime.[12] Bornkamm left the German Christians after the Sports Palace affair of November 1933, in which the main speaker at a large rally held at the Berlin Sports Palace lambasted the Old Testament, the Apostle Paul, and the symbol of the cross as ludicrous and weakening leftovers from Judaism.[13]

It would be easy either to underestimate or to overvalue Bornkamm's SA membership. Some important realities need to be considered. Membership in the SA tended toward volatile fluctuation. Nazi Party membership was "required" of SA members, but many did not in fact join the party.

Though they had a well-deserved reputation for violence prior to 1933, and led a campaign of terror against Communists, Social Democrats, trade unionists, and Jews between March and June 1933, conflicts with Hitler and the party after the Nazi ascent to power eventually led to the bloody Röhm purge, which began on June 30, 1934.

Ernst Röhm, the combative leader of the SA, had aspired for the "brown battalions" to be a militaristic organization. After the Nazis came to power, he tried to overwhelm the party through sheer numbers. Due to the opening of the organization to all "patriotically minded German men," by the beginning of 1934 there were nearly three million members, up six times over their January 1933 numbers.[14] After the "night of the long knives," however, the SA was transformed almost immediately into a politically weak mass organization restricted for the most part to ceremonial functions; towns and villages were freed from SA "bullies." Though some members still perpetrated violence in the mid- and late thirties, it was now more an irritant than a serious political threat. Their membership steadily declined after June 1934. Yet there remained a latent "high readiness" for violence during this time, as evidenced by SA participation in Kristallnacht.[15]

Bornkamm then appears to have joined the SA during a massive membership drive in which all "patriotic" German men were encouraged to join. There is also no indication that he condoned violence as a legitimate means of political expression. Yet, his membership in an organization with a reputation for violence and rowdyism is still intriguing when seen in connection with his views on the Nazi State, the Church, the German Volk, and the Jewish people.

What Do We Expect from the German Protestant Church of the Future? (1939)

Bornkamm expounds his general thinking about Jews and Judaism most clearly in a small book titled *Was erwarten wir von der deutschen evangelischen Kirche der Zukunft?* (What Do We Expect from the German Protestant Church of the Future?) First he discusses the essence of the church, stating that the "ultimate realities" upon which the church and its work exist are "the Word of God and the *Völker*." At the heart of the Gospel are the "Word of God in Jesus Christ" and the "message of the Apostle, the word to the *Völker* according to the mission of the Lord: 'Go forth and teach all *Völker.*"[16] Commenting on the biblical passage upon which this latter principle is based, he argues, "We accentuate the Greek linguistic usage, when we say 'to the *Völker,*' and prudently do not say: to mankind. Because mankind is an abstraction." While the individual person is addressed by the Gospel, he is at the same time "insolubly associated" as an individual with his Volk, by which he is "uniquely shaped and formed." One cannot miss the echoes of Althaus here.

Bornkamm uses the term *Volk* in multiple and differentiated ways. Unlike an "earthly" Volk, the people of God cannot be counted in a census, has no nationality, and claims no national borders. The essence of the church must be seen as völkisch, in Bornkamm's neoconservative, carefully qualified sense. This precision distinguishes his work (and that of others like Althaus) from the more polemical compositions of radical German Christians such as Meyer-Erlach and Sasse.[17]

In the second part of the book, he discusses the "path and shape" of the Protestant church. Bornkamm here argues in part that the "fight against Christianity" (by the "house of Ludendorff" and others) made it difficult for some Christians to appreciate the "genuine religious faith" of "countless members of the National Socialist movement." Bornkamm posits a middle ground between a "deep and passionate confidence" in the "creaturely powers" of Volk and Führer that "attacks or replaces unconditional faith in the Creator" and a Christianity that fails to recognize "the genuine" in the ranks of the National Socialist movement. In other words, passionately devoted Christians and passionately devoted Nazis should learn from each other.[18]

Yet, it is not only to committed individual members of the Nazi movement that he lends qualified support. The Nazi state has a God-given role to play. In one passage, he weaves together the "tremendous breakthrough of national state thinking" (*Nationalstaatsgedanken*) and the "powerful and undeniable truth of racial thinking" (*Rassegedanken*) in explicit support of the foreign policy of the Third Reich. He rejects Luther's view of "defensive wars" as no longer sufficient for coming to terms with the moral question of war and deems the deployment of national power for "creation of the German *Volksstaat* [the state of the German people]" as "justifiable" on Christian moral grounds.

This racial thinking places the task before German Protestants "of clearly separating equality before God and differences of human beings among themselves" and of bringing them into balance in the "right way."

The personal responsibility of the individual does not "eliminate his integration" into the "binding powers" of state and Volk. The carefully constructed logic leads to unspoken but critical conclusions. The quiescent Protestant Christian, bound to his Volk (which is an order of creation), is morally justified in supporting an aggressive Nazi war.

What, then, does Bornkamm expect of the Protestant church when it comes to Jews and Judaism? His argument here does contain some nonrational content, including a discussion of a "much-debated research problem" related to whether a distinction exists between the depiction of Judaism in the words of Jesus and Paul.[19] Yet, Bornkamm does not rely solely on such claims.

Bolshevism, which he describes as the "common denominator" of the powerful "onslaught" of "life-destroying powers," is the "menace of the stateless." It is "no wonder," then, "that it gets its main leaders from stateless Judaism."[20] In espousing the belief that a dangerous Bolshevism is led by Jews, Bornkamm forwards an idea that has obvious currency among his fellow Germans. This is not the only passage in which he expresses irrational antisemitic sentiments. In 1935, he had published a work titled *Vom christlichen zum nationalen Sozialismus* (From Christian to National Socialism), in which he spoke of a "Jewish press" that controlled "left liberalism" in Wilhelmine Germany and of Jewish domination in communist thinking.[21]

He furthers the argument about Bolshevism with both precision and intensity. Bolshevism is far more than a "political system or a political confession of faith"; it is religious in nature, and thus requires a "counteracting" religious force, which he identifies with Christianity, Bolshevism's "mortal enemy." A truly Christian Volk "will never become Bolshevistic." Instead, it will engage itself in the "world struggle against Bolshevism." The preface to this work was written sometime in November 1938, in close proximity to Kristallnacht, from which time this "world struggle" was thrust violently into the public sphere.[22]

"Volk and Race in Martin Luther" (1933)

According to Leopold Cordier, who was then dean of the theology faculty at Gießen, the church training seminar that formed the basis for the book *Volk, Staat, Kirche* (Volk, State, Church) took place in June 1933 with the support of the Hessian regional Protestant church. Along with faculty and

A pile of Hebrew prayer books and other Jewish religious texts damaged by fire at the synagogue in Bobenhausen II, District Vogelsberg, during Kristallnacht. *United States Holocaust Memorial Museum, courtesy of Jewish Community of Giessen.*

regional church representatives, some clergy from Hesse and representatives of the Faith Movement of German Christians were also invited to attend. Attendance "surpassed expectations." Part of the stated purpose of the seminar was to "strengthen the relationship of Volk and state to Church and Gospel."[23]

Heinrich Bornkamm's short yet potent contribution to *Volk, State, Church*, titled "Volk und Rasse bei Martin Luther" (Volk and Race in Martin Luther), was the first lecture in the seminar. He addresses here the very topical issue of Volk and race from the perspective of church history, especially the history of the German Protestant Reformation and its founder, Martin Luther. He argues early in the piece that the terms *Volk* and *race* did not mean the same for Luther as they did for his 1933 Gießen audience. Luther "of course" did not know of a concept called "race." Nevertheless,

Bornkamm argues, the realities of the concepts, though "concealed" under other terms, were still recognizable to him.

Despite the nuances, Luther must have known "something" of the "biological and historical unity of a state." Though Luther came on the scene prior to the advent of nation-states and talk of races, he must have had "at least a notion" of the "biological basic elements in the structure of mankind" that overlap borders of state and Volk, "which we call races." Here Bornkamm espouses an interpretation of Luther's *Judenschriften* that closely parallels Nazi conceptions of Volk and race.[24]

For Bornkamm, it is essential to understand that Luther's "picture of *Volkstum*"—especially German *Volkstum*—was formed at a time of awakening "völkisch consciousness":

> One must free oneself from the idea that national-consciousness has been a matter of course, as we assume, ever since the nation-states of the nineteenth century. . . . Not only did the Romans sense racial antagonism, but also the Germanic peoples, who now for the first time felt a higher unity among the tribes.[25]

Bornkamm thus blurs the boundaries of periodization even further. Not only did Luther know something of Volk and race, but the Germanic peoples also sensed racial antagonism and, concurrently, the unity of their tribes. Both came prior to the advent of the modern nation-state, the supposed marker for "national-consciousness."

Though Luther of all "foreign" peoples opposed the Jews and the Turks, it is the Jews whose "foreignness of race" stirred the "strongest and most concrete" feeling. Due to circumstances, Luther judged the Jewish people differently at different times. Bornkamm traces this progression in the career of the reformer. He covers in some detail Luther's works against the Jewish people, giving his greatest attention to *On the Jews and Their Lies,* including an outline of Luther's accusations and his seven recommendations.[26]

With four observations, he summarizes Luther's "assumptions and motifs" about the "Jewish Question." First, Luther regards the fight against "the Jews" as a "religious dispute." Specifically, their "crime" is blasphemy against Christ. Yet, the goal of Luther's fight is the "conversion of individual Jews"—even if the prospects of this occurring are dim. Second, Luther believes that the authorities have to intervene officially against such "public blasphemy." Luther rejected forced conversion, which is not the goal of the intervention of the authorities. Their aim is rather "to preserve the land." In light of what Bornkamm stated elsewhere about the Nazi state, it can be inferred that he believed Nazi anti-Jewish policy to be a means to preserve the Volk against public blasphemy.

Third, even though forced conversion is rejected, the conversion of individual Jews is nevertheless the goal of such "public suppression." He asserts that even the "severe suggestions" in *On the Jews and Their Lies* should serve to rescue Jews from (as Luther puts it) "the flames and embers." Just *how* such public suppression is to serve the conversion of Jews is not elucidated. Fourth, it is not only Jewish blasphemy of Christ but their usury that "disgusts" Luther. In one of the more strident passages in the text, Bornkamm claims that Luther's disgust is bound together with his wrath that Germany has been "sucked dry" by this seemingly "devil-possessed Volk." Luther's "revulsion," says Bornkamm, "comes from the same depths of Luther's Volk sentiment as his angry defense against all *vermin* of Germany, Rome and its courtesans, as well as every other usurer."[27]

Finally, Bornkamm argues that Luther viewed both the Volk and the authorities as "direct creations of God." As an order of creation, "the authorities are like all other estates (father, mother, lord, farmhand) a 'divine' estate." God, in fact, "saves" his work of creation through the authorities.[28] This choice of words is provocative in that it is the same reformational language used to describe the spiritual work that God does for sinners. Does Bornkamm believe that God will "save" Germany through the Nazi authorities?

While it is beyond dispute that Bornkamm wanted to present his analysis of Volk and race in Luther's works as an essentially religious enterprise, his historical outlook, based in his theology, would not let him cleanly separate the racial from the religious. For Bornkamm, though Luther did not understand race in quite the same way as did Germans living in the 1930s, he did have at least a notion of this idea. In Bornkamm's view of German history, völkisch consciousness was present even in the Middle Ages.

Like Paul Althaus, Heinrich Bornkamm was a prominent figure in Protestant Christianity during the entire Nazi era. His role as president of the Protestant League granted him significant influence among German Protestants. First as full professor of church history and rector of Gießen University, and then as full professor and chair of church history at Leipzig, Bornkamm was a highly formidable theological force. Despite the fact that neither of the Bornkamm texts considered here may be regarded as classics, the renown of their author would have added weight to their carefully argued conclusions.

Bornkamm's departure from the German Christians in late 1933 had more to do with theological commitments and church politics than with any lack of loyalty to the Nazi state or uneasiness about Nazi anti-Jewish policy. Despite the marginalized position of the SA after June 1934, its reputation for brawling and violence never fully disappeared, as was evidenced on November 9 and 10, 1938. Thus, even if he left the group at the end of 1934, his membership would seem a less than respectable choice for an otherwise upstanding academic theologian.

Bornkamm's *What Do We Expect from the German Protestant Church of the Future?* is a carefully crafted, theologically based piece on pressing social and cultural happenings in Nazi Germany. Supporting his argumentation about many of these issues is an accommodation to contemporary culture that is buoyed by theological reasoning. In one instance, for example, he appeals craftily to the "Greek linguistic usage" in a key New Testament passage to support an "orders of creation" paradigm regarding the Volk, which fits very nicely with a conservative, nationalistic view in broader German society.

Though not a Nazi himself, clearly Bornkamm seeks a rapprochement between Protestant Christians and "genuine" Nazis. Some leading Nazis have indeed attacked Christianity. For Bornkamm, though, this is no reason to fail to recognize the genuinely religious ones in their ranks.

Bornkamm seeks no such détente with Judaism. Whether speaking of German Protestants who are insolubly associated with their Volk or of a religiously inspired Bolshevism led by stateless Jews, Bornkamm's assessment of Jews and Judaism—both nonrational and irrational—is exceptionally negative. His brief discussion of "racial thinking" in which he seeks to differentiate between equality before God and differences among peoples in a "balanced" manner, more than subtly implies subjugation of individuals or groups of people who are not properly integrated into their Volk. When one connects this idea with "national-state" thinking and his rejection of Luther's defensive war position, the result is a seemingly reasoned, divinely sanctioned defense of the increasingly aggressive foreign and domestic policies of the Nazi regime.

In "Volk and Race in Martin Luther" (1933), Bornkamm is keen to discuss Luther's views in *historical* terms. What makes the printed lecture so striking is the author's willingness to regard Luther's anti-Jewish attitude as explicitly völkisch in nature. Despite the lack of "race" language in Luther's writings, the concept was clearly there for Bornkamm, even if it was "concealed." While these conclusions are strained, Bornkamm nonetheless sensed correctly the historical unity between the irrational antisemitic and nonrational anti-Judaic logic behind Luther's sixteenth-century call for measures against Jews and that of Protestants—Nazi-aligned Protestants like himself and otherwise—living in Germany in the 1930s.

Employing Althaus's orders of creation theology, he weaves the strands of nation and Volk alongside direct and affirmative appeal to Luther's harshest anti-Jewish pronouncements. When taken together, his conclusions imply that the Nazi authorities could be used by God to save Germany, and indeed his creation, from Jewish blasphemy and usury. For all of these reasons, Bornkamm's positions on Volk and race, perhaps better than any of the theologians discussed in this book, serve to demonstrate how the nonrational/irrational rubric better explains the writings of the theologians than does the racial/religious divide. Although he does not explicitly elevate race to the same theological plane as he does Volk, the interrelatedness of the two concepts imbues the former notion with at least a semi-religious aura. Bornkamm's Luther could quite nicely serve a Nazi state seen as ordained by God with the function of rescuing his creation.

Walter Holsten, Moringen Pastor

Born in 1908 in Osnabrück, Walter Holsten began his ministerial and academic career on the cusp of the Nazi ascent to power, receiving his doctorate in Göttingen in 1932. He became curate at Elverhausen the following year and then pastor in Moringen, near Göttingen, in September 1934. Four years later, he began serving as pastor in Hasbergen. After completing his *Habilitation* in 1946, he became professor of religion and missions at Mainz University the next year. Holsten achieved professor emeritus status in 1973 and died in Mainz in 1982.[29]

One piece of correspondence written while Holsten served at Moringen, which since 1933 had housed one of the first concentration camps in Nazi Germany, reveals theological reasoning aimed at reforming "enemies" of the Nazi state. In August 1936, Holsten told the Reich Church Committee (*Reichskirchenausschuss*) that pastoral care should be granted to prisoners in "protective custody camps" on the grounds that imprisonment and education alone could not turn enemies of the state into citizens. What was needed was preaching and pastoral care that were "based in God" and that could impart the "right internal position" toward Volk and state.[30]

Holsten's impact on greater German Protestantism from 1933 to 1945 seems on the surface to be far less significant than that of more well-known theologians such as Bornkamm and Althaus. He was merely one pastor among thousands and held no important positions in the German Protestant Church. Yet, his influence regarding Luther's views of Volk, Jews, and Judaism is highly significant.

Althaus, in an article titled "Der Wahrheitsgehalt der Religionen und das Evangelium" (The Validity of the Religions and the Gospel), twice referenced Holsten's *Christentum und nichtchristliche Religion nach der Auffassung Luthers* (Christianity and Non-Christian Religion According to Luther).[31] Both this work and Martin Luther's *Schriften wider Juden und Türken* (Writings against Jews and Turks)—which included extensive commentary by Holsten—also appeared on a short list of texts and monographs recommended by Dr. Friedrich Werner, director of the main office of the German Protestant Church in Berlin, in an April 1939 memo to the leaders of all the regional Protestant churches.[32] Given the weight attached to these works by theologians and church officials alike, I will consider them here at some length.

Christianity and Non-Christian Religion According to Luther (1932)

Tellingly, Holsten begins *Christianity and Non-Christian Religion* by describing the "present era of theology and church history" as a decisive fight between Christian and non-Christian religions.[33] What follows will not simply be a lesson in historical theology without contemporary relevance. He could not have known just how relevant these words would appear one year, three years, or six years later.

Holsten places Luther's critique of other religions and philosophies in a reformational context in which the reformer continually referred to the nascent conflict with Catholicism. Commenting on "paganism" in the biblical era—which Holsten regards as "false religion," in contrast to "true religion" or (Old Testament) Judaism—he makes a keen observation about Luther's view of the Jewish people, averring that "Luther could not at all express himself about Israelite paganism without simultaneous reference to Catholicism."[34]

Later, he offers an extended discussion of Luther's views on post-biblical Judaism. Holsten recognizes that both devotees and opponents of antisemitism gladly take the support of Luther in their endeavors, calling the subject "hotly disputed" territory. The "persistent accusation" that Luther raises against Jews concerns their "disobedience" toward Scriptural authority. In elevating the thinking of their rabbis, they parallel Catholic elevation of the pope and his decrees over Scripture.

Concurring with Luther, Holsten contends that when it comes to biblical interpretation, it is the "Christ of the Scriptures" that separates Judaism from Christianity. Enmity against "the true Messiah" rules them. Luther would rather end up in heaven with Augustine and other church fathers—even with their "uncertain Hebrew knowledge and some linguistic errors"—than with the devil, despite the "philological precision and erudition" of the Jews.[35]

Holsten recounts many of the accusations of both *On the Ineffable Name* and *On the Jews and Their Lies,* including the purported Jewish blasphemies of Christ and Mary and the "mad fantasies" about the magical source of Jesus' miracles. He does not gloss over the antisemitic passage where Luther argues that Jews, who have been "accused" of well-poisoning, the kidnapping, ritual abuse and killing of Christian children, and host desecration, are quite capable of such shameful deeds. He examines a passage in *On the Ineffable Name* in which Luther accuses Jewish doctors of attempting to kill ailing Christians through "inconspicuous" means.[36] The absence of any consideration of how these passages demonstrate Luther's irrationality indicates Holsten's lack of embarrassment with their content.

He also treats Luther's "practical approach to the Jews." In a fairly brief discussion of Luther and mission to Jews (*Judenmission*), he stresses the pessimistic approach of the later Luther. "'This or that Jew'" may be converted, but on the whole, Jewish conversion is impossible. Even so, there is still a "glimmer of hope" for some individual Jews in *On the Ineffable Name.* Yet, the antithesis between the "early" and the "later" Luther finds its flashpoint in the demands pertaining to treatment of Jews in *On the Jews and Their Lies.* Unlike the "missionary" attitude of Luther in the earlier period, the later period is characterized by an often "brutal" treatment of Jews. Although conversion is desired, Christians must also protect themselves against their "aggressive pride and unbelief."[37]

In the anti-Jewish program, "every vestige of love seems razed." Because so much is at stake, Luther utters the demands not only once, but repeats them with "detailed explanation" of their necessity. Holsten divides the measures into "civil" and "religious" categories. Measures such as the razing of synagogues and the seizing of prayer books and Talmuds are encroachments on Jewish religious liberty. The forbidding of usury, confiscation of gold and silver, and the like are considered suppression of civil liberty.[38]

The Moringen pastor admits that the contradiction between the early and the later Luther's attitude toward Jews is "extremely strange." Yet, there is a "latent unity" at the basis of this contradiction. For, though the measures appear to be very *un*-merciful, they are actually rooted in "sharp mercy." Whoever practices such mercy is like a doctor who, "in order to rescue the suffering from dangerous disease carries out a painful operation," mercilessly cutting and burning off the metastasis.[39]

Without Luther's later approach, Christians would understand his earlier attitude only superficially, not in its reformational "depth and acridity." Here, Holsten clearly defends the acerbity of the reformer's later writings about Jews and Judaism. He concludes by attempting to distance himself from the "modern" antisemites, who would wish to invoke Luther but fail to recognize that Luther rooted his demands in (sharp) "mercy and not hate." The "Jewish Question," while primarily a religious matter, nevertheless reaches into the political sphere.[40]

Holsten leaves very few stones unturned in his extensive textual analysis. Yet, underneath this keen, often elegant analysis is an implicit agreement with the reformer's severe recommendations—rooted in "sharp mercy"—that becomes explicit in his brief conclusion. Despite his convoluted efforts to distinguish between Luther's approach and that of modern antisemites, he ends up merely shifting the primary motivation of anti-Jewish suspicion from the social and political spheres to the religious. Yet, even at that, he still supports these theological precursors of the Nuremberg Laws, which beginning only three years later would legally cement the ostracism of Jews from German society. Ultimately, Holsten argues for a muted Christian witness to Jews—with low expectations for its effectiveness—coupled with Christian support for government-sanctioned restrictions of Jewish religious and civil liberty.

"Comments" on Luther's *Writings against Jews and Turks* (1938)

Holsten's comments on Luther's *Writings against Jews and Turks* were of considerable importance as an interpretive tool for German pastors and theologians serving during the Nazi regime. The collection first appeared in 1936; the second (unmodified) edition was published in 1938. His comments are especially instructive insofar as they reveal his own attitude toward the "Jewish Question" several years after his work on Christianity and non-Christian religions. In the midst of increasing oppression and marginalization of Jews in the Third Reich, did his views soften, harden, or remain the same?

Holsten's detailed textual comments appear at the end of a work that includes the texts of all of the *Judenschriften* covered in chapter two here, as well as *On the Last Words of David* (1543). There is a short introduction to each work as well. I will discuss some of the more relevant notations and introductory comments.

Though some of the most revealing comments are lengthy, other shorter comments illuminate a great deal as well. Holsten twice consults a dubious source without censure, in the first instance directing the reader to consult Wilhelm Grau's *Antisemitismus im späten Mittelalter* (Antisemitism in the Late Middle Ages) on the matter of Christian mission to Jews in medieval times. Grau, a Catholic, was acting director of the Research Section of the Jewish Question in the Reich Institute for the History of the New Germany, in Munich, from 1935 to 1938. In 1940, Alfred Rosenberg appointed him director of both the Frankfurt Judaica Library and the Frankfurt branch of Rosenberg's planned Nazi University.[41] All of these institutions were ostensibly "scholarly" venues for promoting antisemitic Nazi propaganda. Despite a tone that reveals a general suspicion of Jewish actions and beliefs, Grau's work manages to come across as fairly even-handed. Yet, this apparent impartiality at times is betrayed by conclusions that are not based on credible evidence.[42]

Commenting on a passage from *Against the Sabbatarians,* Holsten repeats a theme common among the more conservative German Protestant theologians and pastors, noting that Luther differentiated "sharply" between Israel as "Volk of God and *the Jews after (and against) Christ. . . ."* The "struggle against the Jews," he says, is not a fight against God's Volk of the Old Covenant and "not at all a fight against the O.T."[43] Holsten here reaffirms his commitment to the present fight against "the Jews," something he had made explicit in his earlier work.

In a concluding comment on the same work, he says, "Obviously the Jewish Question had not been a scholarly question for Luther, but rather [his heart] was full of it, and out of its fullness broke a river of thoughts.

Will this not anyway be the case everywhere one really lives from the Scriptures?" This is probably an allusion to the words of Jesus in the Gospel of Matthew, and is no doubt intended as an encouragement to personal piety.[44] Yet, it is tied to an evaluation of the "Jewish Question" that was—for both Luther and Holsten—overwhelmingly negative.

Holsten begins his introduction to *On the Jews and Their Lies* by noting that the work "is that writing to which Luther owes his fame as a prominent antisemite." It might be called the "arsenal" from which antisemitism got its weapons. Yet, the "Jewish question" is no mere academic inquiry, but rather one that "had its place in his heart." Luther's heart "beat for the Word of God alone." Once again, Holsten seeks both to cloak Luther's antisemitism in pious attire and to distance himself from the "modern" antisemites.

Here, as in the previous work, Christians are encouraged to practice a "sharp mercy" toward Jews. *"Hard measures against the Jews are thus justified and required,* if a genuine mercy is behind them." Christians might be surprised, he avers, that these measures are rooted for Luther in "Christian" rather than "national or other" considerations. Yet, here is where the "Christian" and the "political" meet for Luther.[45] Holsten's support for at least the principles of Nazi anti-Jewish policy is perhaps nowhere clearer than when he states that it is "the obligation of the authorities and of Christianity not to tolerate or through tolerance to encourage" a religion whose essence contradicts the truth. "Anti-Christianity" is an attack on the existence of the Volk *"and therefore demands a national approach."*[46]

Holsten relies quite heavily on the German Christian theologian Erich Vogelsang, and he also twice makes reference to Althaus's work on modern Judaism. In the first appeal to the Erlangen theologian, he notes that a "friendly attitude of modern Jews to Jesus" should not be regarded as their turning to Christ. In the second instance, Holsten comments at length on Luther's proposed measures against Jews. The reader is encouraged to consult Althaus regarding the purportedly disparate attitudes toward work and usury held by Luther and the Jewish people.[47]

Discussing a passage from *On the Jews and Their Lies*, Holsten accentuates Luther's distinction between people as they are "before the world" and as they are "before God," quoting Vogelsang at length: "Human beings and peoples and races are thus not—[as with] the rationalism of the philosemites—all equally valuable, equal in nobility, in intelligence, in talent, in strength." The differences between peoples and races nevertheless do not matter "in the light of eternity, in the court of God," a fact that "the Jews and many antisemites do not understand."[48] Here, via Vogelsang, Holsten makes a further distinction between Christian condemnation of Jews and that of "many antisemites."

While Luther argues that the Jewish people "could not know what God's commandment is," Holsten complains that Stuttgart Protestant pastor Eduard Lamparter sees a "providential task" for Judaism in that it both stresses and protects the "ethical element in the spiritual belief in God." Following Vogelsang once again, he argues that Lamparter in his "Enlightenment liberalism" does not understand Luther's "fight against the Jews" or "the true relationship, the antagonism between Judaism and Christianity."[49]

Holsten also links Judaism to Bolshevism, complete with an appeal to Göttingen theologian Emanuel Hirsch, committed member of the German Christians and the Nazi Party and supporting member of the SS: "One can well say that the messianic expectation of post-biblical Judaism comes to maturity in Bolshevism" and (in Hirsch's words) may represent an "'irreligious variety of Jewish religion.'" "Jewish-led Bolshevism," Holsten continues, "has no affinity with the messianic expectation of the O.T."[50]

Holsten, seemingly the coolly authoritative scholar, here takes the irrational position that Bolshevism is "Jewish-led." Somehow, the messianic expectation of post-biblical Judaism "comes to maturity in Bolshevism." He does not expand on what Bolshevism has to do with this caricatured "Jewish" variety of messianic expectation. The answer lies in the text upon which Holsten is commenting. In this context, Luther says of the Jewish people, "On no more bloodthirsty and vengeful Volk has the sun ever shone. . . ." They wait on their Messiah, who would "murder and kill the whole world by his sword."[51] Holsten is indicating that this murderous Jewish messianic expectation comes to fruition in Bolshevism.

Though he held no important church-political positions within the German Protestant Church, Holsten's ideas about Luther, Christianity, and other religions traveled far and wide through Protestant circles in Nazi Germany. He apparently never joined the German Christians, the Nazi Party, or any affiliated Nazi organizations. His influence stemmed more from his writings than from his biography.

There are several relevant judgments that can be made about *Christianity and Non-Christian Religion According to Luther*. First, in Holsten's view, Luther constantly mingled his criticism of Judaism with a negative valuation of Catholicism. Yet, Holsten singles out only *Jewish* danger to the German nation. If Holsten believes Catholicism to be a danger to Germany, he does not indicate it explicitly. He recognizes that for Luther both Catholicism and Judaism were a "religious" danger to Protestant Christianity. Yet, Luther did not recommend sociopolitical measures against Catholics. Holsten did not recognize the inconsistency, which was rooted in his (and the reformer's) irrational hatred of *Jews*.

In his acute analysis of Luther's views on Jews and Judaism, Holsten does not shy away from some of the reformer's harshest judgments. Christian support for repressive anti-Jewish government measures, which Holsten admits appeared "unmerciful," was an important way to exhibit "sharp mercy." The measures were rooted, as he saw it, in a religious reality that only needed to enter the political realm out of necessity. Such sharp mercy was not hate, he insists. This, even given the fact that it was based not in scholarship, but from Luther's "overflowing" heart. With these kinds of arguments, he attempts to extricate himself from the openly antisemitic crowd.

By the time the "Comments" on Luther's *Writings against Jews and Turks* appeared, Holsten's judgments about the Jewish people seem to have hardened. Here, he quotes as serious scholarship the committed Nazi Wilhelm Grau's work on antisemitism in the Middle Ages and believes Bolshevism to be led by Jews and tied somehow to post-biblical Judaism and its purportedly murderous, false messianic expectation. Further, Holsten appeals to Erich Vogelsang's works and those of Vogelsang's fellow Nazi and German Christian Emanuel Hirsch, in which such irrational hatred of Jews is espoused.[52]

In both works, Holsten consistently supports Luther's anti-Jewish sociopolitical proposals. This is historically significant, of course, in light of the anti-Jewish legal measures that were being implemented in Nazi Germany between the appearance of the earlier work (1932) and the second edition of the latter work (1938). Yet, Holsten consistently tries to portray these measures as solely inspired by religion. In contrast to many German Christians, Holsten's approach to Luther's *Judenschriften* upholds traditional conservative Lutheran orthodoxy. He cannot help, however, espousing anti-Enlightenment sentiment and irrational theories about "Jewish-led" Bolshevism. His work demonstrates once again the dance between the irrational and the nonrational in Protestant scholarship about Jews and Judaism.

Heinrich Hermelink, Marburg Church Historian

Heinrich Hermelink was born in 1877 near Mangalore, India, the eldest son of Protestant missionaries. At the age of seven, he began a long-time friendship with Hermann Hesse (who later became a celebrated poet and author) while the two studied at the boys' school of the Basel Mission, a center for Swabian pietism.[53] Hesse's father worked at the time as a teacher at the mission.[54]

Hermelink studied theology at Tübingen, from 1896 to 1902. Five years later, he completed his *Habilitation* in theology at Leipzig. While studying theology, he worked in a variety of academic jobs, lecturing in church history at Leipzig from 1905 to 1914. Beginning in 1909, he also served as minister in a congregation in Thekla, a prosperous suburb of Leipzig, a post he held until 1914.[55] In that same year, he became professor of church history in Kiel. In 1915, he was named full professor at Bonn.

As a captain in the First World War, Hermelink was seriously wounded and then became a chaplain in Warsaw. He earned the Iron Cross Second Class. From 1916 until 1935, when he was pressured to retire, he was professor of church history and history of dogma at Marburg. For the next three years, he served as a rectory representative in Eschenbach (near Göppingen in Württemberg) and from 1939 to 1942, in a similar capacity in Miesbach (Upper Bavaria). These positions were obtained, respectively, with the help of bishops Theophil Wurm and Hans Meiser. From 1942 to 1945, he held his last such position near Munich, before receiving several university teaching appointments after the war. He died in Munich in February 1958.[56]

Like many of his Marburg colleagues, including Friedrich Heiler and Martin Rade, Hermelink was actively involved with the nascent international ecumenical movement of the 1920s and 1930s. In 1925, he took part in the Life and Work conference in Stockholm. Two years later, he participated in the Faith and Order conference in Lausanne.[57]

In April 1934, Hermelink was notified by the Reich Education Ministry that he was to be transferred to another university. When consulted by that ministry about Hermelink's situation, Berlin church historian Erich Seeberg recommended against dismissing him altogether.[58] Instead, he counseled "on 'social' grounds 'because of his 8 children'" to "'stick him at Gießen,'" where he would conceivably replace Heinrich Bornkamm, who was transferring to Leipzig, as chair of church history.[59]

During the summer, a series of protest letters flooded in from interested parties. Several Dutch theologians and more than one hundred English theologians wrote of their displeasure at the dislocation of both Hermelink and his colleague, Friedrich Heiler. The Sekretariat des Weltbundes für freies Christentum und religiöse Freiheit (Secretariat of the World Federation for Free Christianity and Religious Freedom), which claimed nearly twenty million members and was based in the Netherlands, expressed its "great astonishment" about the dislocations, and warned of serious damage to the reputation of Marburg University abroad.[60]

At the end of February 1935, Emil Balla, who was at that time dean of the theology faculty, received an order from the Reich Culture Ministry to induce Hermelink to request release from his duties or be forced into retirement. Hermelink yielded to this pressure and submitted his petition for release to the proper authorities one week later. He cited the government's position in the brief petition: "According to the wish of the government orally conveyed to me by the dean of the theology faculty I hereby request my release from my position as full professor of church and dogma history on the theological faculty of the Philipps-Universität in Marburg."[61] The Reich Culture Ministry suspended him from his post two weeks later, and finally released him from his responsibilities in late July.[62]

Hermelink believed his forced retirement to be due to his political activities, which included his work on behalf of the German Democratic Party (DDP) and his stance as a "well-known anti-Nazi."[63] According to his friend Theodor Heuss, who later became the first president of the Federal Republic of Germany (West Germany), he had founded a group called the Marburg Student Company, in order to save the state of Hesse from the "spreading of the consequences of the Hitler putsch."[64] While members of the Holl school railed against the supposed weakness and immorality of Weimar democracy, Hermelink embraced "middle-class liberal beliefs" which included acceptance of the new postwar realities.[65]

His dislocation must also be seen in the context of his role as a member of the theology faculty at Marburg. He, along with Rudolf Bultmann and the rest of the theological faculty, had signed the Marburg *Gutachten*. In autumn 1933, after some in the German Christian movement recommended the implementation of the Aryan Paragraph in the German Protestant Church, the Marburg theological faculty responded with an advisory opinion (*Gutachten*) in which they described the policy, which forbade the employment of civil servants of "non-Aryan" origin, as inconsistent with Christian teaching. A leading member of the faculty and prominent figure in the Confessing Church, Hans von Soden, was ousted from his post, but was later reinstated.[66]

Hermelink's article "Zur Theologie Luthers" (On Luther's Theology; 1943) is a thorough survey of literature about Luther's theology during the preceding decade, the first ten years of the Third Reich. He takes up Erich Seeberg's three-volume work *Luthers Theologie*, which he regards as the "most noteworthy publication in the Luther literature of the last decade," in the most depth. Yet, it is his treatment of works by Erlangen church historian Hans Preuss, Werner Petersmann, Theodor Pauls, and Hansgeorg Schroth that reveal his posture toward "Luther and the Jews."

In 1935, Hermelink had dealt with earlier works by Preuss, in a journal article on modern Luther research. Preuss published a series of four books about the reformer from 1931 to 1942. In *Martin Luther, Der Künstler* (Martin Luther, the Artist; 1931) and *Martin Luther, Der Prophet* (Martin Luther, the Prophet; 1933), Preuss does not "escape the danger of canonizing" Luther despite being a "conscientious historian."[67]

In the 1943 article, the last two works in Preuss's series receive harsher criticism from the now Munich-based historian and churchman. Hermelink skewers *Martin Luther, Der Deutsche* (Martin Luther, the German; 1934), which attempts to portray a "German nature" that is based on "racial-theory and psychological reflection on the Volk." He hopes that in future editions "all kinds of far too time-contingent judgments (in particular in the volume about 'the German' in 1934!)" might be improved. The work *Martin Luther, Der Christenmensch* (Martin Luther, the Christian Man; 1942) would be improved by removing the "interspersed condemnations of everything 'Anglican' and 'Western.'" He notes that Preuss "discusses only briefly" Luther's judgments about "the Jews."[68]

Hermelink next examines a work by Werner Petersmann and Theodor Pauls on the supposed "de-Judaizing" of German Luther research. Contra Preuss, who argues that Luther's evaluation of the Jewish people was essentially a "religious" question, Petersmann and Pauls have made the church's traditional condemnation of Jewish "heresy" a more "contentious" thing.[69] Directly from Pauls's compilation it can be seen how little of the polemical language used by Luther against the "Judaizing anti-Christianity" of the Roman Catholic "pope-church" and the "sabbatarian and anti-Trinitarian heretics of the enthusiasts (*Schwärmer*)" is "applicable to today's Jewish question."

Though a bit oblique, with this assertion, Hermelink seems to try at least to narrow the application of Luther's thinking about Jews and Judaism only to those works and passages that address Jews directly. (He may be implying, for example, that *Against the Sabbatarians* was not addressed to Jews and thus should not be applied to them.) Like Luther's polemics against Roman Catholics and radical reformers, so Pauls's "sharpened headings" over Luther's statements are of little use in addressing the "Jewish Question." While not a full-frontal attack on Pauls's strident work, there is no doubt that Hermelink is uncomfortable with its invective.

Pauls is "absolutely right" that Luther's position toward Judaism did *not* undergo "multiple temporary 'transformations.'" Rather, "gruff condemnation" and "the obligation 'to offer the Christian faith to them again'" consistently go hand in hand. But, for Hermelink, the "concentration of the attack and the escalation of the national-political undertones in the polemical writings and table pronouncements [table talk] of the one year from August 1542 until August 1543 remain strange." Hermelink is uncomfortable not only with Pauls's treatment of Luther—he is baffled by the increasingly political and visceral attack on the Jewish people in the reformer's works during what the Marburg church historian regards as one fateful year.[70]

Continuing his brief literature review, Hermelink later discusses Hansgeorg Schroth's booklet on Luther's "Christian antisemitism." Schroth here seeks to distinguish Luther's "salvation-historical antisemitism" from "modern antisemitism." As with Pauls, Schroth's work demonstrates for Hermelink

> how little the present-day racial-political treatment of the Jewish Question, despite apparent agreement in methods (burning of the synagogues and Jewish houses, removal of Jewish books, prohibition of rabbinic teaching with capital punishment, confiscation of all "cash and treasure in silver and gold," among others), can be justified by Luther's position against the Jews.[71]

To the attentive reader, Hermelink's explicit mention of some of Luther's sixteenth-century recommendations in the context of the Marburg historian's rejection of a modern "racial-political" approach to the "Jewish Question" could have served as a reminder of the mass violence and injustice that had taken place, and was still being perpetrated against Jews by the Nazi regime in Germany and across Europe. Yet, Hermelink does not upbraid Petersmann, Pauls, or Schroth directly for their underlying antisemitism. It is only the polemical language and racial motivation that draw his explicit censure.[72]

Born in India as the son of Protestant missionaries, Marburg church history professor Heinrich Hermelink was exposed from an early age to how people lived in nations and cultures outside of Germany. This international exposure and outlook extended to his work in the burgeoning ecumenical movement. No doubt the protest letters of Dutch and English theologians were written to defend principles of academic and religious freedom. Yet, to have received the overwhelming support that he did, Hermelink must also have been well-loved and well-respected.

As a middle-class liberal and a democrat, his thinking (along with that of many of his colleagues at Marburg) ran counter to the prevailing mindset in German Protestantism, which was dictated by the conservative, nationalistic "Holl school." While his self-designation as an "anti-Nazi" is not supported by evidence of active political resistance, his views garnered only suspicion from local and national Nazi authorities. His support for the Marburg *Gutachten* demonstrated his opposition toward the aryanization of the church, and placed him and his colleagues in direct conflict with the leading lights of völkisch Protestantism on the Erlangen theological faculty, including Althaus and Werner Elert.[73] No doubt his political and internationalist views, along with his support for "non-Aryans," contributed to the loss of the post that he had held for nearly twenty years.

Hermelink emphasizes the continuity of Luther's position toward the Jewish people; he sees the "national-political overtones" of the reformer's 1543 *Judenschriften* as a baffling aberration. Only when he speaks of the "*apparent* agreement in methods" between Luther's position and the unfolding "racial-political treatment" in Nazi Germany do we have subtle hints of discomfort with the implications of Luther's antisemitic recommendations. There is no heroic word for Jews in Hermelink's extant writings. Yet, Hermelink clearly is ill at ease with völkisch Christianity. Also present are a consistently expressed rejection of irrational nationalistic antisemitic argumentation and a complete lack of xenophobic assertions against Jews—both of which were highly unusual for a Protestant theologian in Nazi Germany.

Conclusions

That the majority of clergy joined either the Confessing Church or the German Christians cautions against the idea of a vast unaffected Protestant "middle" without strong ideas, principles, or biases. A lack of formal affiliation during the Church Struggle need not suggest a lack of ideological association. In a German Protestant culture that valued obedience to authority very highly, the ideological influence of these clergy on their parishioners should not be underestimated. The same could be said of academic theologians from within the Protestant ranks, some of whom published widely, many of whom preached regularly in Protestant churches, and all of whose responsibility it was to train prospective ministers in theology.

Clergy and academic theologians from the unaffiliated Protestant "middle" addressed the subject of "Luther and the Jews" less directly and less often than did their counterparts in the Confessing Church and the German Christians. Yet, when they did, like many of their contemporaries in the Confessing Church, their portrayals were generally marked by predominantly nonrational anti-Judaic argumentation, careful scholarship, and evenhandedness. It would be a mistake, however, to view their contributions as necessarily neutral or moderate. Accommodation with National Socialism and the association of Jews with Bolshevism—ideas that were most prevalent in German Christian circles—are found in these pages as well. While overt antisemitism may have been more rare in this grouping, the doctrine of the orders of creation—particularly its corollary, the elevation of the German Volk—provided potent cover for anti-Judaic and antisemitic sentiments. The careful nature of the theological scholarship practiced by these individuals would have sharpened the effects of the antisemitic and anti-Judaic content present in their writings, especially for the more urbane members of their readership.

The scholarly engagement with Luther's *Judenschriften* of the three individuals covered here once again exhibit both commonality and difference. The crucial cooperation between scholar and pastor is demonstrated by German Christian and regional church participation in Bornkamm's lectures. Both Holsten's commentary on the *Judenschriften* and Hermelink's review essays would have been read by very few average citizens, but would have been invaluable tools for Lutheran pastors who preached to and taught laypersons about issues found in the reformer's works. Bathed in conservative nationalism, theologians such as Bornkamm embraced Althaus's influential orders of creation theology as the foundation by which to address relevant cultural issues, including the "Jewish Question."

The works of two of these unaffiliated Protestant pastors and theologians projected, in varying degrees, a demeaning disposition toward Jews and Judaism, providing nonrational anti-Judaic and irrational antisemitic arguments against besieged German (and indeed European) Jews to the Protestant "middle" and beyond. Their writings furthered the notions of Jews as the chief source of anti-Christian Bolshevism, as a people inferior to the German Volk and as enemies of Christ. Only in the case of Heinrich Hermelink do we see the exercise of subdued opposition to irrational antisemitism.

CONCLUSION

Heinrich Fausel delivered a farewell sermon to his Heimsheim congregation in January 1947. He had ministered in this small village community in southwest Germany for nearly twenty years, a period that encompassed the demise of the Weimar Republic, the rise to power of Hitler and the Nazis, the Second World War, and the Holocaust. Disaster had struck Heimsheim in April 1945. In just a few short days, fires resulting from French aerial and artillery bombardment destroyed 80 percent of the community's buildings, leaving many farmers with nothing, and those made homeless sought shelter in the remaining buildings. French forces occupied the community from late April until mid-July, using the school building as their quarters.[1]

It was "God alone," urged Fausel in the homily, who had "permitted bandits, maniacs, and criminals to rule over us, and allowed these fools to pull us into the abyss with them." God in fact was angry, not only with these "fools," but with the Germans, for having believed the "foolish delusion" of faith in human progress, that human beings with their strength "can do everything and can achieve everything." It was He who had in fact inflicted "new terrors and wars" on them in order that their hearts might experience a "healing shock."

Yet, the homily is not marked by fire and brimstone alone. Fausel also offers comforting words in the midst of the very real suffering that his Württemberg parishioners had endured. "He [God] also protected us and held His hand over us in the middle of the catastrophe." Had He not allowed them at least to remain alive in the midst of the firestorm and the "hail of bombs?" To those who may have lost their houses or their livestock—and even those with bullet-riddled limbs—Fausel would say, "do not sin, because at least you still have your life, heart, spirit and soul. . . ." Whatever they may have lost, God had preserved their lives.[2]

With his sermon, Fausel seems to have discharged his duty as a curer of souls in an honorable manner. He recognizes the pain and suffering of his congregation, and points them to God as their refuge. Yet, even now, some twenty months after the fall of the Nazi regime, with no risk of recriminations, he has nothing at all to say about the "catastrophe" that had befallen millions of Jews and other victims of Nazism. Nothing of *their* suffering, their loss of goods and property, their degradation in the concentration camps, or their murder at the hand of the "bandits, maniacs and criminals."

The Württemberg Ecclesiastical-Theological Society's April 1946 Declaration on the Jewish Question was one of the most forceful Protestant declarations of guilt in the early postwar period. Fausel was one of the prime movers of the Society, which consisted of between fifty and one hundred participants, including a number of non-theologians. The Society had begun in 1929 as a rather loose association of pastors who sought to improve the theological content of church liturgy in general and of preaching in particular. Four of the five signatories of the declaration, including Fausel, had participated in rescuing Jews, as part of the Württemberg "Rectory Chain."[3] In comprehensive fashion, these five men, on behalf of the Society, confessed explicitly their guilt for numerous sins.

The most salient passage of the declaration is quite remarkable in its frankness. It reads in part:

We retreated despondently and idly as the members of the Volk of Israel among us were dishonored, robbed, tormented, and killed. We permitted the exclusion of fellow Christians who originated according to the flesh from Israel, from the offices of the church, even allowing the ecclesiastical refusal of the baptism of Jews. We did not object to the prohibition of Jewish mission. We did not resist the militaristic falsification of the love of fatherland.

All of this revealed them to be, among other things, "weak in faith" and "remiss in love."[4] As noted earlier, Fausel's participation in Herta Pineas's rescue and his signature on the Society's 1946 Declaration reveal a general sense of collective guilt for the dreadful fate that had been visited on millions of Europe's Jews. Thus, the inconsistency of Fausel's position toward the Jewish people continued into the early postwar period at least.

When we consider the paranoid screeds of Wolf Meyer-Erlach and Martin Sasse, we are confronted with propagandistic and openly antisemitic uses of the reformer's works by committed members of both the Nazi Party and the German Christians. The writings of fellow German Christian Erich Vogelsang are much more sophisticated, but nonetheless are similarly disparaging of Jews. The writings and actions of Confessing Church pastor Heinrich Fausel are utterly inconsistent. At times, he appears to be a philosemite, at times an antisemite. Clearly, there is some diversity among the responses to Luther's *Judenschriften* in the writings of the pastors and theologians we have encountered here. Yet, when we consider the writings of this part of the German population in their totality, some patterns do emerge.

A significant minority of Protestant theologians, pastors, and bishops from varying church-political and theological affiliations, stages in life, and geographical regions in Germany indeed consulted and expounded upon Luther's *Judenschriften*. In the process, they often reinforced the cultural antisemitism and anti-Judaism of many Protestants in Nazi Germany. They mined these treatises for material that was pertinent to surrounding events, including the Nuremberg Laws, Kristallnacht, and the Second World War, appealing to them in all sorts of publications—from church gazettes and theological journals to apologetic pamphlets and books. Their writings either focused directly on the topic of "Luther and the Jews" or utilized the reformer's anti-Judaic and antisemitic arguments to bolster pieces about topical and theological issues, including the place of the Old Testament in Christian theology, the dangers of Bolshevism, and the validity of the practice of baptizing Jews. Some, including figures as diverse as German Christian theologian Erich Vogelsang, Confessing Church pastor Walter Gabriel, and Protestant "middle" pastor Walter Holsten, could openly espouse anti-Enlightenment attitudes in reputable theological writings.

While acknowledging this commonality, I also differentiated the manner in which these works were employed across the Protestant theological landscape. Theologians, pastors, and bishops who were members of the German Christian movement unswervingly embraced Luther's irrational antisemitic rhetoric as their own, often coupling it with romanticized portraits of German superiority, anti-Bolshevism, and an anti-modern outlook. Frequently, the writings of these generally pro-Nazi and theologically radical men were peppered with appeals to antisemites such as nineteenth-century court preacher and Christian Social Party founder Adolf Stöcker, chief Nazi Party ideologue Alfred Rosenberg, and Hitler. Vogelsang serves as something of an exception. While he savaged both Enlightenment thought and liberal theology, he nonetheless couched such rhetoric in predominantly nonrational biblical-theological reasoning.

Clergy and theologians who were members of the Confessing Church usually stressed Luther's nonrational arguments against Jews. They either kept silent about Luther's irrational rhetoric or implicitly approved state involvement in accord with Luther's social agenda. Most of these theologically conservative and generally Nazi-wary individuals were swift to distinguish their rhetoric from the "racial" antisemitism utilized by both the Nazis and the German Christians. In short, they preferred anti-Judaic arguments over antisemitic ones. Yet, despite their desire to paint their arguments as essentially "religious," some included antisemitic reasoning in their writings as well. Berlin Confessing Church apologist Hansgeorg Schroth, for example, warned against the "Jewish-Bolshevist" enemy, while Heinrich Fausel lamented a "terrifying foreign invasion" threatening the German Volk. Only a small minority, including members of the Württemberg "Rectory Chain" and the "Grüber Office," demonstrated sympathy for Jews.

Pastors and theologians who chose not to affiliate formally with either the Confessing Church or the German Christians demonstrated consistently anti-Judaic and occasionally antisemitic appropriation of Luther's writings about Jews and Judaism. In the exceptional case of Marburg church historian Heinrich Hermelink, we witnessed muted but undeniable discomfort with what he regarded as racially motivated antisemitism, and even with Luther's later *Judenschriften*, but no positive word on Jews and Judaism as such. The influential Erlangen systematic theologian Paul Althaus employed a neoconservative orders-of-creation theology, which he married to a politically conservative nationalism in service of the German Volk. In his writings, Jews are occasionally targeted, but appeals to the reformer's writings are curiously absent. Pastors and theologians from this "middle" grouping often made use of long-standing xenophobic images, including the caricature of the Jew as usurer. Like their counterparts in the Confessing Church, many of their theological writings are characterized by at least a modicum of erudition. Yet, it is this very veneer of respectability that would have heightened the effects of the antisemitic and anti-Judaic content of their writings, especially for the more educated members of their reading audience. In the end, all three of these major factions within German Protestantism offered even more traction to the antisemitic notions of Hitler and the Nazis than was already present in Germany—both in the church and in broader society.

Yet, surely the most significant finding here is not the mere presence of such works in the German Protestant literature of the period. More important are the implications of the application of Langmuir's approach for the study of antisemitism and anti-Judaism as it appears in theological writings. The typical emphasis in the historical literature about the Holocaust on *discontinuities* between pre-modern anti-Judaism and modern antisemitism frequently conceals the *continuities* of thought that in fact traverse both periods. While the ruptures are seen as necessary to draw crucial distinctions about the manner of thinking about Jews in changing historical situations, one need not abandon such historical contextualization to appreciate the continuities.

The importance of the application of the component of Langmuir's theory on history, religion, and antisemitism appropriated here—his distinction between the nonrational, irrational, and rational elements in theological thought—lies in its explanatory power. It confronts us with the challenge to render with care the often meticulously constructed thought of theologians and clergy; in other words, to engage its substance, regularly deemed in nebulous fashion as "theological" and thus somehow unknowable. If theological argumentation can be evaluated by its constituent parts, particularly when it touches upon realms more familiar to the study of history—the social, cultural, political, and intellectual—the results may be fruitful indeed. Separating the elements of theological formulations by viewing them in terms of rationality, Langmuir's schema allows us to enter the seemingly impenetrable arena of academic theology, providing a common language by which religious discourse can be understood.

When tempted to confine particular ways of thinking about Jews to this or that historical era, all of this should give us pause. Apart from helping us to understand better the nature of theological rhetoric, Langmuir's approach can, through the category of rationality, enable us to nuance our conception of both "racial" and "theological" versions of anti-Jewish rhetoric. As a result, we can detect antisemitism in the early modern era and anti-Judaism in the modern epoch (and vice versa). Crucially, we can discern that these modes of thinking often have been intertwined in theological writings about Jews and Judaism, both in the sixteenth century and in the twentieth. Despite very different historical circumstances, unmistakably similar patterns of thought about Jews existed among Protestants in Luther's Germany and in Hitler's.

This examination of the interpretation and application of Luther's views on Jews and Judaism on the part of Protestant theologians and clergy provides an intellectual window on the social history of an important segment of the populace in Nazi Germany. With material from Luther's *Judenschriften* as one important part of their intellectual-theological arsenal, many German Protestant pastors, bishops, and academic theologians seized upon an old idea—indeed one much older than Luther—and overlaid it with more up-to-date connotations, with great effectiveness. Such antisemitism and anti-Judaism thus circulated widely through the largest theological confession in Germany. The extent to which these ideas inflamed antisemitic hatred in the Protestant population cannot be determined easily, if at all. Yet, thousands had access to the potent ideology contained in these writings, much of which resembled antisemitic Nazi propaganda aimed at dehumanizing Jews, who suffered and died by the millions in Hitler's Third Reich.

NOTES

Introduction

1. USHMM Fausel Collection, 42, Unpublished Lecture Manuscript, "Die Judenfrage," January 10, 1934; Röhm and Thierfelder, *Ausgegrenzt, 1933–1935*, vol. 1 of *Juden-Christen-Deutsche, 1933–1945*, 165.

2. Röhm and Thierfelder, *Vernichtet, 1941–1945*, vol. 4/I of *Juden-Christen-Deutsche, 1933–1945*, 182ff., 198–199; Richarz, *Jewish Life in Germany*, 448–460.

3. *That Jesus Christ Was Born a Jew* (1523), *Against the Sabbatarians* (1538), *On the Jews and Their Lies* (1543), *On the Ineffable Name and on the Lineage of Christ* (1543), and *On the Last Words of David* (1543). All of these works appeared in the so-called "*Weimarer Ausgabe*," or Weimar Edition of Luther's works. Hereafter, WA. See chapters one and two here; Luther's commentaries, sermons, and "table talk" also contain material about Jews and Judaism.

4. E.g., Ericksen, *Theologians under Hitler*; Gailus, *Protestantismus und Nationalsozialismus*; Heschel, *Aryan Jesus*; Gutteridge, *Open Thy Mouth*. The seminal work on the subject in the English language is Conway, *The Nazi Persecution of the Churches*.

5. In reality, *Gleichschaltung* meant compulsory compliance with the Nazi party and its goals. See Max Weinreich's seminal *Hitler's Professors*; Steinweis, *Studying the Jew*.

6. See, e.g., Friedländer, *The Years of Persecution*, 83–84. Others have distinguished between "traditional" and "modern" antisemitism, with the former term

the approximate equivalent of (pre-modern and early modern Christian) anti-Judaism. See Evans, *Coming of the Third Reich*, 27 and Albert Lindemann, whose formulation is more precise: "premodern religious anti-Semitism" and "modern racist anti-Semitism." See Lindemann, *Esau's Tears*, 26ff.

7. Langmuir, *History, Religion, and Antisemitism*, 105–107, 130, 275, 276.

8. Ibid., 152, 252–255. Aquinas is cited as an excellent example of nonrational thinking.

9. Ibid., 152–153; Langmuir, *Toward a Definition*, 101.

10. Langmuir, *History, Religion, and Antisemitism*, 130.

11. See chapter two here.

12. Langmuir, *History, Religion, and Antisemitism*, 155.

13. Ibid., 276.

14. Browning, *Origins of the Final Solution*, 1–11. Browning here skillfully integrates into his discussion of antisemitism a distinction that Langmuir makes between xenophobia and chimeric antisemitism; Lindemann, *Esau's Tears*, 29; Burrin, *Nazi Anti-Semitism*, 17–19; Alex Novikoff, "The Middle Ages," in Lindemann and Levy, *Antisemitism: A History*, 63–78, especially 76–77.

15. Herf, *The Jewish Enemy*, 3.

16. Kershaw, *The "Hitler Myth*," 229.

17. See chapter two here.

18. Tal, "'Political Faith' of Nazism Prior to the Holocaust," in Tal, *Religion, Politics, and Ideology*, 18.

19. Burleigh, *The Third Reich*, 10.

20. For enlightening (if brief) discussions of the issue, see, e.g., Kertzer, introduction to *The Popes against the Jews*, 3–21; Spicer, *Antisemitism, Christian Ambivalence, and the Holocaust*, ix–xxi.

21. Richard Gutteridge addresses "Luther and the Jews" in an appendix to *Open Thy Mouth*, but the short section serves more to contextualize Luther's treatises than to explain their reception in Nazi Germany. See Gutteridge, *Open Thy Mouth*, 315–325; Kurt Meier addresses the subject directly but not comprehensively in a significant chapter-length study. See chapter two here; Bergen, *Twisted Cross*, 28, 159. Bergen refers to appropriation of Luther's treatises on at least two occasions, but this phenomenon is not central to the thesis of the book.

22. On Bonhoeffer's stance toward Jews and Judaism, see, e.g., Barnes, "Dietrich Bonhoeffer"; Eberhard Bethge, "Dietrich Bonhoeffer und die Juden," in Kremers, *Die Juden und Martin Luther*, 211–249.

23. Skinner, "Meaning and Understanding in the History of Ideas," in Tully, *Meaning and Context*, 29–67, here 30, 45; emphasis added; Tully, "The Pen Is a Mighty Sword: Quentin Skinner's Analysis of Politics," in ibid., 7–25, here 12–13.

24. Barth, the chief author of the Barmen Declaration, prominent member of the Confessing Church and professor of theology at Bonn until 1935, was a favor-

ite target of the German Christians. By elevating German *Volkstum,* along with "its history and its political present" to a "second source of revelation" (i.e., besides the "Holy Scripture"), argues Barth, the German Christians "reveal themselves as believers in 'another god.'" See Barth, *Lutherfeier 1933,* 20, in Hinz-Wessels, *Die Evangelische Kirchengemeinde Bonn,* 391–392; Bergen, *Twisted Cross,* 175–176; Niemöller was pastor of a prestigious church in Berlin-Dahlem and one of the founders of the Confessing Church. He only recognized the error of his own negative views toward Jews after the Second World War. See, e.g., Gerlach, *Witnesses.*

25. On Althaus, see chapter one here; on Bornkamm, see chapter six; on Sasse, see chapter five.

26. See, e.g., Ericksen, *Theologians under Hitler,* Heschel, *Aryan Jesus,* Gerlach, *Witnesses* and Bergen, *Twisted Cross.* Analysis of the antisemitism of major figures is present in all of these works, but references to Luther's *Judenschriften* are scant.

27. Volkov, "Antisemitism as a Cultural Code," 45–46.

28. The economic stresses did not only further the ascent of antisemitism during Weimar. The rise of the Nazi party in Germany was "immeasurably aided" by the economic depression that took hold after 1929. See Fulbrook, *History of Germany, 1918–2000,* 37ff.

29. Volkov, "Antisemitism as a Cultural Code," 45–46.

30. This unaffiliated "middle" grouping is often referred to as "neutrals" in the literature on German Protestantism during the Third Reich. See, e.g., Bergen, "Storm Troopers," 46; Hockenos, *A Church Divided,* 4. While they generally chose neutrality in their church politics, their theological ideas often could resemble those in either the Confessing Church or German Christian wings of the German Protestant Church. Thus, I prefer the terms *middle* and *unaffiliated* over *neutral.*

31. Throughout this book I translate the German term *evangelisch* as "Protestant." While some translate it as "Evangelical," this might be misleading because *evangelisch* has a specifically confessional association with the three main Protestant traditions in Germany (Lutheran, Reformed, and United), whereas to most Americans "Evangelical" generally connotes conservative, mainly Protestant, Christian churches that promote active proclamation of the Christian Gospel to those who do not share their faith.

32. Baranowski, *Confessing Church,* 45–46; Bergen, *Twisted Cross,* 7, 178.

33. Bergen, *Twisted Cross,* 229; Heschel, "Nazifying."

34. Bergen, *Twisted Cross,* 7, 176–178.

35. Some exceptions to this general rule of opposition to Nazism existed. See, e.g., Kaufmann, "Einleitung II," 46–47.

36. Point twenty-four of the Nazi party program called for a "positive Christianity" that crossed confessional boundaries, as long as it did not "endanger" the state or "conflict with the customs and moral sentiments of the Germanic race." Rosenberg, *Das Parteiprogramm,* 15ff., 57ff.

37. Baranowski, *Confessing Church*, 56ff.

38. The Aryan Paragraph forbade the employment of civil servants of "non-Aryan" origin. The term *Aryan*, borrowed by Hitler and the Nazis from eighteenth- and nineteenth-century racial theorists, was a fiction that described the supposedly "pure" German master race. While it originally referred to a group of people in ancient India, in Nazi Germany it came to mean the opposite of *Jew*. See Ericksen and Heschel, *Betrayal*, 25, 31, 51; Bergen, *War and Genocide*, 36–37; on the Confessing Church, Barmen, and the Jewish people, see, e.g., Gerlach, *Witnesses*; Barnett, *For the Soul of the People*, 54.

39. See chapter one here.

40. Fulbrook, *History of Germany, 1918–2000*, 15–36; Ericksen, *Theologians under Hitler*, 26.

41. Ericksen and Heschel, "German Churches."

42. On both the Luther Renaissance and the publication of Luther's works after the First World War, see chapter one here.

43. Gerlach, *Witnesses*, 154–160.

44. See, e.g., Barnett, *For the Soul of the People*, 65–68; Shelley Baranowski, "Confessing Church and Antisemitism," 98; Doris Bergen occasionally differentiates between "moderate" and "radical" German Christians, but cautions against this distinction as it relates to the movement's singular approach to the Jewish people. See Bergen, *Twisted Cross*, 19, 55, 160–161.

45. On the Confessing Church and Dahlem, see Barnett, *For the Soul of the People*, 65–68; on the German Christians and the Sports Palace affair, see Bergen, *Twisted Cross*, 17–18, 174.

46. See chapter six here.

47. Baranowski, "Consent and Dissent," 65; Bergen, *Twisted Cross*, 7–8.

48. Friedländer, *The Years of Persecution*, 27–28.

49. Gerlach, *Witnesses*, 24, 64ff.; Barnett, *For the Soul of the People*, 34–35, 128–133.

50. A fact that Althaus was keen to emphasize. Even so, Althaus sidesteps neither Luther's call to the authorities to "follow Jesus by emptying themselves of their power" nor the reformer's wish that all rulers would be Christians. See Althaus, *Ethics of Martin Luther*, 112–154, esp. 122–124.

51. And, indeed by historical actors such as Karl Barth, Reinhold Niebuhr, and Thomas Mann. See especially the essays by Tracy, Brady, and Gritsch in Tracy, *Luther and the Modern State*; Brady, "Luther's Social Teaching."

52. See, e.g., Ericksen, *Theologians under Hitler*, 25, 84, 115, 178; Tal, *Christians and Jews in Germany*, 292, 305.

53. Tracy, "Luther and the Modern State: Introduction to a Neuralgic Theme," in Tracy, *Luther and the Modern State*, 15; the "Luther-Bismarck myth" is the now discredited idea promulgated by some early twentieth-century German historians that the emergence of Germany as a modern state was a predetermined progres-

sion from Luther to Bismarck. Brady, "Luther and the State: The Reformer's Teaching in Its Social Setting" in Tracy, ibid., 41–42.

54. See, e.g., Friedländer, introduction to *The Years of Persecution*, 1–6.

55. See chapter six here.

1. Protestantism in Nazi Germany

1. Oberman, *Roots of Anti-Semitism*, 22; on anti-Judaism and antisemitism, see the introduction here.

2. Lazare, *Antisemitism: Its History and Causes*, 8, 56–95, 116–118, 176. He crystallizes his view when he states on p. 176, "At the bottom of the anti-Semitism of our own days, as at the bottom of the anti-Judaism of the thirteenth century are the fear of, and the hatred for, the stranger."

3. Arendt, *Origins of Totalitarianism*, xi, 3.

4. Langmuir, *History, Religion, and Antisemitism*, 276; see also Poliakov, *From the Time of Christ to the Court Jews*, vol. 1 of *The History of Anti-Semitism*; Lindemann, *Esau's Tears*.

5. Langmuir, *History, Religion, and Antisemitism*, 157–158; emphasis added.

6. See below and Pulzer, *Rise of Political Anti-Semitism*; Volkov, "Antisemitism as a Cultural Code."

7. Langmuir, *Toward a Definition*, 328.

8. See chapter two here.

9. Berger and Luckmann, *Social Construction of Reality*, 27.

10. Robert Ericksen's *Theologians under Hitler* does this better than many other works, but still the approach there is not history of ideas as such.

11. Volkov, *Germans, Jews, and Antisemites*, 67–68; emphasis added.

12. Volkov, "Antisemitism as a Cultural Code," 25–26; on Stöcker, see below.

13. Ibid., 26–27; see also Evans, *Coming of the Third Reich*, 25–26.

14. Volkov, "Antisemitism as a Cultural Code," 27–28.

15. Ibid., 34–35; emphasis in original.

16. Ibid., 35; Eley, "What Produces Fascism."

17. Volkov, "Antisemitism as a Cultural Code," 36–37.

18. Langmuir, *History, Religion, and Antisemitism*, 145–147.

19. Volkov, "Antisemitism as a Cultural Code," 37–43. Treitschke's infamous phrase, "the Jews are our misfortune," became forever associated with the Berlin historian and later served as a Nazi slogan. He may have borrowed the phrase from Luther. In *On the Jews and Their Lies*, Luther says "the Jews" are "a heavy burden to us, like a plague, pestilence, and vain misfortune in our land." See WA 53:417–552, here 520; Treitschke, "Unsere Aussichten"; Meyer, "Heinrich Graetz and Heinrich von Treitschke."

20. Volkov, "Antisemitism as a Cultural Code," 45–46.

21. Evans, *Coming of the Third Reich*, 25. The party began in 1878 as the Christian Social Worker Party. Uwe Puschner, "Stoecker, Adolf," in *Biographisch-Bibli-*

ographisches Kirchenlexikon, 10:1507–1511. Hereafter, BBK; Günter Brakelmann, "Adolf Stoecker und die Sozialdemokratie," in Brakelmann, Greschat, and Jochmann, *Protestantismus und Politik,* 84–122, here 104–105. Despite Stöcker's Protestant bona fides, he sought to ally himself with the atheist Wilhelm Marr. See Jochmann, "Stoecker als nationalkonservativer Politiker und antisemitischer Agitator," in *Protestantismus und Politik,* 123–198, here 149.

22. Lehmann, "The Germans as a Chosen People," 266.

23. Bornkamm, *Vom christlichen zum nationalen Sozialismus,* 10.

24. Evans, *Coming of the Third Reich,* 26, 189, 218. Evans notes that Fritsch's *Handbuch der Judenfrage,* originally published in 1888, had amazing staying power, reaching its fortieth edition in 1933.

25. Biddiss, "History as Destiny," 79–87. See also Evans, *Coming of the Third Reich,* 33–34.

26. Burleigh and Wippermann, *Racial State,* 36.

27. Chamberlain, *Foundations of the Nineteenth Century,* 1:541, in Biddiss, "History as Destiny," 84.

28. Burleigh and Wippermann, *Racial State,* 24–25.

29. Grimm, "Luther Research since 1920," 106–107.

30. E.g., Vogelsang, *Luthers Hebräerbrief-Vorlesung* (1930); Georg Buchwald, *Luthers Werke für das christliche Haus* (1924); Otto Clemen, *Luthers Werke in Auswahl* (1912–1933).

31. Reinhold Lewin's work on the subject was published before the war, but exercised—and continues to exercise—considerable influence in Luther studies. See Lewin, *Luthers Stellung zu den Juden* (1911); Falb, *Luther und die Juden* (1921); Steinlein, *Luthers Stellung zum Judentum* (1929); Holsten, *Christentum* (1932).

32. Kupisch, "The 'Luther Renaissance,'" 41ff.; Bainton, "Interpretations of the Reformation," 76.

33. Kupisch, "The 'Luther Renaissance,'" 45–46. I will return to both Hirsch and Vogelsang in chapter three.

34. Stayer, *Martin Luther, German Saviour,* xi–xii, 49.

35. Evans, *Third Reich in Power,* 220–222.

36. In the German academic system, the *Habilitation* is the second doctorate.

37. Hetzer, *"Deutsche Stunde,"* 236–237. This work is an in-depth examination of Althaus's antisemitism in the context of his political theology; Ericksen, "Political Theology," 548–549; Friedrich Wilhelm Bautz, "Althaus, Paul," BBK, 1:130–131.

38. The number of students pursuing the study of theology at Erlangen averaged approximately six hundred during the 1930s. In 1933–1934, nearly 30 percent of the student body was registered in the faculty of theology. Kaufmann, "Einleitung II," 32–33; Hetzer, *"Deutsche Stunde,"* 239–240.

39. Hetzer, *"Deutsche Stunde,"* 153–154; Althaus, *Kirche und Volkstum;* Althaus, *Evangelium und Leben,* 113–143.

40. Klaus Scholder, in Barnes, *Nazism, Liberalism, and Christianity*, 107; Ericksen, "Political Theology," 548.

41. Barnes, *Nazism, Liberalism, and Christianity*, 107; van Norden, *Politischer Kirchenkampf*, 33; Althaus, *Deutsche Stunde*, 5; Ericksen, "Political Theology," 552.

42. Gerlach, *Witnesses*, 69ff.; Ericksen, "Political Theology," 548, 562; Paul Althaus and Werner Elert, "Theologische Gutachten über die Zulassung von Christen jüdischer Herkunft zu den Ämtern der deutschen evangelischen Kirche," *Theologische Blätter*, 12, 11 (1933): 321–323 in Ericksen, ibid; because of his moderation, Althaus was (privately) advanced as a candidate for Reich bishop by Württemberg bishop Theophil Wurm. When publicly disagreeing with Emanuel Hirsch over a theological dispute about Christ's resurrection and the message of Easter, Althaus "impugns neither Hirsch's methods nor his motives. . . ." See Ericksen, *Theologians under Hitler*, 79–119, here 79–82.

43. Ericksen, *Theologians under Hitler*, 109–112; Hetzer, "*Deutsche Stunde*," 23ff.; Vollnhals, *Evangelische Kirche und Entnazifizierung*, 171–179.

44. Ericksen, "Political Theology," 548; Althaus, "Die Stimme des Blutes," 157–168.

45. Althaus, "Die Stimme des Blutes," 157, 166.

46. Ibid., 158–159, 166–168.

47. Ibid., 162; John 1:11.

48. Althaus, "Die Stimme des Blutes," 163; Matthew 27:25.

49. Althaus, "Die Stimme des Blutes," 162, 163; Matthew 23:37; there are, infrequently, occasions in Althaus's work where this racial component becomes evident. See, e.g., Althaus, "Kirche, Volk und Staat," in Gerstenmaier, *Kirche, Volk und Staat*, 18, in Ericksen, "Assessing the Heritage," 25. "Race is not already Volk, the biological unity is not already historical unity. But the unity of race in a significant sense and its protection is an essential condition for the formation and preservation of the Volk."

50. Hitler's "Röhm purge," for example, took place in June 1934; Althaus, *Theologie der Ordnungen* (Gütersloh: Bertelsmann, 1934). A second, expanded version appeared in 1935 (Gütersloh: Bertelsmann, 1935). I cite the 1934 edition exclusively here.

51. Ibid., 7, 10, 14; on Althaus's rejection of natural law theology, see Tilgner, *Volksnomostheologie*, 179ff.; Ericksen, *Theologians under Hitler*, 99–101.

52. Althaus, *Theologie der Ordnungen*, 25–26.

53. Althaus, *Völker vor und nach Christus*, 3.

54. Ibid., 5.

55. Ibid., 9.

56. Ericksen demonstrates that he did not give "explicit endorsement" to the Nazi regime after 1938, with Kristallnacht possibly serving as a flashpoint. Significantly, though, Althaus never retracted his pro-Nazi statements or "meaningfully protested the mistreatment of Jews." See Ericksen, "Assessing the Heritage," 23–24.

57. See, e.g., Luther, *Von weltlicher Obrigkeit, wie man ihr Gehorsam schuldig sei,* in WA 11.

58. Wolfgang Altgeld, "Religion, Denomination, and Nationalism," in Smith, *Protestants, Catholics, and Jews,* 52–53; Brinks, "Luther and the German State."

59. Hoover, "German Christian Nationalism."

60. Jantzen, "Propaganda, Perseverance, and Protest," 298; Barnes, "Dietrich Bonhoeffer," 114–116.

61. Steigmann-Gall, *Holy Reich,* 235.

62. Barnes, *Nazism, Liberalism, and Christianity,* 23–24, 108–109.

63. Eckart, in Scholder, *Preliminary History and the Time of Illusions, 1918–1934,* vol. 1 of *Churches and the Third Reich,* 90.

64. Bergen, "Storm Troopers," 47; Scholder, *Churches and the Third Reich,* 1:116; Lamparter, *Das Judentum.*

65. Gerlach, *Witnesses,* 112. See also 258, n. 55, 56 and chapter three here.

66. Ibid., 147–148; see also chapter five here.

2. "Luther and the Jews"

1. Alan Dershowitz, *Chutzpah* (Boston: Little, Brown, 1991), 107, in Carter Lindberg, "Tainted Greatness," in Harrowitz, *Tainted Greatness,* 15–35, here 15. Luther did in one passage in *On the Jews and Their Lies* state about the Jewish people, "We are at fault in not slaying them." Yet, this statement was not part of his seven-point sociopolitical program for them in Germany (see below). As onerous as Luther's recommendations were, it surely is an exaggeration to argue that he viewed it the duty of Germans to murder all Jews. See Luther, *Von den Juden,* 522.

2. Oberman, *Roots of Anti-Semitism,* 94.

3. Luther did not use the term *Judenschriften,* and these writings were intended as Christian apologetics; that is, the defense of the Christian faith. According to Kenneth Hagen, the term originated with the introduction to *Von den Juden und ihren Lügen* (WA 53) by Ferdinand Cohrs and Oskar Brenner, and connoted writings "*against* the Jews" (introduction to *Von den letzten Worten Davids* [WA 54]). Thus, this was not a self-conscious literary category, but a later characterization of Luther scholars, church historians, and modern historians. See Hagen, "Luther's So-Called *Judenschriften,*" 137.

4. Oberman, *Roots of Anti-Semitism,* 84–85; Margaritha was a contemporary of Luther and will be an important figure in our later discussion. See below.

5. Gow, *The Red Jews,* 46–47; Poliakov, *History of Anti-Semitism,* 1: 73–83.

6. Stern, *Josel of Rosheim,* 32–35, 99.

7. Poliakov, *History of Anti-Semitism,* 1: 58–60.

8. The following account is condensed from Oberman, *Roots of Anti-Semitism,* 97–99.

9. Ibid. Such luminaries as Luther, Müntzer, Karlstadt, and even Northern Renaissance artist Albrecht Dürer all had their works printed by Höltzel.

10. Hobbs, "Bucer," 137; Stern, *Josel of Rosheim*, 165.

11. Hobbs, ibid.; Stern, *Josel of Rosheim*, 156–157, 175.

12. Stern, *Josel of Rosheim*, 166–167.

13. Ibid., 168–169, 173–174. Hobbs evaluates Bucer's legacy regarding Jews and Judaism as distinctly less positive than the legacies of Osiander and Capito, despite his confessed indebtedness to some Jewish interpreters of the Hebrew Scriptures. Hobbs, "Bucer," 169.

14. The lengthy title of the tract is translated by Oberman as *Whether It Be True and Credible That the Jews Secretly Strangulate Christian Children and Make Use of Their Blood.* See Oberman, *Roots of Anti-Semitism,* 35.

15. Reuchlin (1455–1522) was a trailblazing Christian Hebraist who was condemned by the pope for giving Christian interpretations to both the Hebrew Bible and the Kabbalah. He was also Melanchthon's great uncle. See Oberman, *Roots of Anti-Semitism,* 11–12.

16. Kammerling, "Andreas Osiander," 219–247; Stern, *Josel of Rosheim,* 180–183.

17. Rowan, "Luther, Bucer, and Eck," 86.

18. Stern, *Josel of Rosheim,* 183.

19. Rowan, "Luther, Bucer, and Eck," 87–88.

20. See, e.g., Robert Bireley, "The Catholic Reform, Jews, and Judaism in Sixteenth-Century Germany," in Bell and Burnett, *Jews, Judaism, and the Reformation,* 249–268, here 250ff.

21. Osiander's relatively friendly position toward Judaism must also be understood in light of both his concurrent attack on Roman Catholicism and the subsequent judgment of Melanchthon and other reformers that his doctrine of justification was heretical. Kammerling, "Andreas Osiander," 219, 247; Oberman, *Roots of Anti-Semitism,* 72.

22. Oberman, *Roots of Anti-Semitism,* 101.

23. See below.

24. Stern, *Josel of Rosheim,* 173.

25. Ibid., 170–173.

26. Edwards, *Luther's Last Battles,* 135; the correspondence with Philipp centered on the issue of the Landgrave's infamous bigamy. Melanchthon makes clear that Luther had not promised to write about bigamy, occupied as he was with completing a series of writings about Jews. See Wengert, "Philip Melanchthon and the Jews," 125–127.

27. Oberman, *Roots of Anti-Semitism,* 48–49.

28. E.g., Nicholas of Lyra and Paul of Burgos. Luther, *Von den Juden,* 417, 480. See also Wilhelm Maurer, "Luthers Stellung zur Judenfrage," in Maurer, *Kirche und Synagoge,* 41.

29. Luther, *Von den Juden,* 513, n. 12; Martin H. Bertram, introduction to Luther, "On the Jews," in *The Christian in Society IV,* ed. Franklin Sherman, trans.

Bertram, vol. 47 of Lehman et al., *Luther's Works,* 130. Hereafter, LW; Stern, *Josel of Rosheim,* 98–99.

30. Stern, *Josel of Rosheim,* 98–99, 103. Josel says, "'Thereafter Margaritha allied himself with Luther and they became as thorns in our [i.e., the Jews'] side.'"

31. Luther, *Von den Juden,* 513.

32. Luther, *Von den Juden,* 485; Oberman, *Roots of Anti-Semitism,* 104, 105, 109; this picture was particularly pronounced in the latter years of Luther's life. See, e.g., Kaufmann, *Luthers "Judenschriften,"* 8–9.

33. See, e.g., Martin Luther, *Luther's Correspondence,* 2: 185–187; Luther, "Lectures on Romans, 1516," in *Lectures on Romans,* ed. Hilton C. Oswald, trans. Jacob A. O. Preus, LW 25:380; Luther, "Luther Proposes to Write against the Jews," in *Table Talk,* ed. and trans. Theodore G. Tappert, LW 54:426.

34. Walther I. Brandt, introduction to Luther, "That Jesus Christ Was Born a Jew," in *The Christian in Society II,* ed. and trans. Walther I. Brandt, LW 45:197–198; Luther, *Daß Jesus Christus ein geborener Jude sei,* in WA 11:307–336, here 314.

35. Luther, *Daß Jesus Christus,* 320–321; Isaiah 7:14.

36. Luther, *Daß Jesus Christus,* 315, 336.

37. Ibid., 320ff., 325–326, 335–336; Genesis 49.

38. Bertram, introduction to Luther, "Against the Sabbatarians: Letter to a Good Friend," in LW 47:59–61; Kaufmann surmises that the term "Sabbatarians" should be understood in a polemical sense, a "bogey man that grew out of the Christian fear that Jews would make proselytes of Christians." He argues further that, in the context of "the shifting Jewish policies" of both Saxony and Hesse, the treatise was an "effective rhetorical and polemical means" of countering toleration of Jews in Protestant territories. Kaufmann, "Luther and the Jews," 89–90.

39. Luther, *Wider die Sabbather,* in WA 50:312–316, 322–324, 336–337.

40. Bertram, introduction to Luther, "On the Jews," 133. The pamphlet is no longer extant. Thus, we can only postulate the source of some of the teachings and practices that Luther cites in this tract.

41. Luther, *Wider die Sabbather,* 337; Luther, *Von den Juden,* 417.

42. What follows is a summary of Bertram's outline, introduction to Luther, "On the Jews," 133–135; *On the Jews and Their Lies* appears in WA 53:417–552; see also LW 47:121–306. My translations of WA here are generally very close to LW.

43. Luther leveled scathing attacks against not only Jews, but against Catholics, Muslims, and "fanatic" or "enthusiast" Protestants as well. See, e.g., Edwards, "Toward an Understanding," 3; for a helpful view of Luther's use of scatological language, see Oberman, "*Teufelsdreck.*"

44. Luther, *Von den Juden,* 441, 442, 512, 520. The image of "whore" applied to the Jewish people here is similar to Old Testament prophetic pejoratives for the Israelites in times of waywardness. See e.g., the book of Hosea. Luther may also intend it as an ironic jab at them, since they supposedly call the Virgin Mary the same.

45. Luther, *Von den Juden*, 478, 441.

46. Ibid., 489; Nicholas of Lyra (ca. 1270–1349) was a Franciscan Hebraist and biblical scholar who "drew from Jewish traditions in his biblical exegesis more systematically than any Latin Christian scholar since Jerome. . . ." Klepper, *Insight of Unbelievers*, 1.

47. Luther, *Von den Juden*, 461–462, 478, 482, 489, 502. Protestant theologian Gerhard Kittel made a similar claim about the Talmud in 1943, extracting a text about capital punishment out of its context. See Steinweis, *Studying the Jew*, 73ff., especially 75; Luther lived in a "small-scale environment" that was "far from the few prospering urbane residues of Jewish life and Jewish erudition in the Reich" and thus had few personal contacts with Jews. See Kaufmann, *Luthers "Judenschriften*," 10–11; Lewin, *Luthers Stellung*, 8ff., 15–25.

48. Luther, *Von den Juden*, 491. Luther is here again reliant upon Paul of Burgos and Nicholas of Lyra; ibid., 502. While some medieval Jews did spread "scurrilous stories" about Christians, the kind of tales that Luther and Margaritha attribute to them are highly dubious. Langmuir, *History, Religion, and Antisemitism*, 282.

49. Luther, *Von den Juden*, 513–517.

50. Ibid., 482, 520, 522.

51. See, e.g., Trachtenberg, *The Devil and the Jews*, 57–155; Hsia, *Myth of Ritual Murder*, 131–136.

52. Luther, *Von den Juden*, 522–526.

53. Edwards, *Luther's Last Battles*, 133.

54. Falk, *The Jew in Christian Theology*, 163–224. It is sometimes argued that the work is difficult to translate (a fact that is not lost on Falk) but the vulgar content surely must have given great pause to other publishers of Luther's works.

55. Luther, *Vom Schem Hamphoras und vom Geschlecht Christi*, in WA 53:580ff.; Edwards, *Luther's Last Battles*, 132–133; Holsten, "Erläuterungen," 559.

56. Luther, *Vom Schem Hamphoras*, 610ff.

57. Ibid., 608; emphasis added; ibid., 613.

58. Ibid., 601, 618, 619, 636–637, 647. The "Judas piss" verbiage is introduced on 636 in a violently facetious image. As ugly as this language is, Luther did not, as Jerome Friedman charged, call for the "wholesale murder" of Jews on the basis that they "were biologically not human since they did not originate from the seed of Adam and Eve. . . ." See Friedman, "Reformation in Alien Eyes," 36. Friedman offers no proof for this claim. In the paragraph where the above quotations appear, Friedman references *On the Jews and Their Lies*, *On the Ineffable Name*, and *On the Last Words of David*.

59. Edwards, *Luther's Last Battles*, 8–9.

60. Maurer, "Luthers Stellung"; others who view Luther's attitude toward Jews as essentially theological include Haynes, *Reluctant Witnesses*, 45–48; Günther Ginzel rejected the division of anti-Judaism ("as 'merely' religiously conditioned antipathy") and antisemitism ("as political-völkisch Jew-hatred") as it is com-

monly applied to the modern era as the "belittlement of a widespread anti-Jewish attitude." Ginzel, "Martin Luther: 'Kronzeuge des Antisemitismus,'" in Kremers, *Die Juden und Martin Luther*, 189–210, here 189.

61. Augustine famously taught that the Jewish people served as a witness to the world of what happens when people disobey God. See Augustine, *City of God*, 18:46, 827. Even so, his view of the Jewish people may have been much less adversarial than is commonly understood. See Fredriksen, *Augustine and the Jews*; Augustine, "In Answer to the Jews."

62. Maurer, "Luthers Stellung," 42.

63. Ibid., 44–45. This Protestant missionary endeavor to Jews does not appear to have happened in any great measure until nearly two centuries after Luther's death. See Clark, *Politics of Conversion*, 1.

64. Luther, "Lectures on Romans: Glosses and Scholia," in LW 25:9, 17. Luther here comments upon two passages from the New Testament epistle to the Romans. See Romans 1:18 and 2:5.

65. Maurer, "Luthers Stellung," 48; Luther, *Von den Juden*, 541.

66. Maurer, "Exkurs 9. Luther und die Juden," in *Kirche und Synagoge*, 89.

67. Oberman, *Roots of Anti-Semitism*, 14, 21, 25, 29.

68. Ibid., 14, 25, 38, 40, 43.

69. Ibid., 50.

70. Edwards, *Luther's Last Battles*, 139–141.

71. Meier covers the reception and interpretation of Luther's *Judenschriften* in some detail, from Lewin's seminal 1911 work through the 1960s. Meier notes here that Rabbi Lewin posited an "abrupt transformation" of Luther's position toward the Jewish people, a view that Wilhelm Grau, Wolf Meyer-Erlach, and others "placed in the service of the NS-Zeitgeist." Erich Vogelsang and Theodor Pauls, who also toed an antisemitic line, stressed the continuity of the reformer's position. See Meier, "Zur Interpretation von Luthers Judenschriften," in *Kirche und Judentum*, 127–153, here 143. On Vogelsang and Meyer-Erlach, see chapter three here.

72. Ibid., 143.

73. Even so, I concur with Susannah Heschel's assertions that Meier's portrayals of both the German Christians and the Eisenach Institute are misleading, particularly with respect to the anti-Judaic and antisemitic goals of the Institute and of the German Christians as a marginal movement within German Protestantism. See Heschel, *Aryan Jesus*, 93–94; chapter five here.

74. Edwards, *Luther's Last Battles*, 9.

75. Ibid., 15. Contra Edwards, Oberman contends that Luther used scatological language throughout his entire career; this kind of crudity had "absolutely nothing to do with disappointment or senility in the last years of life." See Oberman, "*Teufelsdreck*," 444; in a fascinating study, Lyndal Roper touches briefly on the issue of Luther's "anality" in the context of the representations of the reformer's body. See Roper, "Martin Luther's Body," 352–354.

76. Edwards, *Luther's Last Battles*, 17–19, 8–9.

77. Ibid., 17.

78. Ibid., 125. Edwards here regards *Against the Sabbatarians* as his first "major attack on the Jews."

79. Maurer, for example, argues that Luther's theological view of Jews underwent little change during his lifetime. See "Luthers Stellung," 42–43.

80. Oberman believed that Edwards bought into a misleading form of psychohistory regarding the "old" Luther. See Oberman, "*Teufelsdreck*," 438; Edwards, "Luther's Attacks on the Jews," 11.

81. Halpern-Amaru, "Luther and Jewish Mirrors," 95. See also Gilman, "Martin Luther and the Self-Hating Jews." Gilman essentially argues that Luther had contradicting and ambiguous views of Jews that are demonstrated in converts like Pfefferkorn and Margaritha.

82. Halpern-Amaru, "Luther and Jewish Mirrors," 101. Presumably, the former image is closer to that presented in *That Jesus Christ Was Born a Jew* and the latter in *On the Jews and Their Lies* and *On the Ineffable Name*.

83. Halpern-Amaru, "Luther and Jewish Mirrors," 99–100.

84. Bainton, *Here I Stand*, 42, 62.

85. For helpful analysis of the deleterious effects of this "psychogram," see Oberman, "*Teufelsdreck*," 435–439.

86. Luther, "Lectures on Romans," 3.

87. Baron, "John Calvin and the Jews," 391; there were no Jews in Geneva, a fact that may explain in part why Calvin took up no anti-Jewish social program as Luther did. See Detmers, "Calvin, the Jews, and Judaism," 198–199.

88. Bertram, introduction to Luther, "On the Jews," 135. See also Stern, *Josel of Rosheim*, 195, 199–200, 203–204.

89. Stern, *Josel of Rosheim*, 216; Wallmann, "Reception of Luther's Writings"; Kaufmann, "Luther and the Jews," 102.

3. Confessing Church and German Christian Academic Theologians

Portions of this chapter, as well as excerpts from the introduction and chapter one, appeared previously in modified form in Christopher J. Probst, "'An Incessant Army of Demons': Wolf Meyer-Erlach, Luther, and 'the Jews' in Nazi Germany," *Holocaust and Genocide Studies*, 23, 3 (2009): 441–460.

1. For a full discussion of the Eisenach Institute, see Heschel, *Aryan Jesus*. In addition to Meyer-Erlach, several more of its members appear here. See especially chapter five.

2. Of the four, Erich Vogelsang was perhaps the most influential. Still, he did not have the same clout at the time as did, for example, the older, more established Althaus. Despite a modicum of success, none of his works could be considered "classics" in German Protestant theology.

3. Burleigh and Wippermann, *Racial State,* 78–80, 214; Evans, *Third Reich in Power,* 297.

4. Grüttner, *Studenten im Dritten Reich,* 87–100; Evans, *Third Reich in Power,* 291–292.

5. Burleigh's summary of the conclusions of the *Deutschland-Berichte der SOPADE* (1937) entry dated April 4, 1937, 497–499, in Burleigh, *The Third Reich,* 252.

6. Follow the example of the Hessian regional church's cooperation with the theology faculty of Gießen University. See chapter six here. See also Eike Wolgast, "Nationalsozialistische Hochschulpolitik und die evangelisch-theologischen Fakultäten," in Siegele-Wenschkewitz and Nicolaisen, *Theologische Fakultäten,* 45–79, here 59.

7. Hartshorne, "The German Universities and the Government," 232; Hartshorne became a key part of early OMGUS (Office of the Military Government of the United States) efforts to denazify German universities after the war. See Remy, *The Heidelberg Myth,* 128ff.

8. Weinreich, *Hitler's Professors,* 7.

9. Steinweis, *Studying the Jew,* 14–15; the first tier included films such as *Der ewige Jude,* as well as publications such as the *Völkischer Beobachter* and *Der Stürmer.* The SS newspaper *Das Schwarze Korps* falls into the second category in Steinweis's schema.

10. Ibid., 15; Grau, a Catholic, was acting director of the Institute's Research Department on the Jewish Question (Forschungsabteilung Judenfrage) in Munich from 1935 to 1938. See von Papen, "Vom engagierten Katholiken."

11. Koonz, *The Nazi Conscience,* 48, 68.

12. Due to the growing influence of German Christian theologians under the Nazi regime, Confessing Church theologians were increasingly marginalized; the theological responses of this wing of German Protestantism thus appeared, for the most part, outside of the theological faculties of the universities, in journals and circulated church newsletters.

13. Some simply stressed Luther's stature as a Germanic hero. Siegfried Leffler, who co-founded the Church Movement of German Christians (Kirchenbewegung Deutsche Christen) with Julius Leutheuser in 1927, effuses over Luther as the great German. It is Luther—this "son of the German Volk"—who would go "into the Most Holy as priest and theologian and speak there with God . . ." on behalf of the German people. This remarkable language echoes the New Testament book of Hebrews, which describes the saving work of Christ, who enters the Most Holy place alone as high priest on behalf of his people. See Heschel, "Nazifying," 588; Leffler, *Christus im Dritten Reich,* 69–73; Hebrews 9:11–12. Walter Grundmann was professor of New Testament and Völkisch Theology at Jena University and director of the Eisenach Institute. In typical German Christian fashion, he reinforces Luther by appealing to National Socialists and vice versa. He finds it "extraordinarily significant" that the high-profile Nazi educational theorist Ernst Krieck reflects on

the "problem of history" by appealing to Luther, saying, "'Our faith goes the way of Luther, which was the way of devout Teuton blood.'" Ernst Krieck, *Volkscharakter und Sendungsbewußtsein* (Leipzig: Armanen, 1939), 90, in Walter Grundmann, "Das apokalyptische Geschichtsbild und das deutsche Geschichtsdenken," in Grundmann, *Germanentum, Christentum und Judentum*, 2:99; Krieck was professor of pedagogy and philosophy at Heidelberg. Remy, "We are no longer the university," 25–28.

14. Jens Wolff, "Vogelsang, Erich Paul Friedrich," in BBK, 17:1507–1521; the chair at Gießen was previously held by Heinrich Bornkamm, whom I will discuss here in chapter six. Vogelsang was also considered for two other church history chairs, one at Göttingen in 1937 and the other at Vienna in 1939. Königsberg is now known as Kaliningrad, in present-day Russia.

15. Another important topic with which he grappled was Luther's relationship to German mystics and mysticism. Ibid., 1513–1515; Meier, *Kirchenkampf*, 1:286; *Der junge Luther*, ed. Erich Vogelsang, vol. 5 of *Luthers Werke in Auswahl*.

16. Vogelsang, "Das Deutsche in Luthers Christentum," 83–84; emphasis added.

17. Ibid., 84–87.

18. Ibid., 87–88, 92, 102.

19. Stayer, *Martin Luther, German Saviour*, 127. Stayer also asserts that Vogelsang remained "silent on Nazi racist beliefs." While Vogelsang generally does come across as more moderate, primarily using nonrational language to combat Judaism, there are several places in Vogelsang's works where he does not "remain silent" on Nazi racist beliefs. See below.

20. Pauls, *Luther und die Juden*. Pauls was a Nazi Luther researcher who earned his doctorate in philology and until 1938 served as director of a secondary school for boys and girls in Senftenberg. In 1938, he became professor at the University for Teacher Education in Hirschberg-Riesengebirge (Lower Silesia; present-day Jelenia Góra, Poland). While Pauls did not sit on a Protestant theological faculty, he had a running engagement with Protestant theology via the German Christians, most notably by publishing *Luther and the Jews* in 1939, which was part of a long series of ostensibly scholarly works about "positive Christianity." Pauls offered the work as a "gift" to the Eisenach Institute. See von der Osten-Sacken, "Der Nationalsozialistische Lutherforscher Theodor Pauls: Vervollständigung eines Fragmentarischen Bildes," in von der Osten-Sacken, *Das Mißbrauchte Evangelium*, 136–137.

21. Vogelsang, *Luthers Kampf*, 6.

22. Ibid., 7–9, 11; Matthew 27:25.

23. Vogelsang, *Luthers Kampf*, 12–17.

24. Ibid., 18, 25.

25. Ibid., 20, 23; emphasis in original.

26. Ibid., 27–28; Luther, *Von den Juden*, 526.

27. Falk, *The Jew in Christian Theology,* 196, 250; Luther, *Vom Schem Hamphoras,* 615.

28. Vogelsang, *Luthers Kampf,* 31.

29. Ibid., 35.

30. His injuries may have had lasting effects. In a 1920 letter, Swiss theologian Eduard Thurneysen says to Karl Barth that Meyer's war injuries shattered his nerves, causing his "'often somewhat noisy nature and a lack of power of concentration.'" See Barth, *Karl Barth—Eduard Thurneysen, Briefwechsel,* 1:431ff., in Raschzok, "Wolf Meyer-Erlach," 172.

31. Grüttner, *Biographisches Lexikon,* 120; Raschzok, "Wolf Meyer-Erlach," 171ff.; Dr. Jürgen König, archivist at *Landeskirchliches Archiv der Evangelisch-Lutherischen Kirche in Bayern* (hereafter, LKA Nuremberg), e-mail message to author, August 11, 2010.

32. Raschzok, "Wolf Meyer-Erlach," 173–174; Heschel, *Aryan Jesus,* 212. Heschel describes the latter play as "violent and sexually and racially charged," citing a graphic example that makes the point in the clearest of fashions.

33. UAJ Meyer Personnel File. A personnel questionnaire dated June 16, 1945, lists May 15, 1933 as the date of his entry into the NSDAP. Another undated, unsigned "CV" lists April 21, 1933. The latest date listed in this CV is April 1, 1935, when he became rector at Jena. Another document titled "Personalbogen!" signed on September 17, 1935 lists May 1, 1933. See also Heschel, "Nazifying," 592, n. 22.

34. UAJ Grundmann Personnel File. Wolf Meyer-Erlach, "Gutachten über Dozent Dr. Grundmann—Jena. Jena, 23. Oktober 1937." He commends here Grundmann's "scholarly deportment" which, he says, is "completely beholden to National Socialism"; Schenk, "Der Jenaer Jesus," 184–186; Heschel, "Nazifying," 592–593.

35. UAJ Meyer Personnel File, "Entlassungs-Urkunde."

36. Grüttner, *Biographisches Lexikon,* 120; Raschzok, "Wolf Meyer-Erlach," 175; Heschel, *Aryan Jesus,* 270.

37. See Bergen, *Twisted Cross,* 153. In a June 12, 1945 letter of self-defense, he says he was expelled from Saxony in 1938 "on the personal order of *Gauleiter* Mutschmann by the highest office of the Gestapo." The Lord Mayor's office in Pirna on the Elbe indeed communicated to the National Church Movement of the German Christians that a meeting scheduled in Pirna for November 13, 1938 could only take place without Meyer-Erlach as the speaker, on the basis that the governor of the state of Saxony had banned Meyer-Erlach from the territory. The reason for the ban is not stated. Sonne, *Die politische Theologie,* 243. See also UAJ Meyer Personnel File, "Betreff: Verfolgung durch die Partei"; according to Raschzok, he was also interrogated by the Gestapo in Berlin in 1940. See "Wolf Meyer-Erlach," 188.

38. Heschel, *Aryan Jesus,* 149ff.; the closing of the *Apologetische Centrale* (Apologetics Center, or AC) by the Gestapo in December 1937 and of the Confessing Church seminaries (decreed by Himmler in August 1937) might be classified more justifiably as "persecution." On the closure of the AC, see chapter four here; on

the closing of the Confessing Church seminaries, see Barnett, *For the Soul of the People*, 86–88.

39. UAJ, BA 2149. The letter is dated June 20, 1945. He makes similar claims in a letter dated June 2, 1945.

40. He lost the post of rector in 1937, and then the office of University preacher in 1939. See UAJ Meyer Personnel File, "*Rundschreiben* Nr. 40, Jena, den 31 October 1937"; Raschzok, "Wolf Meyer-Erlach," 175; UAJ Meyer Personnel File, "Betreff: Verfolgung durch die Partei."

41. UAJ Meyer Personnel File, undated, unsigned "CV." See n. 33.

42. On Richter, see UAJ, J 90 "Promotionsakten der Theologischen Fakultät, 1938 und 1939"; regarding Schmidt-Clausing, see UAJ, J 92 "Promotionsakten der Theologischen Fakultät, 1941–1947"; the institute had been created the previous year and was to be part of Rosenberg's planned Nazi University. See Steinweis, *Studying the Jew*, 12–13.

43. UAJ, J 92; upon leaving the post of rector in late 1937, he writes to employees and professors at Jena that he "reported for duty" to his office "as a soldier of the Führer." He likewise retires "as a soldier of the Führer." UAJ Meyer Personnel File, "*Rundschreiben* Nr. 40, Jena, den 31 October 1937."

44. *General Anzeiger*, Würzburg, 219, September 23, 1929, in Steinlein, "Luther und das Alte Testament," 184.

45. See below. Since he speaks of "parental" objections, perhaps he was talking about his time as pastor in Würzburg, since it is doubtful he would have had heard much objection from parents of his university pupils.

46. Meyer-Erlach, *Universität und Volk*, 17–18.

47. Meyer-Erlach, "Luther und Gustav Adolf," 10–12.

48. Meyer-Erlach, *Der Einfluss der Juden*; Meyer-Erlach, *Ist Gott Engländer?*; Heschel, "When Jesus Was an Aryan," 74, 203 n. 28; Friedländer, *The Years of Extermination*, 161.

49. Meyer-Erlach, *Der Einfluss der Juden*, 10–13. This, despite the fact that traditional Christian theology identifies the God of Israel as one and the same with the Christian God.

50. Ibid., 29.

51. Meyer-Erlach, *Verrat an Luther*, 18–19, emphasis added; Luther, WA 18:75; on Luther's love for the Old Testament, see *Gerhard Schmidt, Nuremberg Seminary Rector*, below.

52. UAJ Meyer Personnel File, undated, unsigned "CV." See n. 33 above. He lists "Luther" as his "subject area specialty" (*Spezialgebiet*); UAJ *Personal-und-Vorlesungs Verzeichnis 1935–1940*. He taught the former course in 1939 and the latter in 1940; LKA Eisenach A 921 "Entjudung der Kirche 1939–1947," "Institut zur Erforschung und Beseitigung des Jüdischen Einflusses auf das deutsche kirchliche Leben: Die Arbeitskreise," 1.

53. Meyer-Erlach, *Der Einfluss der Juden*, 8–10.

54. Meyer-Erlach, *Juden, Mönche und Luther,* 32.

55. Ibid., 38–39. *"wissenschaftlich kühl, sauber und sachlich";* i.e., purely academic, rational rather than emotive. Thanks to my friends, Drs. Roland Löffler, Tanja Hetzer, and Rudolf Muhs, for help with this translation.

56. Ibid., 60.

57. Thomas A. Brady, Jr. says that Thomas Mann sealed the "Luther-to-Hitler myth" with a lecture at the Library of Congress only three weeks after the Allied victory in the Second World War. See "Luther's Social Teaching," 270–271.

58. Biographical information about Steinlein in the historical literature is scant. I am indebted to Dr. Jürgen König, archivist at LKA Nuremberg, for these biographical details. Dr. König, e-mail message to author, May 23, 2006.

59. Mensing, *Pfarrer und Nationalsozialismus,* 72–73, 92–93, 95, 275; on the völkisch (nationalist) movement in 1924, including the Völkischer Block, see Kershaw, *Hitler, 1889–1936: Hubris,* 224–228.

60. Steinlein, "Luther und die Juden," 121. Steinlein gives no particulars about this article. He also appears to make reference to the same article in *Ludendorffs Phantasien,* 27.

61. Steinlein, *Luthers Stellung zum Judentum;* Steinlein, "Luthers Judenschriften," 24–25.

62. Evans, *Coming of the Third Reich,* 201–202; Steinlein musters his greatest powers of scholarship and sarcasm against spurious claims made by Ludendorff. The result is at times a very scholarly and at other times quite comical defense of Luther and the Protestant church. The Ansbach pastor pulls no punches. Despite Ludendorff's spurious claims, and Steinlein's spirited and sardonic rebuttals of the same, it would be a mistake to miss the gravity of Steinlein's position on the "Jewish Question" in the pages of this work. He does not flinch in referring to Luther's writings about Jews—without further comment, and on multiple occasions—as "antisemitic." He also goes to great lengths to demonstrate that there has been no suppression of Luther's *Judenschriften.* In fact, he shows that Protestant scholars have been very careful to preserve and publish them. He proudly demonstrates—contra Ludendorff—that Luther's antisemitic advice has indeed been heard and heeded. See, e.g., Steinlein, *Ludendorffs Phantasien,* 4, 7, 10, 20–21, 24–27.

63. Meier, "Zur Interpretation von Luthers Judenschriften," 136, n. 34.

64. Steinlein, "Luthers Stellung zur Frage der Judentaufe"; Steinlein, "Luther und das Alte Testament."

65. Steinlein, "Luther und das Alte Testament," 172–173.

66. Ibid., 177–178.

67. Ibid., 198, 200.

68. Steinlein, "Luthers Stellung zur Frage der Judentaufe," 842. Steinlein does not mention the players by name, but does say that the baptism took place in Magdeburg in March, and that the subject of the sacrament was a Jew accused of sex-

ual crimes, leaving little doubt that he is discussing the case of Albert Hirschland, which I examine here in chapter four.

69. Ibid., 842–844.

70. Luther, *Von den Juden,* 551, in ibid., 846.

71. WA 51:187ff.; Steinlein, "Luthers Stellung zur Frage der Judentaufe," 846.

72. In *Frau Dr. Ludendorffs Phantasien über Luther und die Reformation* (1932), however, Steinlein refers to Luther's Judenschriften as "antisemitic." See n. 62 above.

73. On the establishment of the Confessing Church seminaries, all of which were in the Prussian provinces, see, e.g., Bethge, *Dietrich Bonhoeffer,* 419–424.

74. Biographical sketch courtesy of Dr. König, LKA Nuremberg, e-mail messages to author, August 3, 2007 and August 11, 2010.

75. Schmidt, "Luther und das Alte Testament."

76. Ibid., 712–715.

77. Bergen, "Storm Troopers," 52–54.

78. Schmidt, "Luther und das Alte Testament," 712.

79. Ibid., 713, 714; Gerlach, *Witnesses,* 112.

80. Schmidt, "Luther und das Alte Testament," 712–713. Schmidt's representation of Luther's view is reductionist. As demonstrated in chapter two here, the reformer buttressed his nonrational view of Jews with irrational and xenophobic elements.

4. Confessing Church Pastors

1. Gerhard Schäfer, *Die Intakte Landeskirche, 1935–1936,* vol. 4 of *Die Evangelische Landeskirche in Württemberg,* 377.

2. Richard Evans aptly describes *Der Stürmer* (The Stormer), which was edited by Julius Streicher, as a "sensational popular newspaper . . . which rapidly established itself as the place where screaming headlines introduced the most rabid attacks on Jews, full of sexual innuendo, racist caricatures, made-up accusations of ritual murder and titillating, semi-pornographic stories of Jewish men seducing innocent German girls." Evans, *Coming of the Third Reich,* 188–189; The *Bruderrat* (Council of Brethren) was an advisory council of the Confessing Church. These councils existed on both the regional and national levels and consisted of both lay and clergy representatives. See Gerlach, *Witnesses,* 287; EZA 50/3, "Evangelium und Taufe!" *Der Provinzialbruderrat der Provinz Sachsen,* 73–74. Internal evidence suggests that the newsletter was written not long after August 1935. The latest date explicitly referenced is August 15, but there is also reference to a legal letter sent to the editor of *Der Stürmer,* also present in EZA 50 and dated August 23; "Zur Frage der Judentaufe: Bericht zu den Angriffen gegen Pfarrer Zuckschwerdt—Magdeburg," *Württembergische Bekenntnisgemeinschaft Rundbrief,* October 16, 1935, 11–12; "Der Rasseschänder von Magdeburg," *Der Stürmer,* Special Edition 2, August 1935.

3. Gerlach discusses the Zuckschwerdt-Hirschland affair, as well as several other cases of such baptisms. See Gerlach, *Witnesses*, 116–118.

4. "Evangelium und Taufe!" *Der Provinzialbruderrat der Provinz Sachsen*, 73.

5. Ibid.

6. Ibid.

7. Eberhard Röhm and Jorg Thierfelder, *Entrechtet, 1935–1938*, vol. 2/I of *Juden-Christen-Deutsche, 1933–1945*, 48.

8. EZA 50/3, "Hofmann Rechtsanwalt u. Notar" to "Die Schriftleitung des 'Stürmer,'" August 23, 1935, 89–90, here 89.

9. Ibid., 89–90; EZA 50/3, "Hofmann Rechtsanwalt u. Notar" to "Den Rat der Evangelische Kirche der altpreussischen Union," August 23, 1935, 88. The recipient, the Old Prussian Union Church, "included eight regional churches (East Prussia, Brandenburg, Pomerania, Mark Posen-West Prussia, Silesia, Saxony, Westphalia, Rhineland)." Gerlach, *Witnesses*, 288.

10. The apostle deals with the relations between Jews and non-Jews ("Gentiles") in the Roman church quite extensively in this epistle, but especially in chapters 9–11.

11. "Zur Frage der Judentaufe," 11–12; emphasis added. The nationalistic overtones are further evidenced by Zuckschwerdt's appeal to Hirschland's military service.

12. Ibid., 12.

13. See, e.g., "Kundgebung der Bekenntnissynode der evangelischen Kirche der altpreußischen Union: 500 Pfarrer verhaftet," *Der Präses der Bekenntnissynode der Deutschen Evangelischen Kirche: Bad Oeynhausen*, March 28, 1935, 2. According to this article, approximately five hundred pastors were arrested and briefly detained in March 1935 for planning to read a statement critical of the religious aspects of Nazism from their pulpits. Other documents put the number of arrested pastors at 715. See Gerlach, *Witnesses*, 80.

14. Even so, clergy from every wing still wrote and preached about traditional Protestant Christian beliefs that did not necessarily bear directly on the issue of how one was to treat Jews. Sin, justification, righteousness, salvation, and the relationship between church and state are just a few.

15. Helmreich, *German Churches under Hitler*, 156, 495, n.120.

16. With the ascent of the Hitler regime most Protestants were heartened, seeing this turn of events as a national revival. See Lehmann, "The Germans as a Chosen People," 268–269; Bergen, *Twisted Cross*, 12.

17. Helmreich, *German Churches under Hitler*, 156, 495, n. 120.

18. Baranowski, "Consent and Dissent," 65.

19. In this brief discussion, I am following Kulka, "German Population and the Jews," 271–281.

20. Ibid., 274. Despite some dissent from religious people, including Protestants, this book, along with much of the relevant historical literature, demon-

strates that most were either unsympathetic or antagonistic towards German Jews; the "majority opinion in the 1930s," Kershaw elaborates, consisted of "apathetic and latent discriminatory attitudes" that were "closely related, and formed together a broad and fluid spectrum." Kershaw, "German Popular Opinion," 369.

21. "Akademische Tagung der 'Deutsche Christen,'" *Evangelium im Dritten Reich*, February 10, 1935, 46.

22. "Achtung, Theologen, Laien," *Evangelium im Dritten Reich*, March 22, 1936.

23. The writer describes among other things Wolf Meyer-Erlach's talk about Luther and the Jews. "Eisenach 1937," *Deutscher Sonntag*, November 7, 1937, 303.

24. "Eine Stimme des Dankes," *Deutscher Sonntag*, January 8, 1939, 14.

25. "Erklärungen der nichttheologischen Synodalen," *Der Präses der Bekenntnissynode der Deutschen Evangelischen Kirche: Bad Oeynhausen*, June 21, 1935, 8.

26. Gailus, "Overwhelmed by Their Own Fascination," 482.

27. Much more research—via a "social history of ideas" approach—is needed, however, to demonstrate conclusively the views of the average person in the pews of German Protestant churches. I am indebted to Richard Steigmann-Gall for suggesting this helpful terminology. Steigmann-Gall, e-mail message to author, November 8, 2004.

28. "Luther und die Judentaufe," *Württembergische Bekenntnisgemeinschaft Rundbrief*, October 16, 1935, 12–13.

29. *Von den Juden und ihren Lügen: Martin Luther, Luthers Flugschriften für unsere Zeit*. Booklet 3 (Dresden: Landesverein für Innere Mission, 1931).

30. "Luther und die Judentaufe," 13. The Saxony article also quotes the two Luther passages, along with the biblical citation.

31. "Evangelium und Taufe!" 74.

32. Matthias Wolfes, "Fausel, Heinrich," BBK, 20:475–479; Stephenson, *Hitler's Home Front*, 29.

33. City of Heimsheim website, http://www.heimsheim.de/2209_DEU_WWW.php (accessed July 27, 2011); Stephenson, *Hitler's Home Front*, 91.

34. Wolfes, "Fausel," 475–479.

35. USHMM Fausel Collection, 6, Unpublished Sermon Manuscript, "Predigt beim Bezirkskirchengesangsfest am S. Cantate," May 14, 1933; emphasis in original.

36. USHMM Fausel Collection, 8, Unpublished Sermon Manuscript, "Predigt in Heimsheim am Neujahr, den 1. Januar 1945."

37. See the introduction here and Fausel, "Die Judenfrage"; Rohm and Thierfelder, *Ausgegrenzt, 1933–1935*, 165.

38. Fausel, "Die Judenfrage," 1.

39. Ibid.

40. Ibid., 4–5.

41. Ibid., 5–6.

42. Ibid., 3–4.

43. Ibid., 7–9.

44. Ibid., 9.

45. Ibid., 9–10.

46. Ibid., 11–13.

47. Ibid., 14.

48. Ibid., 14; Barnett, *For the Soul of the People,* 133ff.

49. Fausel, "Die Judenfrage," 14–15.

50. Röhm and Thierfelder, *Vernichtet, 1941–1945,* 67–72, 182ff., 198–199. According to Hermann Pineas, Herta "had helped in the household of the local parson's wife, Helene Fausel, whose husband at that time had a congregation in Ditzingen." Pineas in Richarz, *Jewish Life in Germany,* 448–460, here 455–456.

51. See the conclusion here.

52. Christiane Mokroß, EZA, e-mail message to author, August 17, 2007; *Pfarrerbuch der Kirchenprovinz Sachsen,* 3:186.

53. Since he was a member of this body, it is plausible that he could have written their piece about Zuckschwerdt and Hirschland. See above.

54. The introduction of the Aryan paragraph had earlier spurred the formation of the Pastors' Emergency League. See Meier, *Kirchenkampf,* 1:304; Gerlach, *Witnesses,* 69ff. The German Christians wholeheartedly supported the implementation of the Aryan Paragraph in the church. The Confessing Church remained divided over the issue.

55. Meier, *Kirchenkampf,* 2:211.

56. Christiane Mokroß, EZA, e-mail message to author, August 17, 2007; *Pfarrerbuch der Kirchenprovinz Sachsen,* 3:186; Meier, *Kirchenkampf,* 3:324–325.

57. Gabriel, *Luther Von den Juden;* on this writing, see also Röhm and Thierfelder, *Entrechtet, 1935–1938,* 49–50.

58. See chapter three here.

59. Gabriel, *Luther Von den Juden,* 3.

60. Ibid., 4.

61. Ibid., 6–10; see also chapter two here.

62. Ibid., 13; emphasis added.

63. Ibid., 14.

64. Ibid., 16–17, 19–21.

65. Ibid., 24–25, 27–28, 41.

66. Ibid., 40–42; emphasis added.

67. Ibid., 42.

68. Ibid., 42–43; emphasis added.

69. Ibid., 43; *Parousia* refers to the doctrine of the return of Christ, and is based on the biblical Greek term παρουσία. The term is used in I Thessalonians 2:19, II Thessalonians 2:1ff., and elsewhere in the New Testament.

70. Gabriel, *Luther Von den Juden,* 43; Gerlach, *Witnesses,* 37.

71. Gabriel, *Luther Von den Juden,* 43; emphasis added.

72. Ibid., 44.

73. Ibid., 45.

74. Dr. Michael Häusler, ADW Berlin, e-mail message to author, August 13, 2007; ADW Berlin CA/PA II 296; Pöhlmann, *Kampf der Geister,* 16.

75. Dr. Häusler, ADW Berlin, e-mail message to author, August 13, 2007; the titles, all published by the AC in Berlin-Spandau, include *Zeugnisse germanischer Religion* (1935), *Ludendorffs Kampf gegen das Christentum* (1936), and *Luther und die Juden* (1935).

76. Since the terms *Volksmission* and *Volksmissionar* could take on different meanings in different contexts—even within German Protestantism—they are difficult to translate. I have translated *Volksmissionar* as "evangelical missionary" here to convey the traditional sense of the word—that of presenting the Christian Gospel to people in the hope that they would recognize Christ as their Savior and convert to Christianity—that was most probable within the Confessing Church context at that time. For an excellent explanation of the terms, see Mark S. Brocker, "Editor's Introduction to the English Edition," *Conspiracy and Imprisonment, 1940–1945,* vol. 16 of *Dietrich Bonhoeffer Works,* 27.

77. Dr. Häusler, ADW Berlin, e-mail message to author, August 13, 2007; Johannes Röhm, ADW Berlin, e-mail message to author, August 28, 2007; ADW Berlin BP 1408; Pöhlmann, *Kampf der Geister,* 209–210. Walter Künneth, who was director of the AC from 1932 until its closure in December 1937, was involved in a prolonged ideological and literary dispute with Alfred Rosenberg over the latter's publication *Protestantische Rompilger.* Künneth responded with two publications, both of which were banned by the Gestapo, who had also banned at least one AC conference in 1934. Künneth, "Evangelische Wahrheit!" and "Wider die Verfälschung des Protestantismus!" See vom Bruch, *Fachbereiche und Fakultäten,* 115–116.

78. Johannes Röhm, ADW Berlin, e-mail messages to author, August 28 and 29, 2007; ADW Berlin BP 1408 and 1173.

79. Wiese,"'Unheilsspuren,'" 129ff.; Dr. Karin Köhler, LKA BB, e-mail message to author, September 7, 2007; LKA BB Bestand 1 ("Konsistorialakten Berlin-West 1945–1976") and 4 ("Kirchliche Erziehungskammer Berlin-West 1936–1986"); Pöhlmann, *Kampf der Geister,* 261.

80. Schroth, "Christentum und Judentum."

81. Ibid., 150.

82. Ibid.; this caricature of Judaism in connection with anti-Christian Bolshevism is also painted by many German Christian figures. See chapter five here. Nazi ideologue Alfred Rosenberg posited an all-powerful Jewish–Bolshevistic conspiracy. Speaking to the Nazi party congress in 1935, he railed against the supposed Zionist conspiracy working behind the world political scene through "capitalistic methods in the democratic West" and "Bolshevistic terror in the European East...." ADW Berlin CA/AC-S 179, *Durchbruch,* Stuttgart, September 18, 1935.

83. Schroth, "Christentum und Judentum," 150.

84. Ibid., 150–151.

85. Schroth, *Luthers christlicher Antisemitismus.*

86. Ibid., 5–6.

87. Ibid., 6. Church historian and Holl protégé Hanns Rückert, discussing Luther's approach to creation and salvation history, posited a "'unity of history and salvation history [*Heilsgeschichte*], of creation and redemption, which is given in the one God whose immeasurable greatness Paul praises. . . .'" See Rückert, "Luther als Deutscher," *Deutsche Theologie*, Luthersonderheft November 1933, 23, in Hamm, "Rückert als Schüler Karl Holls," 308, n. 151.

88. Schroth, *Luthers christlicher Antisemitismus,* 7.

89. Ibid., 9–12, 14; emphasis added.

90. Ibid., 15; Romans 13:1–7, especially v. 4.

91. Schroth, *Luthers christlicher Antisemitismus,* 15–19.

92. Ibid., 19–22.

93. Ibid., 23–25.

94. Ibid., 28; emphasis added.

95. Ibid., 29.

96. Wiese, "'Unheilsspuren,'" 129–130.

97. EZA 50; the VKL (Vorläufige Kirchenleitung, or Provisional Church Leadership of the German Protestant Church) was the "Confessing Church government established at the Dahlem confessional synod in October 1934 as a counterpart to the Church Consistory and Chancellery in Berlin, which were headed by German Christians or 'neutral' leaders." It was a quasi-national group in the sense that Confessing Church pastors in Württemberg and other regional churches viewed it as a sort of "spiritual" leadership for the Confessing Church, but these pastors still fell under the leadership of their respective regional church governments. See Gerlach, *Witnesses,* 288; Barnett, *For the Soul of the People,* 69–70.

98. EZA 50/114, "Luther zur Judenfrage," 75–78.

99. Ibid., 75.

100. Ibid.

101. Ibid.; Luther, *Von den Juden,* 522ff.

102. "Luther zur Judenfrage," 76.

103. Ibid.

104. Ibid.; on the usage of Luther's texts by German Christians, see chapter five here; on the idea of "false canonization" of the reformer, see Steinlein, *Luthers Stellung zum Judentum,* 15.

105. "Luther zur Judenfrage," 77.

106. Ibid., 78; the third option—murdering them—is not discussed. Given the pinpoint theological focus of the manuscript, and nearly complete lack of direct reference to current events, it is hard to determine whether the widespread violence against Jews that began with November 9–10, 1938 was ongoing when it was written.

107. Ibid.

108. Gerlach, *Witnesses*.

109. See, e.g., Hilberg, *Perpetrators, Victims, Bystanders*; Cesarani and Levine, *"Bystanders" to the Holocaust*.

5. German Christian Pastors and Bishops

1. Gailus, "Overwhelmed by Their Own Fascination," 487.

2. Ibid., 485, 491. While Gailus rightly calls the "intact" churches "conformist" with respect to their attitude toward the Nazi state, he might underestimate the penetration of "völkisch" ideology in the Confessing Church and in the Protestant "middle." Throughout the article, he almost exclusively associates "völkisch Protestantism" with the German Christians. Paul Althaus, an influential figure among the Protestant "neutrals," was the leading proponent of a Protestantism whose theology was shaped by "creation orders," of which "the Volk" was crucial. (See chapter one here.) While Berlin apologist Hansgeorg Schroth (chapter four) forcefully challenged völkisch Protestantism, Walter Künneth, a prominent Confessing Church figure, embraced it in a very qualified fashion. See, e.g., "Gutachten Lic. Walter Künneth: Die Kirche und die Judenfrage (11. April 1933)" in Röhm and Thierfelder, *Ausgegrenzt, 1933–1935*, 369–371. On Künneth's work for the "Apologetische Centrale," see Pöhlmann, *Kampf der Geister*, 17–21. Certainly, though, German Christian versions of völkisch theology tended to be much more radical than the varieties espoused by either Althaus or Künneth.

3. Bergen, *Twisted Cross*, 7–8.

4. These are often referred to as the "intact" churches. Yet, contra the prevailing notion that local churches simply replayed national and regional church issues and events, Kyle Jantzen argues that "dissenting pastors consistently found space within which they could influence parishioners against the established church policy of their *Land* Church superiors." See Jantzen, "Propaganda, Perseverance, and Protest," 295–327, here 297; for a thorough if overly sympathetic summary of the history of the Confessing Church, see Wolf-Dieter Hauschild, "Bekennende Kirche," *Religion in Geschichte und Gegenwart*, 4th ed., 1:1241–1245. Hereafter, RGG⁴.

5. Bergen, "The Antidoctrinal Church," in *Twisted Cross*, 44–60.

6. There is also evidence of significant disdain for the violence of Kristallnacht on the part of the German populace. See, e.g., Burleigh, *The Third Reich*, 331ff. This attitude was generally not shared by German Christian clergy.

7. Browning, *Ordinary Men*. My brief mention of major events here is not meant to imply, of course, that nothing important happened in between. Others have described adeptly the progression of Nazi aggression against Jews on the lengthy but contingent path to the *Shoah*.

8. See, e.g., Evans, *Third Reich in Power*, 580–610.

9. Burleigh and Wippermann, *Racial State*, 44–45. Hamburg schoolteacher Luise Solmitz, a non-Jewish woman, was married to a Jewish man. The entire fam-

ily, including their children, practiced Christianity. On September 15, 1935, she wrote that the Nuremberg Laws were "our civil death sentence." Despite some of the privileges afforded to Jews in such "mixed marriages," her husband nonetheless lost his citizenship. See Evans, *Third Reich in Power,* 569–570.

10. See, e.g., chapter three here.

11. Lindemann, *"Typisch jüdisch,"* 747–748.

12. Ibid., 748.

13. ADW Berlin CA/AC-S 68, "Deutsche Christen," vol. 3:1935–1937, Günter Niemack, "Gibt es ein Auserwähltes Volk Gottes?" *Prignitzer Generalanzeiger,* September 21, 1935 (copy of a typed manuscript).

14. Niemack, "Gibt es ein Auserwähltes Volk Gottes?"

15. Ibid.

16. "Rassengesetze und christlicher Glaube," *Evangelium im Dritten Reich,* October 20, 1935. See also examples of the "high point of antisemitic agitation" from August until October 1935 regarding the Reich Party Congress's race legislation in *Der Weckruf.* Luther, Stöcker, and Goebbels were frequently cited. Weitenhagen, *Evangelisch und Deutsch,* 173, n. 410.

17. Evans, *Third Reich in Power,* 580; Burleigh, *The Third Reich,* 323–324.

18. Hitler publicly decreed the end of the pogrom on November 10, but arrests of Jewish men continued until November 16, when Heydrich gave the order for the arrests to stop. Evans, *Third Reich in Power,* 585, 590–591, 597; Burleigh, *The Third Reich,* 328.

19. Evans, *Third Reich in Power,* 590; Goeschel, "Suicides of German Jews," especially 27ff.

20. Evans, *Third Reich in Power,* 599.

21. Schairer, "Die Jahveh-Tempel in Deutschland zerstört!" *Deutscher Sonntag,* November 20, 1938, 346.

22. Schairer, "Jahveh-Tempel," 347.

23. Lindemann, *"Typisch jüdisch,"* 255.

24. Otto Dov Kulka, "Popular Christian Attitudes in the Third Reich to National-Socialist Policies towards the Jews," in *Judaism and Christianity under the Impact of National Socialism, 1919–1945,* ed. Kulka and P. R. Mendes-Flohr (Jerusalem: Historical Society of Israel and the Zalman Shazar Center for Jewish History, 1987), 257, in Burleigh, *The Third Reich,* 332–333; Klapproth was killed in action in Russia in 1943. See *Letters and Papers from Prison,* ed. John W. de Gruchy, vol. 8 of *Dietrich Bonhoeffer Works,* 136, 153, 693; Bethge, *Dietrich Bonhoeffer,* 442, 565, 582.

25. Lindemann, *"Typisch jüdisch,"* 260.

26. EZA 7/3688, H. H., "Pfarrer wollen es nicht glauben: Aber Luther hat wirklich so gegen die Juden geschrieben," *Preußische Zeitung,* December 12, 1938.

27. Ibid.

28. Ibid.

29. EZA 7/3688, Letter from Feix to the Protestant Consistory of the Province of East Prussia in Königsberg, December 6, 1938.

30. EZA 7/3688, G. Feix, "Marienwerder/Wpr. Schulungsbrief Nr. 6, Blatt 2."

31. Ibid.

32. Ibid.; this portion of John 8 is a favorite German Christian New Testament passage. In a heated exchange, Jesus, responding to assertions by his Jewish audience that God is their father, replies sharply, "You belong to your father the devil, and you want to carry out your father's desire. He was a murderer from the beginning, not holding to the truth, for there is no truth in him." John 8:44. Norman Beck argues that this and other such New Testament passages are anti-Judaic. See Beck, *Mature Christianity.* For a different view, see Stephen Motyer's discussion of the usage of the term "Jews" (Ιουδαιοι) in John's Gospel. Motyer, *Your Father the Devil?*

33. Feix, "Schulungsbrief."

34. Numerous other examples of Protestant reactions to Kristallnacht could be given. Pieces in *Nationalkirche—Briefe an Deutsche Christen* and *Deutsches Christentum* also cite Luther's *Judenschriften* shortly after Kristallnacht. See Weitenhagen, *Evangelisch und Deutsch,* 328–329, 331–332.

35. See, e.g., Goldhagen, *Hitler's Willing Executioners,* 111; Gerlach, *Witnesses,* 147–148.

36. Schenk, "Der Jenaer Jesus," 177–178; the *Landeskirchenrat* is the regional "Central Council," the "administration, or governing body, of some regional churches." Gerlach, *Witnesses,* 287.

37. Meier, *Kirchenkampf,* 3:681; 1:473–474.

38. Ibid., 2:61–62, 75–76, 140. See also Bergen, "Storm Troopers," 43–45.

39. Martin Sasse, in *Kirchliches Jahrbuch für die Evangelische Kirche in Deutschland, 1933–1944,* ed. Joachim Beckmann (Gütersloh: Bertelsmann, 1948), 162ff., in Meier, *Kirchenkampf,* 2:342.

40. Meier, *Kirchenkampf,* 3:77; Heschel, "Deutsche Theologen," 75; an invitation to members of the German Christian movement in Eisenach to attend the "2nd main conference" of the Eisenach Institute from March 3 through March 5, 1941 mentions that Sasse would lead the conference's closing worship service. LKA Eisenach DC III 2a, letter from Kurt Thieme to the members of the *Markgemeinde* in Eisenach, February 25, 1941.

41. Meier, *Kirchenkampf,* 3:481; Heschel, "Deutsche Theologen," 73.

42. Martin Sasse, "Aufruf des Thür. Landeskirchenrats," *Deutscher Sonntag,* December 4, 1938, 361. In a November 17 meeting, Sasse spoke about the need for decisive action on the part of Thuringian ministers in light of the "new and decisive chapter" in the "struggle for the solution of the Jewish question." After the meeting, a group of forty-eight Thuringian "*Oberpfarrer*" approved unanimously a resolution that included a rejection of the "attitude" of those like Karl Barth and the Provisional Church Leadership (VKL of the Confessing Church) as "an abuse

of the Gospel for purposes traitorous to the Volk" and of all "glorification of the Jewish Volk in the name of Christianity." See Sasse, "Gegen jüdischen Geist in der Kirche! Gemeinsame Erklärung der Oberpfarrer der Thüringer Ev. Kirche," *Deutscher Sonntag,* December 4, 1938, 361.

43. Sasse, "Aufruf," 361.

44. Dungs, "Martin Luther über die Juden: Weg mit Ihnen!" *Deutscher Sonntag,* January 22, 1939, 29.

45. Sasse, *Martin Luther über die Juden: Weg mit Ihnen!* (Freiburg: Sturmhut, 1938) (no page cited), in Gerlach, *Witnesses,* 147.

46. Sasse, *Martin Luther and the Jews,* 4.

47. Ibid., 3.

48. Ibid., 6, 8, 14.

49. This serves as an exception to Gailus's conclusion that Confessing Church pastors were more likely to have descended from families with theological traditions.

50. Rainer Lächele, "Immanuel Schairer (1885–1963)," in Lächele and Thierfelder, *Wir konnten uns nicht entziehen,*175–187, here 175–176.

51. Ibid., 176–177; Meier, *Kirchenkampf,* 2:132–133.

52. Lächele, "Immanuel Schairer," 176–178, 182.

53. Ibid., 182; *Deutscher Sonntag* ceased publication in September 1939, at the onset of the war. See Meier, *Kirchenkampf,* 3:458; Schairer, *Volk-Blut-Gott; Protestantismus und Nationalsozialismus.*

54. Meier, *Kirchenkampf,* 3:330; in the early years of the Third Reich, Schairer was the regional leader of the German Christians in Württemberg and at least initially enjoyed cordial relations with the regional bishop, Theophil Wurm. See ibid., 1:443.

55. Lächele, "Immanuel Schairer," 182–183; he also defied regional church authorities on at least two occasions, once in 1934 and once in 1935, for holding unauthorized German Christian worship services, which competed with local Protestant services. See Schäfer, *Evangelische Landeskirche in Württemberg,* 4:57; Jantzen, "Propaganda, Perseverance, and Protest," 301–302; on the BDM and NS-Frauenschaft, see, e.g., Stephenson, *Women in Nazi Germany.*

56. Lächele, "Immanuel Schairer," 178, 183–184, 186.

57. Ibid., 184–187.

58. Schairer, "Weltbolschewismus und Weltkirche," *Deutscher Sonntag,* October 10, 1937, 274–277; Johannes Schleuning, "Judentum gegen Christentum: Jüdisch-bolschewistischer Vernichtungskampf gegen die christliche Kirche," *Evangelium im Dritten Reich,* March 28, 1937; see also chapters four and six here.

59. Schairer, "Weltbolschewismus und Weltkirche," 274.

60. Ibid., 274–275.

61. Ibid., 275; Herf, *The Jewish Enemy,* 7, 11–12. Hansgeorg Schroth feared the "annihilation" of both religion and the church. See chapter four here.

62. Schairer, "Weltbolschewismus und Weltkirche," 275; on Schroth, see chapter four here; on Hirsch, chapter six.

63. Ibid., 275.

64. Ibid., 275; Schairer's anti-Bolshevism also resonates with typical Nazi thinking, including similar attitudes found in the "criminal orders" of June 1941. See Bartov, *Germany's War and the Holocaust*, 5–8.

65. Schairer, "Weltbolschewismus und Weltkirche," 276; Luther, *Von den Juden*, 527.

66. Schairer also touches briefly on Luther's relationship to "the Jews" in "Germanisierung des Christentum?" *Deutscher Sonntag*, March 6, 1938, 71.

67. Schairer, "Weltbolschewismus und Weltkirche," 276.

68. Ibid.

69. Ibid.

70. Ibid., 277.

71. Ibid. This is a direct and purposeful contradiction of Jesus' words as recorded in Matthew 5:17, where he says, "Do not think that I have come to abolish the Law or the Prophets; I have not come to abolish them but to fulfill them."

72. Schairer, "Weltbolschewismus und Weltkirche," 277.

73. See the introduction here.

74. On the Protestant League, see chapter six here.

75. Schenk, "Der Jenaer Jesus," 216; Weitenhagen, *Evangelisch und Deutsch*, 1, 210–211, 482–483, 387–388; on the "national church" wing of the German Christian movement, see Bergen, *Twisted Cross*, 114–116; Dungs says that the forwarding of the previous meeting report detailing the work of the Institute to soldiers on the front resulted "again and again" in "joyful testimonies." LKA Eisenach DC III 2a, Dungs, "Zur Werbearbeit," *Institut zur Erforschung des jüdischen Einflusses auf das deutsche kirchliche Leben: Arbeitsbericht 1942/43*, 7–8. This document lists Dungs as the Institute's Advertising Committee Director; Bergen, *Twisted Cross*, 59.

76. Schenk, "Der Jenaer Jesus," 216. Dungs could thus request and receive annual reports on the work of the Institute from Grundmann. Grundmann wrote one such report in friendly yet business-like fashion to Dungs on December 18, 1942. In it, he stressed the work of the "Spinoza Working Group," which detailed the seventeenth-century Dutch Jewish philosopher's (supposedly negative) influence on the "German life of faith" in the eighteenth and nineteenth centuries. LKA Eisenach DC III 2a, "Institut zur Erforschung des jüdischen Einflusses auf das deutsche kirchliche Leben—Der wissenschaftliche Leiter—Jena, den 18. Dezember 1942" (addressed to Dungs); Heschel, "When Jesus Was an Aryan," 72, 74.

77. Weitenhagen, *Evangelisch und Deutsch*, 210–212, 256–257, 328–329.

78. Weitenhagen, *Evangelisch und Deutsch*, 473–474; Stuttgart German Christian pastor Georg Schneider includes Luther, Chamberlain, and Rosenberg in his list of "poets of the Redeemer," who he also describes as "representatives of a völkisch religion." Schneider, preface to *Völkische Reformation*, v–vi.

79. Weitenhagen, *Evangelisch und Deutsch*, 473–474.

80. Dungs, in ibid., 99; emphasis in original; *Der Weckruf,* Cologne, 37, 1935, 586 in ibid., 174, n. 413.

81. Dungs, "Neues zur Judenfrage," *Deutscher Sonntag,* December 12, 1937, 340–341.

82. See chapter three here.

83. Dungs, "Neues zur Judenfrage," 340–341.

84. Ibid.; see chapter three here, n. 55.

85. Ibid.

86. Dungs, "Luther über die Juden," 29; a significant article about a discovery in Luther's personal library of a copy of Salvagus Porchetus's "Victoria adversus impios Hebraeos" is presented in *Deutscher Sonntag.* See "Antijüdisches Buch aus Luthers Besitz," November 6, 1938, 330. The author of the article quite correctly deems it significant because of its impact on Luther's *On the Jews and Their Lies* and *On the Ineffable Name.*

87. Dungs, "Luther über die Juden," 29; Dungs cites the title of Linden's work incorrectly, as *Luthers Kampfschriften gegen die Juden.*

88. Ibid.

89. Dungs's engagement with the so-called Jewish Question did not end in 1939. In June 1941, upon introducing the new de-Judaized songbook "Great God, We Praise You" on the Wartburg in Eisenach, Dungs intoned that a Volk that wanted to "take in hand the ultimate solution of the Jewish Question" could "under no circumstances further tolerate residues of the Jewish-Christian spirit." Dungs, speech manuscript, June 13, 1941, LKA Eisenach DC, C VI 2a, 301, in *Kirche, Christen, Juden in Nordelbien, 1933–1945: Die Ausstellung im Landtag 2005,* eds. The President of the Schleswig-Holstein Legislative Assembly, Annette Göhres and Joachim Liß-Walther (Kiel: Schleswig-Holstein Landtag, 2006), http://www.landtag.ltsh.de/export/sites/landtagsh/downloads/infomaterial/schriften reihe/sr-heft-7_kirche-christen-juden.pdf, 117 (accessed July 19, 2011).

90. The close proximity of the publication dates of many of these writings to important events in the progressing Nazi oppression and violence against Jews both demonstrates the significance of these events and suggests a heightened impact on their German Christian readership. In a "word of warning" concerning the Jewish Question, delivered to "the clergymen of the Lutheran Protestant church of Mecklenburg" during what he calls "decisive days," Mecklenburg bishop Walther Schultz demonstrates the "corrupting acts of Judaism" with reference to lengthy quotations from Luther's *Judenschriften.* There is an "'unavoidable obligation'" for the Church, he cries, to "deploy all powers for the de-Judaizing of the religious legacy of our Volk." His word of warning closes with a firm demand to be faithful to the legacy of Martin Luther. Schultz's words were initially printed just one week after Kristallnacht, and covered in *Deutscher Sonntag* on February 5, 1939, less than one week after Hitler, in a speech to the Reichstag on the sixth anniversary of his appoint-

ment as Reich Chancellor, first publicly threatened the "'annihilation of the Jewish race in Europe.'" "Decisive days" they were indeed. See "Der Landesbischof Walter Schultz zur Judenfrage," *Deutscher Sonntag*, February 5, 1939, 44; Schultz, *Kirchlichen Amtsblatt*, November 16, 1938, in Beste, *Kirchenkampf in Mecklenburg*, 219–220; Evans, *Third Reich in Power*, 604. Hitler framed his threat as a sort of "prophecy"; Jeffrey Herf argues that this speech marked a turning point, as from January 30, 1939 Hitler, "in contrast to his public practice between 1919 and 1939" spoke and wrote "with unprecedented clarity, bluntness, and frequency about acting on his threats to exterminate the Jews of Europe." See Herf, *The Jewish Enemy*, 5.

6. Pastors and Theologians from the Unaffiliated Protestant "Middle"

1. Though the numbers are difficult to assess with certainty, we know that there were approximately 18,000 Protestant pastors in 1934, a number that held steady throughout most of the Third Reich. In 1934, there were 5,256 Confessing Church, approximately 6,000 German Christian, and approximately 7,000 Protestant pastors who were not affiliated with either wing. The number of Confessing Church pastors dipped under 5,000 in 1937, and the ranks of German Christian pastors seem also to have decreased over time. See Helmreich, *German Churches under Hitler*, 156, 495, n. 120; Bergen, *Twisted Cross*, 178.

2. This from a May 1936 document produced by the VKL. On the VKL, see here chapter four, n. 97. By this VKL count, twenty-nine professors of Protestant theology were from the Confessing Church, fifty-two were German Christians, and ninety-one were "others" (*Sonstigen*). See Kaufmann, "Einleitung II," 48–49.

3. Hamm, "Rückert als Schüler Karl Holls," 276–277.

4. Weitz, *Weimar Germany*, 251–296; Ericksen, *Theologians under Hitler*, 1–27, here 26.

5. On the *Anschluß*, see Fulbrook, *History of Germany, 1918–2000*, 75–76; the steep rise in the number of students pursuing studies in Protestant theology can be explained by the large number of vacancies in Protestant rectories waiting to be filled across Germany since the mid-1920s, along with the economic and occupational needs of youth in late Weimar. See Kaufmann, "Einleitung II," 32–33; Evans, *Third Reich in Power*, 295.

6. In 1931, over 100,000 students were enrolled in German universities. By 1939, there were just over 40,000. Kaufmann, "Einleitung II," 34–35; Evans, *Third Reich in Power*, 295.

7. Heinrich Steitz, "Heinrich Bornkamm," 88–89; three of the main figures discussed in this book (Vogelsang, Bornkamm, and Hermelink) were professors of church history. See Kaufmann, "Einleitung II," 35–36.

8. Kaufmann, "'Anpassung,'" 139; *Universitätsarchiv Tübingen*, Bestand 207: Nachlaß Hanns Rückert (1901–1974), http://www.uni-tuebingen.de/UAT/w326/w326fram.htm (accessed July 19, 2011); the leader of the National Socialist Profes-

sors League in Leipzig said that he is "recognized as scholarly" but is also "very opaque politically" and is "slightly gruff and unjust" in his judgment about others. Nowak, "Heinrich Bornkamm," 60.

9. Steitz, "Heinrich Bornkamm," 96; Grüttner, *Biographisches Lexikon*, 26.

10. Grüttner, *Biographisches Lexikon*, 26–27.

11. Besier, *Spaltungen und Abwehrkämpfe*, 3:366–367; Bornkamm, *Was erwarten wir*, 14–16, 26; Bergen, *Twisted Cross*, 114–116.

12. Both the dates of Bornkamm's entry into the SA and the date of his exit from the same can be brought into question. Church historian Kurt Nowak accepted Bornkamm's own account in a personnel questionnaire from Leipzig University in May 1945, stating that his membership lasted from April 1934 to December of that same year. Yet, in a 1937 evaluation of Bornkamm, the leader of the National Socialist Professors League in Leipzig said that he had been a member of the SA "since November 1933." In citing this quotation, Nowak placed a "[*sic!*]" after this phrase, choosing to take Bornkamm's postwar defense as accurate. Although acknowledging the danger of assuming the truth of one of these postwar defenses (*Verteidigungen*), he nonetheless chose to believe Bornkamm rather than a "suspicious observer" like the leader of the Professors' League. Such a judgment must be seen in the context of Nowak's overall characterization of Bornkamm's affinity for National Socialism as an aberration for the church historian. Yet, rhetoric from his 1935 book *From Christian to National Socialism*, as well as occasional comments in his other writings encouraging Protestant Christian rapprochement with Nazism cast doubt upon this overly sympathetic conclusion. See below and Nowak, "Heinrich Bornkamm," 55, 60–62, 70, 77; Kaufmann, "'Anpassung,'" 150–151.

13. See, e.g., EZA 550/60, "Kampf um die Reichskirche: Wachsende Opposition innerhalb der Deutschen Christen—Weitere Austrittserklärungen," *Germania*, Berlin, November 27, 1933. Despite rapturous applause from the 20,000 in attendance, scores of church leaders and other theologians—including Kittel—also split with the Berlin leadership of the Faith Movement of German Christians, primarily because of the theological extremism expressed by Reinhold Krause; Bergen, *Twisted Cross*, 17–18, 174.

14. The Röhm purge involved the dismissal, arrest, and murder of the SA's leaders, marking an end to the once-powerful organization's importance in German politics. See Longerich, *Die braunen Bataillone*, 7, 86, 240, 243–244; Bessel, *Political Violence*, 97, 130.

15. Kristallnacht ("the night of broken glass") took place on November 9 and 10, 1938 and involved the destruction of hundreds of Jewish synagogues and businesses across Germany. See chapter five here. Bessel, *Political Violence*, 130, 147, 148.

16. Bornkamm, *Was erwarten wir*, 13; Matthew 28:19. Bornkamm's translation closely parallels Luther's Bible (1545), which has "Darum gehet hin und lehret alle Völker. . . ."

17. Bornkamm, *Was erwarten wir,* 13–14; on Meyer-Erlach and Sasse, see, respectively, chapters three and five here.

18. Ibid., 23–26.

19. Ibid., 42–43; Günther Bornkamm, *Hat Paulus das Christentum verdorben?*

20. Bornkamm, *Was erwarten wir,* 53.

21. Bornkamm, *Vom christlichen zum nationalen Sozialismus,* 4, 10; despite these consistent public pronouncements about the damaging effects of Jews on German life, Bornkamm offered help to at least one Jewish professor, Margarete Bieber, who was fired as a result of Bornkamm's implementation of the Law for the Restoration of the Professional Civil Service at Gießen, where he was serving as rector. See Nowak, "Heinrich Bornkamm," 70–71.

22. Bornkamm, *Was erwarten wir,* 53–54, 8.

23. Leopold Cordier, preface to *Volk, Staat, Kirche,* 3–4. The three-day seminar was given twice, first in Darmstadt and then in Gießen one week later. See Steitz, "Heinrich Bornkamm," 92; the theological faculties often worked in cooperation with local church governments. Church historian Heinrich Steitz comments, "From the outset not only the education of the Hessian ministers, but also cooperation during their continuing education, was incumbent on the Protestant theological faculty. . . . As prelate, [Dr. Wilhelm] Diehl was chairman of the theological examination commission in Gießen. But Diehl also held lectures in Gießen about Hessian church history. Thus the theology students already became acquainted with their future church superiors." Steitz, ibid.

24. Bornkamm, "Volk und Rasse bei Martin Luther," in *Volk, Staat, Kirche,* 5–19, here 5–6.

25. Ibid., 6–7.

26. Ibid., 12–15.

27. Ibid., 15–17; emphasis added.

28. Ibid., 18; after losing his position at Leipzig after the war, Bornkamm was hired by Heidelberg University in 1947. That year, he repackaged most of his Luther essays and published the collection under the title *Luthers geistige Welt* (Luther's World of Thought). Rather remarkably, Bornkamm simply removed most passages that reflected National Socialist racial theory, and removed or softened the tone of passages that reflected Luther's harshest judgments about Jews. See Hartmut Lehmann's insightful essay, "Heinrich Bornkamm im Spiegel seiner Luther-studien von 1933 und 1947," in Kaufmann and Oelke, *Evangelische Kirchenhistoriker,* 367–380.

29. Dr. Hans Otte, *Landeskirchliches Archiv Hannover,* e-mail message to author, February 15, 2006. The personnel records pertaining to Holsten were destroyed in an Allied bombing raid; Henning Wrogemann, "Holsten, Walter," in RGG⁴, 3:1872.

30. From October 1933 until March 1938, Moringen housed female inmates, including some Jews and many Jehovah's Witnesses and Communists. See Jane Caplan, introduction to Gabriele Herz, *The Women's Camp in Moringen,* 1–55, here 1–5; Holsten, in Besier, *Spaltungen und Abwehrkämpfe,* 887.

31. Althaus, "Der Wahrheitsgehalt der Religionen," 282, 284.

32. At the suggestion of the Reich Minister for Church Affairs, Hanns Kerrl, Werner asked these church authorities to "motivate the ministers" in their area of supervision "in an appropriate way to an engagement with the position of Luther on the Jews. . . ." EZA 7/3688, Werner memo to regional Protestant church authorities, April 22, 1939.

33. Holsten, *Christentum*, 13.

34. Ibid., 74. See also Holsten, "Erläuterungen," 533.

35. Holsten, *Christentum*, 99–101, 102–103, 105.

36. On the passage from *On the Jews and Their Lies*, see chapter two here; Holsten, *Christentum*, 112–116; Luther, *Von den Juden*, 482, 520; Luther, *Vom Schem Hamphoras*, 613, 615, 641.

37. Holsten, *Christentum*, 118–121; Luther, *Von den Juden*, 417, 419; Luther, *Vom Schem Hamphoras*, 579, 634; elsewhere Holsten points to passages in Luther that demonstrate that the reformer no longer sought the conversion of the Jewish people, but only the "fortification" of Christians in their faith. See Holsten, ibid., 100–101; in another place, Holsten notes the presence of hope for conversion of Jews in Luther's letter to Josel of Rosheim (1537). See Holsten, "Erläuterungen," 531–532.

38. Holsten, *Christentum*, 122–123.

39. Ibid., 125; Luther, *Von den Juden*, 522, 526.

40. Holsten, *Christentum*, 125–126.

41. Holsten, "Erläuterungen," 527: text 2, 12; 535: text 39, 27. ("text ##, ##" refers to the page and line number in Luther's text upon which Holsten is commenting); Grimsted, "Roads to Ratibor," 406; von Papen, "Vom engagierten Katholiken."

42. In one such instance, Grau leaves open the question of medieval Jewish ritual murder. It is wrong, he complains, "to accept the fact of ritual murder without reservation," which "the Christian historians above all have done." Yet it is "equally incorrect" to assert, as the Jewish researchers have done, that ritual murders could not possibly have occurred. Grau, *Antisemitismus im späten Mittelalter*, 145.

43. Holsten, "Erläuterungen," 537: text 59, 23; emphasis added.

44. Ibid., 537: text 60, 33; ". . . For out of the overflow of the heart the mouth speaks." Matthew 12:34.

45. Holsten, "Erläuterungen," 537–539; emphasis added.

46. If no "energetic measures" are taken against Jews, he argues, Christians make themselves "jointly guilty for Jewish enmity against Christ." Ibid.; emphasis added; 553–554: text 189, 13ff.

47. Ibid., 530: text 28, 10ff.; 553–554: text 189, 13ff. Both Althaus citations are from "Die Frage des Evangeliums an das moderne Judentum," in vol. 2 of Althaus, *Theologische Aufsätze*.

48. Vogelsang, *Luthers Kampf*, 12, in Holsten, "Erläuterungen," 541: text 66, 33. Holsten appeals to this work in several other places. See, e.g., 544: text 95, 27ff.; 545–546: text 101, 30; 553–554: text 189, 13ff., 19.

49. Holsten, "Erläuterungen," 544: text 95, 27. Holsten expresses incredulity in his reading of Lamparter, referring to him as "Protestant (!) pastor Ed. Lamparter." The Lamparter quotation is from Lamparter, *Das Judentum*, 295; Lamparter fought energetically against antisemitism in Weimar Germany. See Niewyk, *The Jews in Weimar Germany*, 59.

50. Ericksen, "Assessing the Heritage," 26; Holsten, "Erläuterungen," 543: text 81, 25; Hirsch, *Die gegenwärtige geistige Lage*, 24.

51. Luther, *Von den Juden*, in *Schriften wider Juden und Türken*, 81.

52. Yet, he also appealed to Althaus, who was no longer part of the German Christians and who never joined the Nazi party. This illustrates that with respect to Jews and Judaism, as with many other matters, Protestant scholars often crossed party affiliation within the German Protestant Church.

53. Hesse won the Nobel Prize for Literature in 1946. Among his most well-known works are *Siddhartha* (1922) and *Das Glasperlenspiel* (The Glass Bead Game; 1943). See Joseph Mileck, *Hermann Hesse: Life and Art* (Berkeley: University of California Press, 1981); he should not be confused with another Hermann Hesse, a Reformed pastor who directed a Confessing Church seminary in Elberfeld, and appears in some of the literature about the Church Struggle. See, e.g., Helmreich, *German Churches under Hitler*, 497, n. 42; pietism was a Protestant movement that originated with Philipp Jakob Spener (1635–1705) and stressed a personal relationship with Christ and devotion to a godly lifestyle, including prayer and regular study of the Bible. Fulbrook, *Concise History of Germany*, 86ff.

54. Jaspert, "Der Kirchenhistoriker," 220; Hammann, "Heinrich Hermelink," 481.

55. HStAM 310, 1992/55, 6219, "*Auszug* aus dem von Prof. Hermelink ausge-füllten Fragebogen der amer. Militärregierung" [the word "Auszug" (excerpt) is underlined in the original typescript of this document]; HStAM 305a, 1992/55, 4291, personal data sheet without title; Hammann, "Heinrich Hermelink," 482; Friedrich Wilhelm Bautz, "Hermelink, Heinrich," BBK, 2:759–760.

56. He lectured after the Second World War at Munich and Tübingen. It is hard to ascertain how long Hermelink's military service lasted during the First World War. On a questionnaire filled out for the American military authorities after the Second World War, he listed his years of military service as "1914–1918." See HStAM 310, 1992/55, 6219, "*Auszug* aus dem von Prof. Hermelink ausgefüllten Fragebogen der amer. Militärregierung"; Hammann, "Heinrich Hermelink," 487; HStAM 307a, 1972/35, 16, Friedrich Heiler, Hermelink Obituary, *Oberhessische Presse*, February 1958; Bautz, "Hermelink," 759–760; Jaspert, "Der Kirchenhisto-riker," 224; Hermelink also wrote an important documentary work on the Church Struggle, which nonetheless reflected much of the mythology surrounding the Confessing Church in the early postwar period. See Hermelink, *Kirche im Kampf*.

57. Life and Work grew out of the efforts of Swedish archbishop Nathan Söder-blom to create an international conference of churches to work for peace during

World War I. More than six hundred delegates from countries across the globe met in August, 1925 to listen to speeches, to give and hear papers, and to worship. The sequel to Life and Work took place in Oxford in 1937. It was hindered by the absence of the German delegation, whose passports were confiscated by the Gestapo just a few weeks before it commenced. As a result of the Oxford Conference, Life and Work merged with other ecumenical organizations to form the World Council of Churches. While Life and Work focused on ethics and society, Faith and Order centered on theology. See Hammann, "Heinrich Hermelink," 485; Barnes, *Nazism, Liberalism, and Christianity*, 7–10, 47; Gerlach, *Witnesses*, 134–135.

58. Seeberg took over the influential chair for church history at Berlin in 1927 for the recently and suddenly deceased Karl Holl, promoting a third way for Lutheran theology, a "Luther Revolution." He traced what he considered "revolutionary" aspects of Luther's theology and attempted to meld them with National Socialism. He cut a decidedly divisive figure and thus is remembered as much for his pro-Nazi views and his run-ins with fellow Protestants as he is for his attempt to carve his own theological legacy. A controversy that erupted in 1937 between Seeberg and several Holl school devotees led to the departure of sixteen members (including Bornkamm and Hanns Rückert) from the Society for Church History (Gesellschaft für Kirchengeschichte), a key organ of the church history subdiscipline. Seeberg's cantankerousness and refusal to apologize to Bornkamm and Rückert for caustic personal comments in the Society's journal were widely regarded for at least exacerbating the dispute, if not causing it altogether. See Kaufmann, "'Anpassung,'" 200–204, 206–210; Klaus-Gunther Wesseling, "Seeberg, Erich," BBK, 10:1297–1304; Lippmann, *Marburger Theologie*, 174.

59. Seeberg, in Meier, *Die Theologischen Fakultäten*, 79, in Lippmann, *Marburger Theologie*, 174, n. 63; Kaufmann, "'Anpassung,'" 242–243, n. 623.

60. The dean of the theology faculty, Hans von Soden, even composed a letter on behalf of the theology students at Marburg, expressing their "esteem and gratitude" to Hermelink for his work; Heiler taught History and Philosophy of Religion at Marburg from 1920–1935. See Bautz, "Heiler, Friedrich," BBK, 2:660–661; Lippmann, *Marburger Theologie*, 176–178.

61. HStAM 305a, 1992/55, 4291, Hermelink to the Reich Culture Minister, March 6, 1935; Jaspert, "Der Kirchenhistoriker," 238.

62. The release from his duties was retroactive to April 1. HStAM 305a, 1992/55, 4291; Lippmann, *Marburger Theologie*, 175–176.

63. Lippmann, *Marburger Theologie*, 174, 176.

64. Heuss, *Erinnerungen*, 332, in Jaspert, "Der Kirchenhistoriker," 230–231.

65. Hammann, "Heinrich Hermelink," 485–486.

66. See Gerlach, *Witnesses*, 69ff.; the search for Hermelink's replacement entailed some bitter ironies and reflected the tensions of the Church Struggle in the Marburg theological faculty. Max Baur, the rector at Marburg, recommended that the university hire Bornkamm to replace Hermelink, despite the known fact

that Bornkamm was already committed to his new position at Leipzig. In doing so, he cited the possibility of bringing the university under "a National Socialist leadership" that would "certainly affect itself for the blessing of our State." Ernst Wolf, a Confessing Church sympathizer, was also advanced as a candidate. In the end, Ernst Benz, a National Socialist sympathizer, was chosen. See HStAM 310, 1978/15, 3705, Baur to the University Curator, October 5, 1934; Emil Balla, on behalf of the Theological Faculty of Marburg University, to the Reich Education Minister, September 29, 1934; Lippmann, *Marburger Theologie*, 185; Klaus-Gunther Wesseling, "Soden, Hans Freiherr von," BBK, 10:714–722; Kaufmann, "Anpassung," 242–243, n. 623.

67. Hermelink, "Zur Theologie Luthers"; Hans Preuss, *Martin Luther, Der Künstler* (1931), *Martin Luther, Der Prophet* (1933), *Martin Luther, Der Deutsche* (1934), *Martin Luther, Der Christenmensch* (1942) (Gütersloh: Bertelsmann); Hermelink, "Die neuere Lutherforschung," 76–77.

68. Hermelink, "Zur Theologie Luthers," 45–46. Hermelink does, however, praise Preuss's "splendidly selected" quotations from Luther.

69. Hermelink, "Zur Theologie Luthers," 46–47; Petersmann and Pauls, *"Entjudung."* Petersmann was a Breslau pastor and regional chairman of the German Christians in Silesia. On Petersmann and Pauls, see von der Osten-Sacken, "Der Nationalsozialistische Lutherforscher Theodor Pauls," 136–141.

70. Hermelink, "Zur Theologie Luthers," 46–47.

71. Ibid., 47–48.

72. The VKL had appointed a "Theological Committee for the Study of the Jewish Question." The committee was charged with creating a "memorandum and a synod declaration on the Jewish question" that was to serve as a model for a Reich Confessing Synod. In November 1936, the VKL asked Hermelink to provide to the committee "two short summarizing essays about 'The position of the Jews in the Middle Ages and in the reformation time' and about 'The position of Luther on the Jews.'" It is not known whether Hermelink responded to their reply. The committee met in Berlin-Dahlem on February 22, 1937. Hermelink does not appear to have published either essay. The proposed Synod never took place. See Röhm and Thierfelder, *Entrechtet, 1935–1938*, 289, n. 524; Junghans, Bibliography of Heinrich Hermelink's works.

73. See chapter one here.

Conclusion

1. Stephenson, *Hitler's Home Front*, 334–335, 341; Fausel recounts in his sermon that when the French captain said to him on April 28 that they had to vacate everything, he believed that they could no longer return home. USHMM Fausel Collection, 9, Printed Sermon Manuscript, "Rufe getrost, schone nicht!" January 5, 1947.

2. Fausel, "Rufe getrost, schone nicht!" 3, 4, 6.

3. See the introduction and chapter four here.

4. USHMM Evangelische Bekenntnisgemeinschaft in Württemberg Collection, "Erklärung der kirchlich-theologischen Sozietät in Württemberg vom 9. April 1946"; it must be remembered that this statement represents the sentiments of a small minority within German Protestantism, even a small minority in the Württemberg churches. The Stuttgart Declaration of Guilt (October 1945), which confessed vaguely that German Protestants had not witnessed, prayed, believed, or loved vigorously enough, and made equivocating allusions to both German suffering and supposedly widespread Protestant resistance to Nazism—while making no direct mention of Jews—was more representative of how German Protestants dealt with their Nazi past in the early postwar years. And, even it was highly controversial for what it did confess and was probably influenced by international and ecumenical ecclesiastical pressure that was brought to bear on the German participants. See Hockenos, *A Church Divided*, 75–100.

BIBLIOGRAPHY

Archival Sources

Archiv des Diakonischen Werkes der EKD (ADW Berlin)
    ADW/CA/AC "Apologetische Centrale"
    ADW/CA/AC-S "Central Ausschuss für Innere Mission (Materialsammlung
    der Apologetischen Centrale)"
Evangelisches Zentralarchiv Berlin (EZA)
    Bestand 7/3688 "Evangelischer Oberkirchenrat. Akten betreffend: das Judentum
    und die antisemitische Bewegung"
    Bestand 50 "Archiv für die Geschichte des Kirchenkampfes"
    Bestand 550 "Zeitungsausschnittsammlung"
Hessisches Staatsarchiv Marburg (HStAM)
    305a "Rektor und Senat 1527–1978"
    307a "Theologische Fakultät 1799–1971"
    310 "Kurator, Verwaltungsdirektor, Kanzler"
Humboldt Universität, Berlin Theology Faculty Library
Landeskirchenarchiv der Ev.-Lutherischen Kirche in Thüringen (LKA Eisenach)
    A 921 "Entjudung der Kirche 1939–47"
    DC II, III "Deutsche Christen"
Landeskirchliches Archiv Berlin-Brandenburg (LKA BB)
    Bestand 1 "Konsistorialakten Berlin-West 1945–1976"
    Bestand 4 "Kirchliche Erziehungskammer Berlin-West 1936–1986"

United States Holocaust Memorial Museum (USHMM)
    RG 14.065M Evangelische Bekenntnisgemeinschaft in Württemberg Collection,
        Microfilm Copy of Landeskirchliches Archiv Stuttgart, D 31 (Ev. Bekenntnis-
        gemeinschaft ca. 1933–1969)
    RG 14.066M Heinrich Fausel Collection, Microfilm Copy of Landeskirchliches
        Archiv Stuttgart, D 33 (Nachlass Fausel ca. 1933–1965)
Universitätsarchiv Jena (UAJ)
    Bestand BA "Rektor und Senat 1834–1945"
    Bestand D "Personalakten 1900ff."
    Bestand J "Theologische Fakultät 1628–1970"
Wiener Library, London

Published Primary Sources

Periodicals

Deutsche Theologie
Deutscher Sonntag
Durchbruch (Stuttgart)
Das Evangelische Westfalen
Evangelium im Dritten Reich
General Anzeiger (Würzburg)
Germania (Berlin)
Junge Kirche
Korrespondenzblatt für die evangelisch-lutherischen Geistlichen in Bayern
Luther: Vierteljahrsschrift der Luthergesellschaft
Lutherjahrbuch
Luthertum
Neue Allgemeine Missionszeitschrift
Oberhessische Presse
Der Präses der Bekenntnissynode der Deutschen Evangelischen Kirche: Bad Oeynhausen
Preußische Zeitung
Preußischer Jahrbücher
Prignitzer Generalanzeiger
Der Provinzialbruderrat der Provinz Sachsen
Der Stürmer
Theologische Rundschau
Der Weckruf (Cologne, 1934–1936)
Der Weckruf (Krefeld, 1933–1934)
Württembergische Bekenntnisgemeinschaft Rundbrief

Books and Articles

Althaus, Paul. *Die Deutsche Stunde der Kirche.* 2nd ed. Göttingen: Vandenhoeck
    & Ruprecht, 1934.

———. *The Ethics of Martin Luther*. Translated by Robert C. Schultz. Philadelphia: Fortress Press, 1972.

———. *Evangelium und Leben: Gesammelte Vorträge*. Gütersloh: Bertelsmann, 1927.

———. *Kirche und Volkstum: Der völkische Wille im Lichte des Evangeliums*. Gütersloh: Bertelsmann, 1928.

———. "Die Stimme des Blutes." In *Der Gegenwärtige: Predigten von Paul Althaus*, 157–168. Gütersloh: Bertelsmann, 1932.

———. *Theologie der Ordnungen*. Gütersloh: Bertelsmann, 1934.

———. *Theologische Aufsätze*. 2 vols. Gütersloh: Bertelsmann, 1929–1935.

———. *Völker vor und nach Christus: Theologische Lehre vom Volke*. Leipzig: Deichert, 1937.

———. "Der Wahrheitsgehalt der Religionen und das Evangelium: Grundsätze der theologischen Kritik aller Religion." *Neue Allgemeine Missionszeitschrift*, 11, 10 (1934): 277–292.

Althaus, Paul, and Werner Elert. "Theologische Gutachten über die Zulassung von Christen jüdischer Herkunft zu den Ämtern der deutschen evangelischen Kirche." *Theologische Blätter*, 12, 11 (1933): 321–323.

Barth, Karl. *Karl Barth—Eduard Thurneysen, Briefwechsel*. Edited by Eduard Thurneysen and Caren Algner. 3 vols. Zurich: Theologischer Verlag, 1973–2000.

———. *Lutherfeier 1933. Theologische Existenz Heute 4*. Munich: Christian Kaiser, 1933.

———. *Theological Existence Today! (A Plea for Theological Freedom)*. Translated by R. Birch Hoyle. London: Hodder and Stoughton, 1933.

Bonhoeffer, Dietrich. *Dietrich Bonhoeffer Works*. Edited by Victoria J. Barnett. 16 vols. Minneapolis: Fortress, 1995–.

———. *Gesammelte Schriften*. Edited by Eberhard Bethge. 6 vols. Munich: Christian Kaiser, 1958–1974.

Borcherdt, H. H., and Georg Merz, eds. *Schriften wider Juden und Türken*. Vol. 3 of *Martin Luther: Ausgewählte Werke*. 2nd ed. Munich: Christian Kaiser, 1938.

Bornkamm, Günther. *Hat Paulus das Christentum verdorben?* Berlin: Verlag des Evangelischen Bundes, 1937.

Bornkamm, Heinrich. "Volk und Rasse bei Martin Luther." In *Volk, Staat, Kirche: Ein Lehrgang der Theologischen Fakultät Gießen*, 5–19. Gießen: Alfred Töpelmann, 1933.

———. *Vom christlichen zum nationalen Sozialismus*. Frankfurt am Main: Diesterweg, 1935.

———. *Was erwarten wir von der deutschen evangelischen Kirche der Zukunft?* Berlin: Verlag des evangelischen Bundes, 1939.

Chamberlain, H. S. *The Foundations of the Nineteenth Century*. Translated by John Lees. 2 vols. London: John Lane, 1910.

Falb, Alfred. *Luther und die Juden*. Munich: Deutscher Volksverlag, 1921.

Gabriel, Walter. *D. Martin Luther Von den Juden: Luthers christlicher Antisemitismus nach seinen Schriften*. Göttingen: Vandenhoeck & Ruprecht, 1936.

Gerstenmaier, Eugen, ed. *Kirche,Volk und Staat*. Berlin: Furche, 1937.

Grau, Wilhelm. *Antisemitismus im späten Mittelalter*. Munich: Duncker and Humblot, 1934.

Grundmann, Walter. *Die Entjudung des religiösen Lebens als Aufgabe deutscher Theologie und Kirche*. Weimar: Deutsche Christen, 1939.

———, ed. *Germanentum, Christentum und Judentum: Studien für Erforschung ihres gegenseitigen Verhältnisses*. 3 vols. Leipzig: Wigand, 1942–1943.

———, ed. *Die völkische Gestalt des Glaubens*. Leipzig: Wigand, 1943.

Hartshorne, E. Y. "The German Universities and the Government." *Annals of the American Academy of Political and Social Science*, 200 (1938): 210–234.

Hermelink, Heinrich. "Die neuere Lutherforschung." *Theologische Rundschau*, 7 (1935): 63–85, 131–156.

———. "Zur Theologie Luthers." *Theologische Rundschau*, 15 (1943): 13–55.

Hirsch, Emanuel. *Die gegenwärtige geistige Lage im Spiegel philosophischer und theologischer Besinnung*. Göttingen: Vandenhoeck & Ruprecht, 1934.

Holsten, Walter. *Christentum und nichtchristliche Religion nach der Auffassung Luthers*. Gütersloh: Bertelsmann, 1932.

———. "Erläuterungen." In Borcherdt and Merz, *Schriften wider Juden und Türken*, 523–579.

Kattermann, Gerhard. "Luthers Handexemplar des antijüdischen Porchetus in der Landesbibliothek Karlsruhe." *Zentralblatt für Bibliothekswesen*, 5 (1938): 45–50.

Kittel, Gerhard. *Die Historischen Voraussetzungen der jüdischen Rassenmischung*. Hamburg: Hanseatische Verlagsanstalt, 1939.

———. *Die Judenfrage*. Stuttgart: Kohlhammer, 1933.

Künneth, Walter. *Evangelische Wahrheit! Ein Wort zu Alfred Rosenbergs Schrift "Protestantische Rompilger."* Berlin: Wichern, 1937.

Lamparter, Eduard. *Das Judentum in seiner Kultur und religionsgeschichtlichen Erscheinung*. Gotha: Leopold Klotz, 1928.

Landesverein für Innere Mission. *Daß Jesus Christus ein geborener Jude sei: Ein Brief D. Martin Luthers wider die Sabbather an einen guten Freund. Martin Luther, Luthers Flugschriften für unsere Zeit*. (MLLF) Booklet 2. Dresden: Landesverein für Innere Mission, 1931.

———. *Vom Schem Hamphoras und vom Geschlecht Christi: Aus Predigten und Tischreden über die Juden*. MLLF Booklet 4. Dresden: Landesverein für Innere Mission, 1931.

———. *Von den Juden und ihren Lügen*. MLLF Booklet 3. Dresden: Landesverein für Innere Mission, 1931.

———. *Von Kaufshandlung und Wucher*. MLLF Booklet 1. Dresden: Landesverein für Innere Mission, 1931.

———. *Von weltlicher Obrigkeit und wie weit man ihr Gehorsam schuldig sei*. MLLF Booklet 5. Dresden: Landesverein für Innere Mission, 1931.

Leffler, Siegfried. *Christus im Dritten Reich der Deutschen: Wesen, Weg, und Ziel der Kirchenbewegung "Deutsche Christen."* Weimar: Deutsche Christen, 1935.

Lewin, Reinhold. *Luthers Stellung zu den Juden: Ein Beitrag zur Geschichte der Juden in Deutschland während des Reformationzeitalters.* Berlin: Trowitzsch and Sohn, 1911.

Linden, Walther. *Luthers Kampfschriften gegen das Judentum.* Berlin: Klinkhardt, 1936.

Ludendorff, Mathilde. *Der ungesühnte Frevel an Luther, Lessing, Mozart, Schiller im Dienste des allmächtigen Baumeisters aller Welten.* Munich: Ludendorffs Volkswarte-Verlag, 1929.

Luther, Martin. *D. Martin Luthers Werke: Kritische Gesamtausgabe.* 120 vols. Weimar: Böhlau, 1883–2009.

———. *Dr. Martin Luthers Briefwechsel.* Edited by Ernst Ludwig Enders et al. 19 vols. Frankfurt a.M.: Evangelischer Verein, 1884–1932.

———. *Luther's Correspondence and Other Contemporary Letters.* Edited and translated by Preserved Smith. 2 vols. Philadelphia: The Lutheran Publication Society, 1913–1918.

———. *Luthers Werke für das christliche Haus.* Edited by Georg Buchwald. 10 vols. 4th ed. Leipzig: M. Heinsius, 1924.

———. *Luthers Werke in Auswahl.* Edited by Otto Clemen. 8 vols. Bonn: Marcus and Weber, 1912–1933.

———. *Luther's Works.* Edited by H. T. Lehman et al. 56 vols. St. Louis: Concordia, 1955–1986.

Meyer-Erlach, Wolf. *Der Einfluss der Juden auf das englische Christentum.* Weimar: Deutsche Christen, 1940.

———. *Ist Gott Engländer?* 4th ed. Freiburg im Breisgau: Sturmhut, 1940.

———. *Juden, Mönche und Luther.* Weimar: Deutsche Christen, 1937.

———. "Luther und Gustav Adolf." In Grundmann, *Die völkische Gestalt des Glaubens,* 2–21.

———. *Universität und Volk: Rektoratsrede über den Neubau der Deutschen Universität.* Jena: Gustav Fischer, 1935.

———. *Verrat an Luther.* Weimar: Deutsche Christen, 1936.

Noack, Joachim. *Luther und die Juden: Dargestellt nach Luthers Schrift "Wider die Jüden und ihre Lügen" von 1543.* Berlin: M. Lühr, 1933.

Parisius, Hans Ludolf, ed. *Von den Juden und ihren Lügen als Volksgaube.* Munich: Ludendorffs Volkswarte-Verlag, 1932.

Pauls, Theodor. *Luther und die Juden: Aus Luthers Kampfschriften gegen die Juden.* Bonn: Bonn University, 1939.

———. *Luther und die Juden: Der Kampf, 1524–1526.* Bonn: Bonn University, 1939.

———. *Luther und die Juden: In der Frühzeit der Reformation, 1513–1524.* Bonn: Bonn University, 1939.

Petersmann, Werner, and Theodor Pauls. *"Entjudung" selbst der Luther-Forschung in der Frage der Stellung Luthers zu den Juden!* 3rd ed. Bonn: Scheur, 1940.

Preuss, Hans. *Martin Luther, Der Christenmensch.* Gütersloh: Bertelsmann, 1942.

——. *Martin Luther, Der Deutsche.* Gütersloh: Bertelsmann, 1934.

——. *Martin Luther, Der Künstler.* Gütersloh: Bertelsmann, 1931.

——. *Martin Luther, Der Prophet.* Gütersloh: Bertelsmann, 1933.

Rosenberg, Alfred. *Das Parteiprogramm: Wesen, Grundsätze und Ziele der NSDAP.* Munich: Zentralverlag der NSDAP, 1922.

Rückert, Hanns. "Luther als Deutscher." *Deutsche Theologie,* Luthersonderheft (November 1933): 10–23.

Sasse, Martin. *Martin Luther and the Jews.* Freiburg: Baer and Bartosch, 1939.

——. *Martin Luther über die Juden: Weg mit Ihnen!* Freiburg: Sturmhut 1938.

Schairer, Immanuel. *Protestantismus und Nationalsozialismus im Austausch ihrer geschichtlichen Sendung.* Munich: Müller, 1934.

——. *Volk-Blut-Gott: Ein Gruß des Evangeliums an die deutsche Freiheitsbewegung.* Berlin: Martin Warneck, 1933.

Schmidt, Gerhard. "Luther und das Alte Testament." *Junge Kirche,* 5, 17 (1937): 712–724.

Schneider, Georg. *Völkische Reformation: Eine Wegweisung zu christdeutscher Einheit.* Stuttgart: Kohlhammer, 1934.

Schroth, Hansgeorg. "Christentum und Judentum." *Das Evangelische Westfalen,* 14, 11 (1937): 150–151.

——. *Ludendorffs Kampf gegen das Christentum.* Berlin: Apologetische Centrale, 1936.

——. *Luther und die Juden.* Berlin: Apologetische Centrale, 1935.

——. *Luthers christlicher Antisemitismus Heute.* Wittenberg: Westdeutscher Lutherverlag, 1937.

Steinlein, Hermann. *Frau Dr. Ludendorffs Phantasien über Luther und die Reformation.* Leipzig: Deichert, 1932.

——. "Luther und das Alte Testament." *Luthertum,* 48 (1937): 172–184, 193–200.

——. "Luther und die Juden" (Book reviews). *Luther: Vierteljahrsschrift der Luthergesellschaft,* 19 (1937): 121–123. Reprint, Amsterdam: Swets and Zeitlinger/ John Benjamins, 1971.

——. "Luthers Judenschriften in volkstümlicher Ausgabe." *Korrespondenzblatt für die evangelisch-lutherischen Geistlichen in Bayern,* 16 January 1933, 24–25.

——. *Luthers Stellung zum Judentum.* Nuremberg: Landesverein für Innere Mission, 1929.

——. "Luthers Stellung zur Frage der Judentaufe." *Junge Kirche,* 3, 18 (1935): 842–846.

Treitschke, Heinrich von. *Luther und die deutsche Nation.* 2nd ed. Berlin: G. Reimer, 1883.

——. "Unsere Aussichten." *Preußischer Jahrbücher,* 44 (1879): 559–576.

Vogelsang, Erich. "Das Deutsche in Luthers Christentum." *Lutherjahrbuch,* 16 (1934): 83–102.

———, trans. *Luthers Hebräerbrief-Vorlesung von 1517/18.* Berlin: de Gruyter, 1930.

———. *Luthers Kampf Gegen die Juden.* Tübingen: J.C.B. Mohr, 1933.

Walther, Wilhelm. *Luther und die Juden und die Antisemiten.* Leipzig: Dörffling and Franke, 1921.

Secondary Sources

Altgeld, Wolfgang. "Religion, Denomination, and Nationalism in Nineteenth-Century Germany." In Smith, *Protestants, Catholics, and Jews,* 49–66.

Arendt, Hannah. *The Origins of Totalitarianism.* 6th ed. London: Deutsch, 1986.

Augustine. *Concerning the City of God against the Pagans.* Translated by Henry Bettenson. New York: Penguin, 1984.

———. "In Answer to the Jews." In *Saint Augustine, Treatises on Marriage and Other Subjects,* vol. 27 of *The Fathers of the Church: A New Translation,* edited by Roy J. Deferrari, translated by Sister Marie Liguori, 387–416. New York: The Fathers of the Church, Inc., 1955.

Bainton, Roland H. *Here I Stand: A Life of Martin Luther.* New York: Abingdon Press, 1950.

———. "Interpretations of the Reformation." *The American Historical Review,* 66, 1 (1960): 74–84.

Baranowski, Shelley. "The Confessing Church and Antisemitism: Protestant Identity, German Nationhood, and the Exclusion of Jews." In Ericksen and Heschel, *Betrayal,* 90–109.

———. *The Confessing Church, Conservative Elites, and the Nazi State.* Lewiston: Edwin Mellen Press, 1986.

———. "Consent and Dissent: The Confessing Church and Conservative Opposition to National Socialism." *The Journal of Modern History,* 59, 1 (1987): 53–78.

Barnes, Kenneth C. "Dietrich Bonhoeffer and Hitler's Persecution of the Jews." In Ericksen and Heschel, *Betrayal,* 110–128.

———. *Nazism, Liberalism, and Christianity: Protestant Social Thought in Germany and Great Britain, 1925–1937.* Lexington: University Press of Kentucky, 1990.

Barnett, Victoria. *For the Soul of the People: Protestant Protest against Hitler.* New York: Oxford University Press, 1992.

Baron, Salo W. "John Calvin and the Jews." In *Essential Papers on Judaism and Christianity in Conflict,* edited by Jeremy Cohen, 380–400. New York: New York University, 1991.

Bartov, Omer. *Germany's War and the Holocaust: Disputed Histories.* Ithaca: Cornell University Press, 2003.

Bauer, Yehuda et al., eds. *Remembering for the Future: Working Papers and Addenda.* 3 vols. Oxford: Pergamon Press, 1989.

Beck, Norman. *Mature Christianity in the Twenty-First Century: The Recognition and Repudiation of the Anti-Jewish Polemic in the New Testament*. New York: Crossroad/Herder and Herder, 1994.

Beckmann, Joachim, ed. *Kirchliches Jahrbuch für die Evangelische Kirche in Deutschland, 1933–1944*. Gütersloh: Bertelsmann, 1948.

Bell, Dean Phillip. "Martin Luther and the Jews: The Reformation, Nazi Germany and Today." In *The Solomon Goldman Lectures*, vol. 7, edited by Dean Phillip Bell, 155–187. Chicago: The Spertus Institute of Jewish Studies, 1999.

Bell, Dean Phillip, and Stephen G. Burnett, eds. *Jews, Judaism, and the Reformation in Sixteenth-Century Germany*. Leiden: Brill, 2006.

Ben-Sasson, Hayim Hillel. "The Reformation in Contemporary Jewish Eyes." *Proceedings of the Israel Academy of Sciences and Humanities*, 4 (1971): 1–88.

Bergen, Doris L. "German Military Chaplains in World War II and the Dilemmas of Legitimacy." *Church History*, 70, 2 (2001): 232–247.

———. "Storm Troopers of Christ: The German Christian Movement and the Ecclesiastical Final Solution." In Ericksen and Heschel, *Betrayal*, 40–67.

———. *Twisted Cross: The German Christian Movement in the Third Reich*. Chapel Hill: University of North Carolina Press, 1996.

———. *War and Genocide: A Concise History of the Holocaust*. Lanham, Md.: Rowman and Littlefield, 2009.

Berger, Peter L., and Thomas Luckmann. *The Social Construction of Reality: A Treatise in the Sociology of Knowledge*. Reprint, New York: Pelican, 1984.

Besier, Gerhard. *Spaltungen und Abwehrkämpfe, 1934–1937*. Vol. 3 of *Die Kirchen und das Dritte Reich*. Berlin: Propyläen, 2001.

Bessel, Richard. *Political Violence and the Rise of Nazism: The Storm Troopers in Eastern Germany, 1925–1934*. London: Yale University Press, 1984.

Beste, Niklot. *Der Kirchenkampf in Mecklenburg von 1933 bis 1945: Geschichte, Dokumente, Erinnerungen*. Göttingen: Vandenhoeck & Ruprecht, 1975.

Bethge, Eberhard. *Dietrich Bonhoeffer: A Biography*. Revised ed. Edited by Victoria J. Barnett. Minneapolis: Fortress, 2000.

Biddiss, Michael. "History as Destiny: Gobineau, H. S. Chamberlain and Spengler." *Transactions of the Royal Historical Society*, 6, 7 (1997): 73–100.

Bienert, Walther. *Martin Luther und die Juden: Ein Quellenbuch mit zeitgenössischen Illustrationen, mit Einführungen und Erläuterungen*. Frankfurt a.M.: Evangelisches Verlagswerk, 1982.

Biographisch-Bibliographisches Kirchenlexikon. 28 vols. Herzberg: Verlag Traugott Bautz, 1990–.

Brady, Thomas A., Jr. "Luther's Social Teaching and the Social Order of His Age." In Dünnhaupt, *The Martin Luther Quincentennial*, 270–290.

Brakelmann, Günter, Martin Greschat, and Werner Jochmann. *Protestantismus und Politik: Werk und Wirkung Adolf Stoeckers*. Hamburg: Christians, 1982.

Bräuer, Siegfried. "Das Lutherjubiläum 1933 und die deutschen Universitäten I." *Theologische Literaturzeitung*, 108 (1983): 641–662.

Brinks, Jan Herman. "Luther and the German State." *Heythrop Journal*, 39, 1 (1998): 1–17.

Brosseder, Johannes. *Luthers Stellung zu den Juden im Spiegel seiner Interpreten: Interpretation und Rezeption von Luthers Schriften und Äusserungen zum Judentum im 19. und 20. Jahrhundert vor allem im deutschsprachigen Raum*. Munich: M. Hueber, 1972.

Browning, Christopher R. *Ordinary Men: Reserve Police Battalion 101 and the Final Solution in Poland*. London: Penguin, 2001.

———. *The Origins of the Final Solution: The Evolution of Nazi Jewish Policy, 1939–1942*. London: Arrow Books, 2005.

Bruch, Rüdiger vom, ed. *Fachbereiche und Fakultäten*. Vol. 2 of *Die Berliner Universität in der NS-Zeit*. Stuttgart: Franz Steiner, 2005.

Burleigh, Michael. *The Third Reich: A New History*. London: Pan Books, 2001.

Burleigh, Michael, and Wolfgang Wippermann. *The Racial State: Germany, 1933–1945*. 14th printing, Cambridge: Cambridge University Press, 2007.

Burnett, Stephen G. "Distorted mirrors: Antonious Margaritha, Johann Buxtorf, and Christian Ethnographies of the Jews." *Sixteenth Century Journal*, 25, 2 (1994): 275–287.

Burrin, Philippe. *Nazi Anti-Semitism: From Prejudice to the Holocaust*. Translated by Janet Lloyd. New York: The New Press, 2005.

———. "Political Religion: The Relevance of a Concept." *History and Memory*, 9, 1–2 (1997): 321–349.

Cesarani, David, and Paul A. Levine, eds. *"Bystanders" to the Holocaust: A Re-Evaluation*. London: Frank Cass, 2002.

Chazan, Robert. *Medieval Stereotypes and Modern Antisemitism*. Berkeley: University of California Press, 1997.

Clark, Christopher M. *The Politics of Conversion: Missionary Protestantism and the Jews in Prussia, 1728–1941*. Oxford: Clarendon Press, 1995.

Conway, John S. *The Nazi Persecution of the Churches, 1933–1945*. London: Weidenfeld and Nicholson, 1968.

Detmers, Achim. "Calvin, the Jews, and Judaism." In Bell and Burnett, *Jews, Judaism, and the Reformation*, 196–217.

Dipper, Theodor. *Die Evangelische Bekenntnisgemeinschaft in Württemberg, 1933–1945: Ein Beitrag zur Geschichte des Kirchenkampfes im Dritten Reich*. Göttingen: Vandenhoeck & Ruprecht, 1966.

Docker, John. "The Enlightenment, Genocide, Postmodernity." *Journal of Genocide Research*, 5, 3 (2003): 339–360.

Dünnhaupt, Gerhard, ed. *The Martin Luther Quincentennial*. Detroit: Wayne State University Press, 1985.

Edwards, Mark U., Jr. *Luther's Last Battles: Politics and Polemics, 1531–46.* Ithaca: Cornell University Press, 1983.

———. "Toward an Understanding of Luther's Attacks on the Jews." In *Christians, Jews, and Other Worlds: Patterns of Conflict and Accommodation,* edited by Phillip F. Gallagher, 1–19. London: University Press of America, 1988.

Eley, Geoff. "What Produces Fascism: Preindustrial Traditions or a Crisis of the Capitalist State?" *Politics and Society,* 12, 2 (1983): 53–82.

Ericksen, Robert P. "Assessing the Heritage: German Protestant Theologians, Nazis, and the 'Jewish Question.'" In Ericksen and Heschel, *Betrayal,* 22–39.

———. "The Political Theology of Paul Althaus." *German Studies Review,* 9, 3 (1986): 547–567.

———. *Theologians under Hitler: Gerhard Kittel, Paul Althaus, and Emanuel Hirsch.* New Haven: Yale University Press, 1985.

Ericksen, Robert P., and Susannah Heschel. "The German Churches and the Holocaust." In *The Historiography of the Holocaust,* edited by Dan Stone, 296–318. New York: Palgrave Macmillan, 2004.

Ericksen, Robert P., and Susannah Heschel, eds. *Betrayal: German Churches and the Holocaust.* Minneapolis: Fortress Press, 1999.

Evans, Richard J. *The Coming of the Third Reich.* London: Penguin, 2004.

———. *The Third Reich in Power: How the Nazis Won Over the Hearts and Minds of a Nation.* London: Penguin, 2006.

Falk, Gerhard. *The Jew in Christian Theology: Martin Luther's Anti-Jewish Vom Schem Hamphoras, Previously Unpublished in English, and Other Milestones in Church Doctrine Concerning Judaism.* Jefferson: McFarland and Company, 1992.

Fredriksen, Paula. *Augustine and the Jews: A Christian Defense of Jews and Judaism.* Paperback edition, New Haven: Yale University Press, 2010.

Friedlander, Henry. "The Manipulation of Language." In *The Holocaust: Ideology, Bureaucracy, and Genocide: The San Jose Papers,* edited by Friedlander and Sybil Milton, 103–113. 2nd printing, Milwood: Kraus International, 1982.

Friedländer, Saul. *The Years of Extermination, 1939–1945.* Vol. 2 of *Nazi Germany and the Jews.* London: Weidenfeld and Nicolson, 2007.

———. *The Years of Persecution, 1933–1939.* Vol. 1 of *Nazi Germany and the Jews.* London: Weidenfeld and Nicolson, 1997.

Friedman, Jerome. "The Reformation in Alien Eyes: Jewish Perceptions of Christian Troubles." *Sixteenth Century Journal,* 14, 1 (1983): 23–40.

Fulbrook, Mary. *A Concise History of Germany.* 2nd ed. Cambridge: Cambridge University Press, 2004.

———. *History of Germany, 1918–2000: The Divided Nation.* 2nd ed. Oxford: Blackwell, 2002.

Gailus, Manfred. "Overwhelmed by Their Own Fascination with the 'Ideas of 1933': Berlin's Protestant Social Milieu in the Third Reich." Translated by Pamela Selwyn. *German History,* 20, 4 (2002): 462–93.

———. *Protestantismus und Nationalsozialismus: Studien zur nationalsozialistischen Durchdringung des protestantischen Sozialmilieus in Berlin.* Cologne: Böhlau, 2001.

Gerlach, Wolfgang. *And the Witnesses Were Silent: The Confessing Church and the Persecution of the Jews.* Translated by Victoria J. Barnett. Lincoln: University of Nebraska Press, 2000.

Gilman, Sander L. "Martin Luther and the Self-Hating Jews." In Dünnhaupt, *The Martin Luther Quincentennial,* 79–87.

Ginzel, Günther, ed. *Antisemitismus: Erscheinungsformen der Judenfeindschaft gestern und Heute.* Bielefeld: Verlag Wissenschaft und Politik, 1991.

Goeschel, Christian. "Suicides of German Jews in the Third Reich." *German History,* 25, 1 (2007): 22–45.

Goldhagen, Daniel J. *Hitler's Willing Executioners.* New York: Vintage Books, 1997.

Gow, Andrew Colin. *The Red Jews: Antisemitism in an Apocalyptic Age, 1200–1600.* Edited by Heiko A. Oberman. Leiden: Brill, 1995.

Graetz, Heinrich. *History of the Jews.* 6 vols. Philadelphia: The Jewish Publication Society of America, 1967.

Grimm, Harold J. "Luther Research since 1920." *Journal of Modern History,* 32, 2 (1960): 105–118.

Grimsted, Patricia Kennedy. "Roads to Ratibor: Library and Archival Plunder by the Einsatzstab Reichsleiter Rosenberg." *Holocaust and Genocide Studies,* 19, 3 (2005): 390–458.

Gritsch, Eric W. "Was Luther Anti-Semitic?" *Christian History, 12, 3 (1993): 38–39.*

Grüttner, Michael. *Biographisches Lexikon zur nationalsozialistischen Wissenschaftspolitik.* Heidelberg: Synchron, 2004.

———. "German Universities under the Swastika." In *Universities under Dictatorship,* edited by John Connelly and Michael Grüttner, 75–112. University Park: Pennsylvania State University Press, 2005.

———. *Studenten im Dritten Reich.* Paderborn: Ferdinand Schöningh, 1995.

Gutteridge, Richard. *Open Thy Mouth for the Dumb! The German Evangelical Church and the Jews, 1879–1950.* Oxford: Blackwell, 1976.

Hagen, Kenneth. "Luther's So-Called *Judenschriften:* A Genre Approach." *Archiv für Reformationsgeschichte,* 90 (1999): 130–158.

Halpern-Amaru, Betsy. "Martin Luther and Jewish Mirrors." *Jewish Social Studies,* 46 (1984): 95–102.

Hamm, Berndt. "Hanns Rückert als Schüler Karl Holls: Das Paradigma einer theologischen Anfälligkeit für den Nationalsozialismus." In Kaufmann and Oelke, *Evangelische Kirchenhistoriker,* 273–309.

Hammann, Konrad. "Heinrich Hermelink als Reformationshistoriker." *Zeitschrift für Theologie und Kirche,* 96, 4 (1999): 480–507.

Harrowitz, Nancy A., ed. *Tainted Greatness: Antisemitism and Cultural Heroes.* Philadelphia: Temple University Press, 1994.

Haynes, Stephen R. *Reluctant Witnesses: Jews and the Christian Imagination.* Louisville: Westminster John Knox, 1995.

Helmreich, Ernst C. *The German Churches under Hitler: Background, Struggle, and Epilogue.* Detroit: Wayne State University Press, 1979.

Henrich, Sarah, and James L. Boyce. "Martin Luther: Translations of Two Prefaces on Islam: *Preface to the* Libellus de ritu et moribus Turcorum (1530), and *Preface to* Bibliander's Edition of the Qur'an (1543)." *Word and World,* 16, 2 (1996): 250–266.

Herf, Jeffrey. *The Jewish Enemy: Nazi Propaganda during World War II and the Holocaust.* London: Belknap Press, 2006.

Hermelink, Heinrich, ed. *Kirche im Kampf: Dokumente des Widerstands und des Aufbaus in der evangelischen Kirche Deutschlands von 1933 bis 1945.* Stuttgart: Wunderlich, 1950.

Herz, Gabriele. *The Women's Camp in Moringen: A Memoir of Imprisonment in Germany, 1936–1937.* Edited by Jane Caplan. Translated by Hildegard Herz and Howard Hartig. Oxford: Berghahn, 2006.

Heschel, Susannah. *The Aryan Jesus: Christian Theologians and the Bible in Nazi Germany.* Princeton: Princeton University Press, 2008.

———. "Deutsche Theologen für Hitler." In von der Osten-Sacken, *Das Mißbrauchte Evangelium,* 70–90.

———. "Nazifying Christian Theology: Walter Grundmann and the Institute for the Study and Eradication of Jewish Influence on German Church Life." *Church History,* 63, 4 (1994): 587–605.

———. "When Jesus Was an Aryan: The Protestant Church and Antisemitic Propaganda." In Ericksen and Heschel, *Betrayal,* 68–89.

Hetzer, Tanja. *"Deutsche Stunde": Volksgemeinschaft und Antisemitismus in der politischen Theologie bei Paul Althaus.* Munich: Allitera, 2009.

Heuss, Theodor. *Erinnerungen, 1905–1933.* 3rd ed. Tübingen: Rainer Wunderlich, 1963.

Hilberg, Raul. *Perpetrators, Victims, Bystanders: The Jewish Catastrophe, 1933–1945.* Paperback edition, New York: HarperPerennial, 1993.

Hinz-Wessels, Annette. *Die Evangelische Kirchengemeinde Bonn in der Zeit des Nationalsozialismus (1933–1945).* Cologne: Rheinland-Verlag, 1996.

Hobbs, R. Gerald. "Bucer, the Jews, and Judaism." In Bell and Burnett, *Jews, Judaism, and the Reformation,* 137–169.

Hockenos, Matthew D. *A Church Divided: German Protestants Confront the Nazi Past.* Bloomington: Indiana University Press, 2004.

Hoover, A. J. "German Christian Nationalism: Its Contribution to the Holocaust." In Bauer, *Jews and Christians during and after the Holocaust,* vol. 1 of *Remembering for the Future,* 62–71.

Hoßfeld, Uwe, Jürgen John, Oliver Lemuth, and Rüdiger Stutz. *"Kämpferische Wissenschaft": Studien zur Universität Jena im Nationalsozialismus.* Cologne: Böhlau, 2003.

Hsia, R. Po-chia. *The Myth of Ritual Murder: Jews and Magic in Reformation Germany*. New Haven: Yale University Press, 1988.

Jantzen, Kyle. *Faith and Fatherland: Parish Politics in Hitler's Germany*. Minneapolis: Fortress Press, 2008.

———. "Propaganda, Perseverance, and Protest: Strategies for Clerical Survival Amid the German Church Struggle." *Church History*, 70, 2 (2001): 295–327.

Jaspert, Bernd. "Der Kirchenhistoriker Heinrich Hermelink." In Jaspert, *Theologie und Geschichte*, vol. 1, 219–239.

———. *Theologie und Geschichte: Gesammelte Aufsätze*. 3 vols. Frankfurt am Main: Peter Lang, 1989–1999.

Junghans, H. Bibliography of Heinrich Hermelink's works, *Theologische Literaturzeitung*, 84, 7 (1959): 551–559.

Kammerling, Joy. "Andreas Osiander, the Jews, and Judaism." In Bell and Burnett, *Jews, Judaism, and the Reformation*, 219–247.

Kaufmann, Thomas. "'Anpassung' als historiographisches Konzept und als theologiepolitisches Programm: Der Kirchenhistoriker Erich Seeberg in der Zeit der Weimarer Republik und des 'Dritten Reiches.'" In Kaufmann and Oelke, *Evangelische Kirchenhistoriker*, 122–272.

———. "Einleitung II: Anmerkungen zu generationsspezifischen Bedingungen und Dispositionen." In Kaufmann and Oelke, *Evangelische Kirchenhistoriker*, 32–54.

———. "Luther and the Jews." In Bell and Burnett, *Jews, Judaism, and the Reformation*, 69–104.

———. *Luthers "Judenschriften" in ihren historischen Kontexten*. Göttingen: Vandenhoeck & Ruprecht, 2005.

Kaufmann, Thomas, and Harry Oelke, eds. *Evangelische Kirchenhistoriker im "Dritten Reich."* Gütersloh: Christian Kaiser, 2002.

Kaye, James, and Bo Stråth, eds. *Enlightenment and Genocide, Contradictions of Modernity*. Brussels: P.I.E.– Peter Lang, 2000.

Kershaw, Ian. "German Popular Opinion and the 'Jewish Question', 1939–1943: Some Further Reflections." In *Juden im Nationalsozialistischen Deutschland–– The Jews in Nazi Germany 1933–1943*, edited by Arnold Paucker, 365–388. Tübingen: J.C.B. Mohr, 1986.

———. *Hitler, 1889–1936: Hubris*. Paperback edition, New York: W.W. Norton and Company, 2000.

———. *The "Hitler Myth": Image and Reality in the Third Reich*. Re-issue, Oxford: Oxford University Press, 2001.

Kertzer, David I. *The Popes against the Jews: The Vatican's Role in the Rise of Modern Anti-Semitism*. New York: Knopf, 2001.

Klepper, Deeana Copeland. *The Insight of Unbelievers: Nicholas of Lyra and Christian Reading of Jewish Text in the Later Middle Ages*. Philadelphia: University of Pennsylvania Press, 2008.

Koonz, Claudia. *The Nazi Conscience*. London: Belknap Press, 2003.

Kremers, Heinz, ed. *Die Juden und Martin Luther—Martin Luther und die Juden: Geschichte, Wirkungsgeschichte, Herausforderung.* Dusseldorf: Neukirchener Verlag, 1985.

Kulka, Otto Dov. "The German Population and the Jews: State of Research and New Perspectives." In *Probing the Depths of German Antisemitism: German Society and the Persecution of the Jews, 1933-1941,* edited by David Bankier, 271-281. Jerusalem: Yad Vashem, 2000.

Kupisch, Karl. "The 'Luther Renaissance.'" *Journal of Contemporary History,* 2, 4 (1967): 39-49.

Lächele, Rainer. *Ein Volk, ein Reich, ein Glaube: Die "Deutschen Christen" in Württemberg, 1925-1960.* Stuttgart: Calwer, 1994.

Lächele, Rainer, and Jörg Thierfelder, eds. *Wir konnten uns nicht entziehen: 30 Porträts zu Kirche und Nationalsozialismus in Württemberg.* Stuttgart: Quell, 1998.

Langmuir, Gavin I. "Continuities, Discontinuities and Contingencies of the Holocaust." In *The Fate of the European Jews, 1939-1945: Continuity or Contingency?,* edited by Jonathan Frankel, 9-29. New York: Oxford University Press, 1997.

———. *History, Religion, and Antisemitism.* Berkeley: University of California Press, 1990.

———. "Prolegomena to any Present Analysis of Hostility against Jews." *Social Science Information,* 15, 4 (1976): 689-727.

———. *Toward a Definition of Antisemitism.* Berkeley: University of California Press, 1990.

Lazare, Bernard. *Antisemitism: Its History and Causes.* Translator not identified. Lincoln, Nebraska: University of Nebraska Press, 1995.

Lehmann, Hartmut. "The Germans as a Chosen People: Old Testament Themes in German Nationalism." *German Studies Review,* 14, 2 (1991): 261-273.

———. "Hans Preuß 1933 über 'Luther und Hitler.'" *Kirchliche Zeitgeschichte,* 12, 1 (1999): 287-296.

———. "Heinrich Bornkamm im Spiegel seiner Luther-studien von 1933 und 1947." In Kaufmann and Oelke, *Evangelische Kirchenhistoriker,* 367-380.

Lindberg, Carter. "Tainted Greatness: Luther's Attitudes toward Judaism and Their Historical Reception." In Harrowitz, *Tainted Greatness,* 15-35.

Lindemann, Albert S. *Esau's Tears: Modern Anti-Semitism and the Rise of the Jews.* Cambridge: Cambridge University Press, 1997.

Lindemann, Albert, and Richard S. Levy, eds. *Antisemitism: A History.* Oxford: Oxford University Press, 2010.

Lindemann, Gerhard. *"Typisch jüdisch": Die Stellung der Ev.-luth. Landeskirche Hannovers zu Antijudaismus, Judenfeindschaft und Antisemitismus, 1919-1949.* Berlin: Duncker and Humblot, 1998.

Lippmann, Andreas. *Marburger Theologie im Nationalsozialismus.* Munich: K.G. Saur, 2003.

Littell, Franklin H. "The Holocaust and the Christians." *Journal of Church and State*, 41, 4 (1999): 725–738.

Locke, Hubert G., and Marcia Sachs Littell, eds. *Holocaust and Church Struggle: Religion, Power, and the Politics of Resistance*. Vol. 16 of *Studies in the Shoah*. Lanham, Md.: University Press of America, 1996.

Longerich, Peter. *Die braunen Bataillone: Geschichte der SA*. Munich: C.H. Beck, 1988.

Maurer, Wilhelm. *Kirche und Synagoge: Motive und Formen der Auseinandersetzung der Kirche mit dem Judentum im Laufe der Geschichte. Franz Delitzsch-Vorlesungen 1951*. Stuttgart: Kohlhammer, 1953.

———. "Die Zeit der Reformation." In *Kirche und Synagoge: Handbuch zur Geschichte von Christen und Juden. Darstellung mit Quellen*, vol. 1, edited by Karl-Heinrich Rengstorf and Siegfried von Kortzfleisch, 363–452. Stuttgart: Klett, 1968.

Meier, Kurt. *Die Deutschen Christen: Das Bild einer Bewegung im Kirchenkampf des Dritten Reiches*. 3rd ed. Göttingen: Vandenhoeck & Ruprecht, 1967.

———. *Der Evangelische Kirchenkampf*. 3 vols. Göttingen: Vandenhoeck & Ruprecht, 1976–1984.

———. *Kirche und Judentum: Die Haltung der evangelischen Kirche zur Judenpolitik des Dritten Reiches*. Göttingen: Vandenhoeck & Ruprecht, 1968.

———. *Die Theologischen Fakultäten im Dritten Reich*. Berlin: de Gruyter, 1996.

Mensing, Björn. *Pfarrer und Nationalsozialismus: Geschichte einer Verstrickung am Beispiel der Evangelisch-Lutherischen Kirche in Bayern*. Göttingen: Vandenhoeck & Ruprecht, 1998.

Meyer, Michael A. "Heinrich Graetz and Heinrich von Treitschke: A Comparison of Their Historical Images of the Modern Jew." *Modern Judaism*, 6, 1 (1986): 1–11.

Möller, Bernd. *Luther-Rezeption: Kirchenhistorische Aufsätze zur Reformationsgeschichte*. Edited by Johannes Schilling. Göttingen: Vandenhoeck & Ruprecht, 2001.

Motyer, Stephen. *Your Father the Devil? A New Approach to John and "the Jews."* Carlisle, England: Paternoster, 1997.

Niewyk, Donald L. *The Jews in Weimar Germany*. 2nd ed. New Brunswick, N.J.: Transaction Publishers, 2001.

Norden, Günther van. *Politischer Kirchenkampf: Die rheinische Provinzialkirche, 1934–1939*. Bonn: Habelt, 2003.

Nowak, Kurt. "Zeiterfahrung und Kirchengeschichtsschreibung. Heinrich Bornkamm im Dritten Reich." *Zeitschrift für Kirchengeschichte*, 103, 1 (1992): 46–80.

Oberman, Heiko A. *Luther: Man Between God and the Devil*. Translated by Eileen Walliser-Schwarzbart. New York: Doubleday, 1992.

———. *The Roots of Anti-Semitism in the Age of Renaissance and Reformation*. Translated by James I. Porter. Philadelphia: Fortress Press, 1984.

———. "*Teufelsdreck:* Eschatology and Scatology in the 'Old' Luther." *Sixteenth Century Journal,* 19, 3 (1988): 435–450.

Osten-Sacken, Peter von der. *Martin Luther und die Juden: Neu untersucht anhand von Anton Margarithas "Der gantz Jüdisch glaub" (1530/31).* Stuttgart: Kohlhammer, 2002.

———, ed. *Das Mißbrauchte Evangelium: Studien zu Theologie und Praxis der Thüringer Deutsche Christen.* Berlin: Institut Kirche und Judentum, 2002.

———. "Der Nationalsozialistische Lutherforscher Theodor Pauls: Vervollständigung eines Fragmentarischen Bildes." In von der Osten-Sacken, *Das Mißbrauchte Evangelium,* 136–166.

Papen, Patricia von. "'Scholarly' Antisemitism during the Third Reich: The Reichsinstitut's Research on the 'Jewish Question,' 1935–1945." Ph.D. diss., Columbia University, 1998.

———. "Vom engagierten Katholiken zum Rassenantisemiten: Die Karriere des Historikers 'der Judenfrage' Wilhelm Grau." In *Theologische Wissenschaft im "Dritten Reich": Ein ökumenisches Projekt,* edited by Georg Denzler and Leonore Siegele-Wenschkewitz, 68–113. Frankfurt: Haag and Herchen, 2000.

Plantinga, Alvin. "Reason and Belief in God." In *Faith and Rationality: Reason and Belief in God,* edited by Plantinga and Nicholas Wolterstoff, 16–90. Notre Dame, Ind.: University of Notre Dame Press, 1983.

Pöhlmann, Matthias. *Kampf der Geister: Die Publizistik der "Apologetischen Centrale," 1921–1937.* Stuttgart: Kohlhammer, 1998.

Poliakov, Léon. *From the Time of Christ to the Court Jews.* Vol. 1 of *The History of Anti-Semitism.* Translated by Richard Howard. Philadelphia: University of Pennsylvania Press, 2003.

The President of the Schleswig-Holstein Legislative Assembly, Annette Göhres, and Joachim Liß-Walther, eds. *Kirche, Christen, Juden in Nordelbien, 1933–1945: Die Ausstellung im Landtag 2005.* Kiel: Schleswig-Holstein Landtag, 2006.

Probst, Christopher J. "Protestant Responses to Martin Luther's 'Judenschriften' in Germany, 1929–1945." Ph.D. diss., University of London, 2008.

Pulzer, Peter G. J. *The Rise of Political Anti-Semitism in Germany and Austria.* Revised ed. London: Halban, 1988.

Raschzok, Klaus. "Wolf Meyer-Erlach und Hans Asmussen: Ein Vergleich zwischen der Praktischen Theologie der Deutschen Christen und der Bekennenden Kirche." In *Zwischen Volk und Bekenntnis: Praktische Theologie im Dritten Reich,* edited by Klaus Raschzok, 167–202. Leipzig: Evangelische Verlagsanstalt, 2000.

Religion in Geschichte und Gegenwart: Handwörterbuch für Theologie und Religionswissenschaft. Edited by Hans Dieter Betz et al. 8 vols. 4th ed. Tübingen: Mohr Siebeck, 1998–2007.

Remy, Steven P. *The Heidelberg Myth: The Nazification and Denazification of a German University.* Cambridge, Massachusetts: Harvard University Press, 2002.

——. "'We are no longer the university of the liberal age': The Humanities and National Socialism at Heidelberg." In *Nazi Germany and the Humanities,* edited by Wolfgang Bialas and Anson Rabinbach, 21–49. Oxford: Oneworld, 2007.

Richarz, Monika, ed. *Jewish Life in Germany: Memoirs from Three Centuries.* Translated by Stella P. Rosenfeld and Sidney Rosenfeld. Bloomington: Indiana University Press, 1991.

Röhm, Eberhard, and Jörg Thierfelder. *Juden-Christen-Deutsche.* 4 vols. Stuttgart: Calwer, 1990–2007.

Roper, Lyndal. "Martin Luther's Body: The 'Stout Doctor' and His Biographers." *The American Historical Review,* 115, 2 (2010): 351–384.

Rowan, Steven. "Luther, Bucer, and Eck on the Jews." *Sixteenth Century Journal,* 16, 1 (1985): 79–90.

Schäfer, Gerhard. *Die evangelische Landeskirche in Württemberg und der National-sozialismus: Eine Dokumentation zum Kirchenkampf.* 6 vols. Stuttgart: Calwer, 1971–1986.

Schenk, Wolfgang. "Der Jenaer Jesus: Zu Werk und Wirken des völkischen Theologen Walter Grundmann und seiner Kollegen." In von der Osten-Sacken, *Das Mißbrauchte Evangelium,* 167–279.

Scholder, Klaus. *The Churches and the Third Reich.* Translated by John Bowden. 2 vols. London: SCM Press, 1987–1988.

Siegele-Wenschkewitz, Leonore. *Neutestamentliche Wissenschaft vor der Judenfrage: Gerhard Kittels theologische Arbeit im Wandel deutscher Geschichte.* Munich: Christian Kaiser, 1980.

——. "New Testament Scholarship and the Nazi-State: Christian Responsibility and Guilt in the Holocaust." In Bauer, *The Impact of the Holocaust and Genocide on Jews and Christians,* vol. 3 of *Remembering for the Future,* 2717–2727.

Siegele-Wenschkewitz, Leonore, and Carsten Nicolaisen, eds. *Theologische Fakultäten im Nationalsozialismus.* Göttingen: Vandenhoeck & Ruprecht, 1993.

Skinner, Quentin. "Meaning and Understanding in the History of Ideas." In Tully, *Meaning and Context,* 29–67.

Smith, David Norman. "The Social Construction of Enemies." *Sociological Theory,* 14, 3 (1996): 203–240.

Smith, Helmut Walser, ed. *Protestants, Catholics, and Jews in Germany, 1800–1914.* Oxford: Berg, 2001.

Sonne, Hans-Joachim. *Die politische Theologie der Deutschen Christen.* Göttingen: Vandenhoeck & Ruprecht, 1982.

Spicer, Kevin P., ed. *Antisemitism, Christian Ambivalence, and the Holocaust.* Bloomington: Indiana University Press, 2007.

Stayer, James M. *Martin Luther, German Saviour: German Evangelical Theological Factions and the Interpretation of Luther, 1917–1933.* Montreal: McGill-Queens University Press, 2000.

Steigmann-Gall, Richard. *The Holy Reich: Nazi Conceptions of Christianity, 1919–1945.* Cambridge: Cambridge University Press, 2003.

Steinweis, Alan E. *Studying the Jew: Scholarly Antisemitism in Nazi Germany.* Cambridge, Mass.: Harvard University Press, 2006.

Steitz, Heinrich. "Heinrich Bornkamm (1901–1977): Theologe und Kirchenhistoriker." In *Gießener Gelehrte in der ersten Hälfte des 20. Jahrhunderts,* edited by Hans Georg Gundel, Peter Moraw, and Volker Press, 87–98. Marburg: Elwert, 1982.

Stephenson, Jill. *Hitler's Home Front: Württemberg under the Nazis.* New York: Continuum, 2006.

———. *Women in Nazi Germany.* Harlow, England: Longman, 2001.

Stern, Selma. *Josel of Rosheim: Commander of Jewry in the Holy Roman Empire of the German Nation.* Translated by Gertrude Hirschler. Philadelphia: The Jewish Publication Society of America, 1965.

Stone, Dan. *Histories of the Holocaust.* Oxford: Oxford University Press, 2010.

———. "Modernity and Violence: Theoretical Reflections on the Einsatzgruppen." *Journal of Genocide Research,* 1, 3 (1999): 367–378.

Sucher, C. Bernd. *Luthers Stellung zu den Juden: Eine Interpretation aus germanistischer Sicht.* Munich: Nieuwkoop B. Degraaf, 1977.

Tal, Uriel. *Christians and Jews in Germany: Religion, Politics, and Ideology in the Second Reich, 1871–1914.* Translated by Noah Jonathan Jacobs. Ithaca, N.Y.: Cornell University Press, 1975.

———. *Religion, Politics and Ideology in the Third Reich: Selected Essays.* London: Routledge, 2004.

Tilgner, Wolfgang. *Volksnomostheologie und Schöpfungsglaube: Ein Beitrag zur Geschichte des Kirchenkampfes.* Göttingen: Vandenhoeck & Ruprecht, 1966.

Trachtenberg, Joshua. *The Devil and the Jews: The Medieval Conception of the Jews and Its Relation to Modern Anti-Semitism.* 2nd paperback edition, Philadelphia: The Jewish Publication Society of America, 1983.

Tracy, James, ed. *Luther and the Modern State in Germany.* Vol. 7 of *Sixteenth Century Essays and Studies.* Kirksville: Truman State University Press, 1986.

Tully, James, ed. *Meaning and Context: Quentin Skinner and his Critics.* Cambridge: Polity Press, 1988.

———. "The Pen Is a Mighty Sword: Quentin Skinner's Analysis of Politics." In Tully, *Meaning and Context,* 7–25.

Voegelin, Eric. *Die politischen Religionen.* Edited by Peter J. Opitz. 2nd ed. Munich: Wilhelm Fink Verlag, 1996.

Volkov, Shulamit. "Antisemitism as a Cultural Code: Reflections on the History and Historiography of Antisemitism in Imperial Germany." In *Leo Baeck Institute Yearbook* 23 (1978): 25–46.

———. *Germans, Jews, and Antisemites: Trials in Emancipation.* Cambridge: Cambridge University Press, 2006.

Vollnhals, Clemens. *Evangelische Kirche und Entnazifizierung 1945–1949: Die Last der nationalsozialistischen Vergangenheit*. Munich: Oldenbourg, 1989.

Wallmann, Johannes. "The Reception of Luther's Writings on the Jews from the Reformation to the End of the 19th Century." *Lutheran Quarterly*, 1, 1 (1987): 72–97.

Weinreich, Max. *Hitler's Professors: The Part of Scholarship in Germany's Crimes against the Jewish People*. 2nd ed. New Haven, Conn.:Yale University Press, 1999.

Weitenhagen, Holger. *Evangelisch und Deutsch: Heinz Dungs und die Pressepolitik der Deutschen Christen*. Cologne: Rheinland-Verlag, 2001.

Weitz, Eric D. *Weimar Germany: Promise and Tragedy*. Princeton: Princeton University Press, 2007.

Wengert, Timothy J. "Philip Melanchthon and the Jews: A Reappraisal." In Bell and Burnett, *Jews, Judaism, and the Reformation*, 105–135.

Wiese, Christian. "'Unheilsspuren': Zur Rezeption von Martin Luthers 'Judenschriften' im Kontext antisemitischen Denkens in den Jahrzehnten vor der Schoah." In von der Osten-Sacken, *Das Mißbrauchte Evangelium*, 91–135.

Wokler, Robert. "The Enlightenment Project on the Eve of the Holocaust." In Kaye and Stråth, *Enlightenment and Genocide*, 59–79.

Zabel, James A. *Nazism and the Pastors: A Study of the Ideas of Three Deutsche Christen Groups*. Missoula, Mont.: Scholars Press, 1976.

INDEX

Page numbers in italics refer to illustrations.

Education Ministry, under Nazis, 61,
163
Edwards, Mark, 50; on Luther's
diatribes as theology, 51–52; on
Luther's physical and mental ill-
ness, 53, 55–56; Oberman's critiques of, 188n75, 189n80
Eisenach Institute (Institute for
Research into and Elimination
of Jewish Influence in German
Church Life), 191n20; German
Christians and, 128, 136, 140,
203n40; goals of, 128, 135, 188n73;
Meyer-Erlach's influence through,
60, 69–70, 73–74
Elert, Werner, 31, 167
emancipation, vs. antisemitism, 8,
22–23
emigration, Jewish, 123
employment, restrictions on Jews', 11,
98, 164–165, 180n38
end-time scenario, Luther's, 46, 102
England, Meyer-Erlach linking Judaism to, 72, 75
Enlightenment, 5–6, 38, 67, 103, 114,
145. See also anti-Enlightenment
thinking
Erlangen University, 31; Althaus's
influence from position at, 9–10, 27,
35; Jews blocked from, 30; theological faculty, 27, 31, 35, 167
Eucharist. See host, sacred, Jews
accused of desecration of
Evans, Richard, 195n2
expulsion of Jews, Luther recommending, 66, 110, 112

Faith Movement of German Christians, 30, 151, 208n13
Fausel, Heinrich, 1–2, 113–115,
172–173, 198n50, 213n1; farewell
sermon by, 170–171; as Heimsheim
pastor, 94–99; lecture on the Jewish
Question, 95–99; sheltering Jewish
woman, 2, 99

Fausel, Helene, 99, 198n50
fear: in irrational antisemitism, 99,
114, 116; at root of antisemitism
and anti-Judaism, 74–75, 181n2
Feix, G., 126
Final Solution. See Holocaust; Jews,
Nazis' treatment of
foreign policy, of Third Reich, 154
The Foundations of the Nineteenth
Century (Die Grundlagen des
neunzehnten Jahrhunderts)
(Chamberlain), 24
Friedman, Jerome, 187n58
Fritsch, Theodor, 24
From Christian to National Socialism
(Vom christlichen zum nationalen
Sozialismus) (Bornkamm), 150

Gabriel, Walter, 99–103, 113–114, 173
Gailus, Manfred, 118–119, 201n2
Gerlach, Wolfgang, 113
German Christians, 26, 79, 93, 135,
178n24, 201n4, 203n40; Bornkamm
leaving, 147, 154; Confessing
Church vs., 9–10, 100, 114, 118–119,
136, 142; hagiographic use of
Luther, 37, 73–74, 123, 142–143,
190n13; influence of, 8–9, 190n12;
irrational antisemitism of, 142,
173; on Kristallnacht, 123, 131,
140, 201n6; Meyer-Erlach in, 68,
73–74; pastors in, 91–92, 131,
207n1; periodicals and publications
of, 20, 91, 130–132, 136–138, 140,
206n90; relations with Nazis, 8–9,
70, 83, 127–128, 136, 190n13; relations with other Protestant groups,
10–11; response to Nuremberg
Race Laws, 120–121; Schairer and,
204nn54,55; as significant minority, 119, 188n73; supporting Aryan
Paragraph, 30–31, 98, 198n54;
theologians of, 63, 81–83, 190n12,
207n2; theology of, 74, 80, 119, 135;
unbalanced use of Judenschriften,

response to, 8, 37; support for, 10,
119, 128–129, 154, 160
Joachim I, Landgrave of Brandenburg,
43, 45
Joachim II, at Frankfort Convention,
45
John Frederick of Saxony, 43, 45
Jonas, Justus, 45–46
Josel of Rosheim, 42–43, 45, 55, 101
Judaism, 65, 72; arguments against
based on Old Testament, 80, 95–96;
Catholicism compared to, 156–157;
Christianity *vs.*, 104–107, 128,
133–135, 161; definitions of, 103,
114; efforts to eliminate influence
in church, 134–135, 140, 147; liberalism linked to, 24, 150; linked
to Bolshevism, 105–109, 114–115,
132–133, 140, 150, 161–162, 169,
199n82; Luther on, 36, 103
Judenordnung (Laws Governing the
Jewish Status) (Philipp of Hesse), 43
Judenschriften (writings about Jews
and Judaism), Luther's, 46–51,
76, 184n3, 206n90; academic
theologians using, 63, 81–83; anti-
Judaism and antisemitism in, 12,
19; anti-Judaism *vs.* antisemitism
in, 5, 41; collections of, 25, 138;
Confessing Church on, 112–117,
173; early *vs.* late writing of, 54–56;
German Christians using, 114,
138–139, 142–143, 173; German
Christians using decontextualized passages from, 119, 129–130,
133–134; Holsten's comments on,
159, 168; influence of, 2–3, 7–8, 58;
intentions in writing, 48, 184n3;
interpretations of, 39–41, 51–53,
96–98, 152, 187n60, 188n71; misin-
terpretations of, 39–41; popularity
of, 137–138, 172; preserved and promoted, *vs.* suppressed, 125, 194n62;
responses to, 8, 73; selectivity in

use of, 80, 82, 140–143; unaffiliated
pastors and theologians using, 145,
173–174; uses of, 13, 14, 37, 63–68,
157, 202n16
justification, doctrine of *(Rechtfertigungslehre)*, 51–53, 57, 185n21

Kirche und Volkstum (Church and
Nationality) (Althaus), 16–17, 27
Kittel, Gerhard, 62
Klapproth, Erich, 124
knowledge, sociological context of,
19–20
Kommende Kirche (Coming Church)
(edited by Dungs), 136
Königsberg Protestant Church Congress (1927), 16–17, 27
Krieck, Ernst, 190n13
Kristallnacht, 148, 202n18, 208n15;
destruction in, 123, *151;* German
Christian pastors on, 120, 128–129,
131; German Christians on, 123,
139–140, 206n90; Jews sent to concentration camps following, 123,
124; Luther's recommendations
anticipating, 12, 14, 117; responses
to, 123–127, 201n6
Künneth, Walter, 199n77, 201n2

labor, forced, 49
Lamparter, Eduard, 38, 161, 211n49
Langmuir, Gavin, 3–6, 13, 18–19, 23,
174–175, 178n14
language, Nazi use of, 5–6, 180n38
Law against the Overcrowding of
German Schools and Universities
(1933), 60
Law for the Restoration of the Profes-
sional Civil Service (1933), 11, 60
Lazare, Bernard, 17
Leffler, Siegfried, 136, 190n13
Leipzig University, Bornkamm at, 147,
153–154
Leutheuser, Julius, 190n13

CHRISTOPHER J. PROBST is a visiting assistant professor of modern European history at Saint Louis University. He received his Ph.D. in modern European history from Royal Holloway, University of London in 2008 and continued his research as a Charles H. Revson Foundation Fellow at the Center for Advanced Holocaust Studies of the United States Holocaust Memorial Museum.